IMAGES
of America

RUSSELL COUNTY

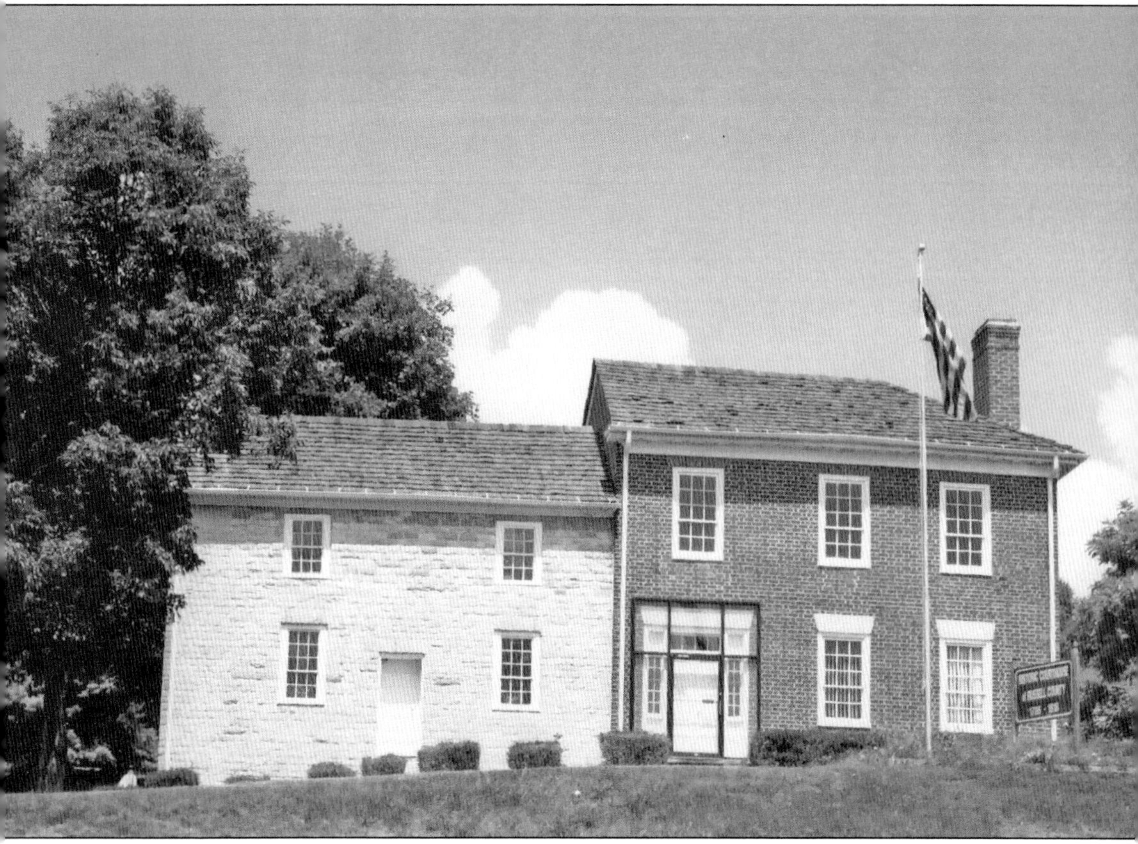

This building is the second Russell County Court House and was built at Dickensonville. It cost the county $2,188.97 to build. This courthouse was used from October 22, 1799, until February 3, 1818. (Courtesy of Andrew Chafin.)

ON THE COVER: A steamroller smooths the streets of Honaker in the early 1920s. Major M. Griffith is driving the team of horses pulling the water wagon. Major Griffith is the grandfather of Claude E. Griffith, the donor of this picture. Claude E. Griffith, known as "Cosmo," is a well-known storyteller and member of the Russell County Genealogy Group. His knowledge and collection of Russell County information is immense. The town of Honaker was incorporated in 1919 and is known as the Redbud Capital of the World. Millions of redbuds bloom in the town each spring. The town is home to the Honaker Heritage Museum, where thousands of Russell County artifacts are on display. (Courtesy of Claude E. "Cosmo" Griffith.)

IMAGES
of America

RUSSELL COUNTY

Andrew Chafin

ARCADIA
PUBLISHING

ISBN 978-0-7385-5394-8

Published by Arcadia Publishing
Charleston, South Carolina

Printed in the United States of America

Library of Congress Catalog Card Number: 2007943009

For all general information contact Arcadia Publishing at:
Telephone 843-853-2070
Fax 843-853-0044
E-mail sales@arcadiapublishing.com
For customer service and orders:
Toll-Free 1-888-313-2665

Visit us on the Internet at www.arcadiapublishing.com

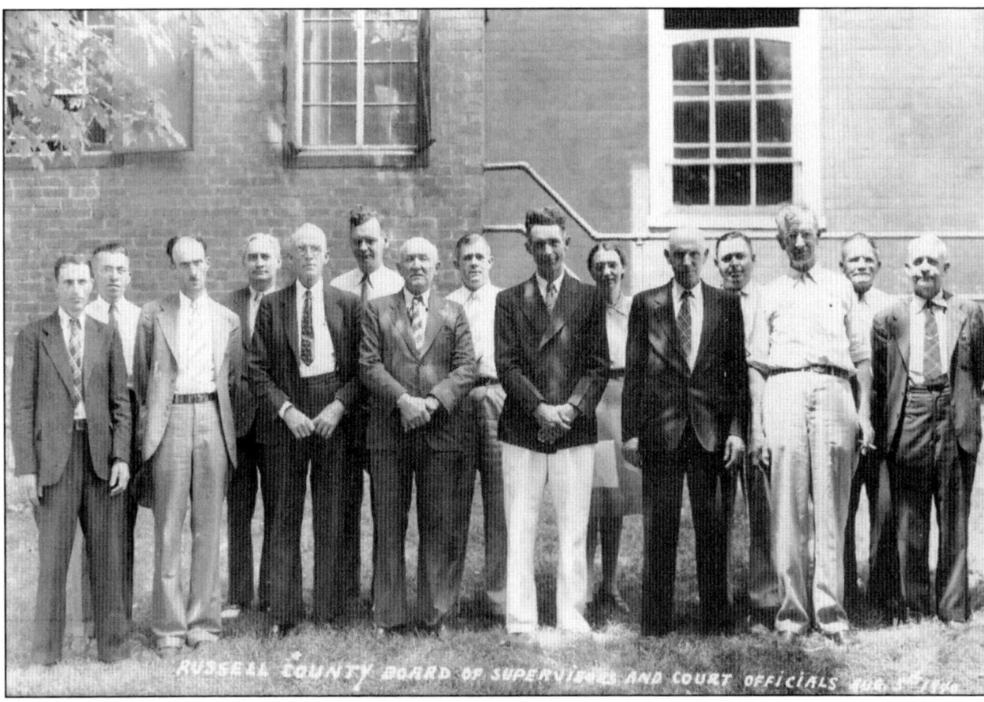

This is the Russell County Board of Supervisors and Court Officials. This picture was taken on August 5, 1940, at the present-day courthouse. Pictured here from left to right are as follows: Bert Price, supervisor; Ellis Hargis, clerk; Joe Hillman, supervisor; Luther Fuller, Commonwealth attorney; Morgan Wallace, supervisor; Grady Jessee, deputy clerk; John Mason, supervisor; Marvin Hess, commissioner of revenue; Newlin White, supervisor; Mary Sue Fuller, treasurer; Farley Hartsock, supervisor; Arthur Combs, sheriff; Robert McCoy, supervisor; Ellis Jessee; and Joe Duff, judge. (Courtesy of Russell County Public Library [RCPL], provided by Russell County Courthouse.)

CONTENTS

ACKNOWLEDGMENTS

Every effort has been made to provide accurate information. Much of the information regarding the photographs was based on information provided by those contributing the photographs and stories passed down from family member to family member, so minor discrepancies may exist. Every attempt was made to obtain a variety of pictures from as many contributors as possible. The long history of Russell County, the size of the county, and the great progress that has occurred in the last 222 years made it impossible to include all that has occurred. This book is intended to be a "backward glance" of life the way it was.

I wish to thank the many Russell Countians who generously came forth with their photographs and stories depicting the county's past. I hope this book justifies their faith in me and reflects life in Russell County in the earlier years in a meaningful manner.

I want to thank Patty J. Nichols for typing, editing, and arranging this book and the many others who gave both their time and their photographs and shared their special stories and recollections, which made this book possible. The special assistance of Diane Fuller and Kathleen Taylor was invaluable. Kelly McBride, director of the Russell County Public Library, and her associate Jennifer Bundy were very helpful, as was Jerry Lark, editor of the *Lebanon News*. Thanks to Claude E. "Cosmo" Griffith for providing the cover photograph. Thanks also to the Honaker Heritage Museum, Russell County Historical Society, Mary Ann Post, Jim Easterly, Jim Baldwin, Jeff Owen, Angie Beavers, Judy Harris, Kelly O'Quinn, Linda Tate, Tammy Caldwell, Randy Williams, Steve Starnes, Sherman Wallace Jr., James C. Jessee, Nellie R. Jessee, Frank R. Finney, Clifford Miller, Tommy Taylor, Patricia Garrett, and all the many others who assisted. Images were provided by the Honaker Heritage Museum (HHM) or the Russell County Public Library (RCPL) unless otherwise noted.

INTRODUCTION

The first county government in America was formed in 1634 at James City, Virginia. One hundred fifty-two years later, on January 2, 1786, three years before George Washington became president, Russell County was formed from a part of Washington County. The county was named for Col. William Russell, who assisted in the drafting of the Declaration of Independence. Russell was a member of the 13th Virginia Regiment. L. P. Summers, a Washington County native, later wrote, "Washington County lost a great extent of country and many valuable citizens when Russell County was formed."

The county lies in the central part of Appalachia, a 13-state region stretching from New York to Mississippi. The land is ancient—perhaps more than a billion years old. Its peaks and valleys were born of cataclysmic eruptions, which ultimately created a landscape forbidding, inviting, and beautiful. Early settlers endured geographic isolation as they shaped the ways of life, the attitudes, products, legends, and realities that would ultimately usher Russell County into the information age of the 21st century.

Daniel Boone maintained his home and family in Russell County from 1773 to 1775 while serving as a lieutenant and captain in the Virginia Militia. As a delegate from Virginia's county of Kentucky, Boone sat with Thomas Jefferson and Patrick Henry in the Virginia legislature.

In 1774, Daniel Boone led the defense of the Clinch River Settlements during Dunmore's War. The war was between the Colony of Virginia and the Shawnee and Mingo Indians. The Virginia-led attack was designed to remove the last obstacle to Colonial conquest of the area.

In 1785, a large group of citizens petitioned the Virginia legislature to form Russell County. Among the petitioners was Ephraim Hatfield, the great-great-great-grandfather of the author of this book. Hatfield moved westward to what is now West Virginia. His offspring were the Hatfields of the great Hatfield-McCoy Feud.

On July 7, 1776, William Russell, then a captain, wrote to Col. William Preston that John Douglas, a sergeant, had been traveling through Native American lands from Abingdon to Lebanon and the Clinch settlements with a friend when they stopped at Moccasin Gap to have lunch. As they took lunch on a large flat rock, a shot rang out from the woods and killed the young Douglas. Years later, a bronze plaque was placed on the rock now known as the John Douglas Wayside.

Colonel Preston's grandson, William Ballard Preston, served in the Virginia General Assembly and in 1849 was appointed secretary of war by Pres. Zachary Taylor. A college in Blacksburg, Preston and Olin Institute, was named for him. It was from this school that Virginia Tech evolved.

The first court in Russell County was held in the home of William Robinson at Castle's Woods (present-day Castlewood) on May 1, 1786. Justices were Alexander Barnett, Henry Smith, David Ward, Andrew Cowan, Samuel Ritchie, Thomas Carter, Henry Dickenson, and John Thompson.

An original courthouse was built of logs by Henry Dickenson at Dickensonville. The courthouse was burned during the Revolutionary War, and Dickenson then constructed a new courthouse at a cost of $2,188.97. The structure, used until 1818, still stands and is called "The Old Courthouse."

A new courthouse was built in the town of Lebanon when the county seat was moved to the town in 1814.

The county has three incorporated towns: Lebanon, Cleveland, and Honaker. Honaker was founded in 1919 and named for Squire Harvey Honaker, postmaster. The town is hailed as the Redbud Capital of the World and hosts a redbud festival each April. The town also is home to the Honaker Museum. The town's estimated population in 2003 was 922.

Cleveland was founded in 1946 and was named for Pres. Grover Cleveland. Its estimated population in 2003 was 142. The town is located on the Clinch River and was once a thriving coal-mining community.

Other communities in Russell County include Hansonville, Dickensonville, Dante, Finney, Castlewood, Drill, Swords Creek, Rosedale, and Belfast.

Other counties formed from Russell were Lee County, in 1793, and Tazewell County, in 1799. In 1815, Scott County was formed from a portion of Russell and Lee Counties. In 1858, Buchanan County was formed from parts of Russell and Tazewell Counties, and in 1856, Wise County was formed from parts of Lee, Scott, and Russell Counties. A portion of southern West Virginia was within the original boundaries of Russell County.

By 1858, Russell County had been reduced from an initial acreage of 3,000 square miles to 483 square miles. In 1790, the population of Russell County was 3,338, which included 190 slaves. The 2000 Census showed the county had a population of 30,242.

In the past two decades, the county has evolved from a sleepy, agricultural community into a teeming industrial and technology center. Companies such as Northrop Grumman, CGI, AT&T, International Automotive Components, and Alcoa have moved to the county during the past few years and now employ thousands of workers.

Danny Brown, chairman of the county board of supervisors, calls the resurgent county "a renaissance of hope and opportunity for our young people."

One

Friends and Neighbors

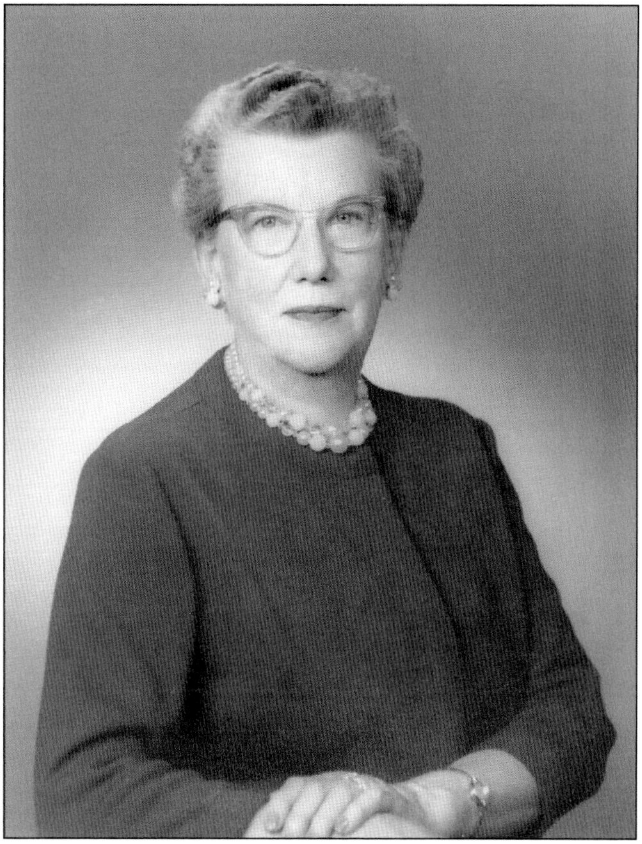

Gaynelle Albert was well known as a local Russell County historian. She was civic minded and participated in Russell County events. She was involved with the Red Cross Chapter, the Women's Club, the PTA, the Garden Club, and the Three Arts Club. Albert was active in the First Baptist Church as a pianist, choir director, Sunday school teacher, and singer of hymns. Albert was one of the original founders of the RCPL, which started in a room of the courthouse in Lebanon. In 1932, she started the first Honaker Community Library. After she passed away, Albert's home was donated to the county. It is now the present-day Honaker Community Library branch of Russell County Public Library. (Courtesy of HHM.)

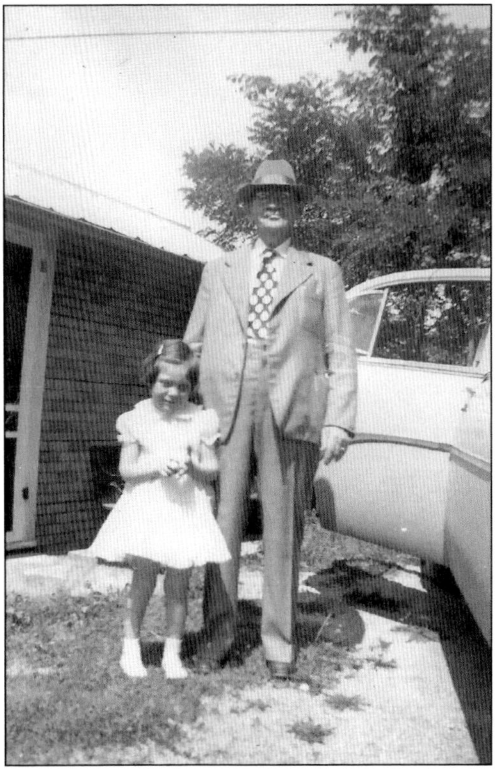

Charmie McNew was a Blackford railroad agent; with him is Diane Fuller. Diane's dad, Clarence Fuller, took McNew to church on Sundays. McNew always gave Diane a stick of chewing gum. McNew worked as an agent at the Blackford Railroad Station until 1958, when the station closed. McNew then transferred to the Honaker Railroad Station. The Blackford Depot was built around 1905 by the Barytes Company, named for the mineral it mined. When the company moved out, the Norfolk and Western bought it. They then built pens and loading chutes to haul the cattle, sheep, and turkeys grown locally to markets in other parts of the country. (Courtesy of HHM, provided by Diane Fuller.)

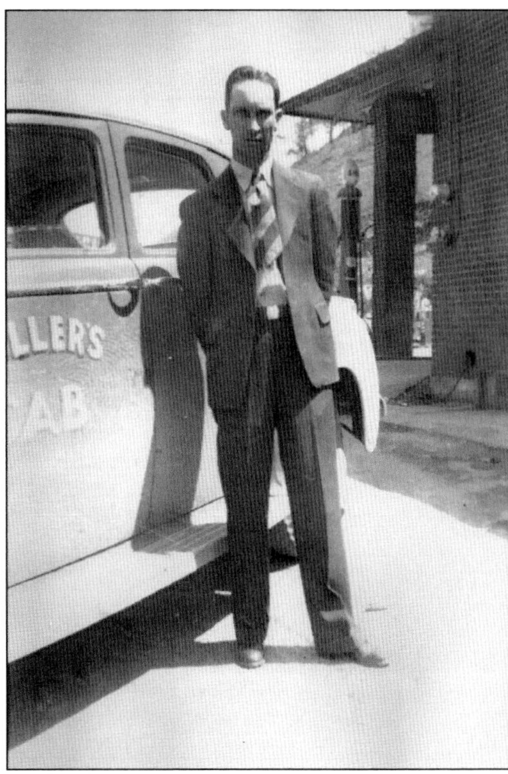

Clarence Fuller first started driving a cab in 1938. In 1939, he purchased his first cab, a Ford, from Naff Wysor. Clarence Fuller always wore a tailor-made suit and had the first air-conditioned taxi in Honaker. He retired from the taxi service in 1986 at the age of 80. His passengers consisted of schoolteachers, schoolchildren, and people coming into town to trade. He would often meet the bus at Oaks Garage to take travelers the remainder of the way to their destination. He would also travel to Abingdon and the Tri-City Airport. Someone said he had "hauled" everyone in the state of Virginia. Locals still tell his kin, "Your dad used to haul me." (Courtesy of HHM, provided by Diane Fuller.)

Judy Fuller, at the age of seven, gets her hair dried at Fuller's Beauty Shop. Her parents, Clarence and Bea Fuller, owned the beauty shop while Lily Monk and Delma Hubbard operated it. Delma Hubbard operated the beauty shop for 30 years. (Courtesy of HHM, provided by Diane Fuller.)

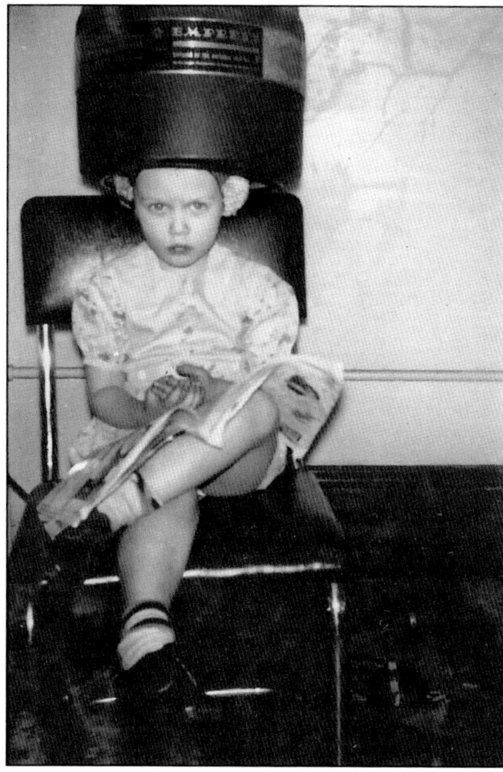

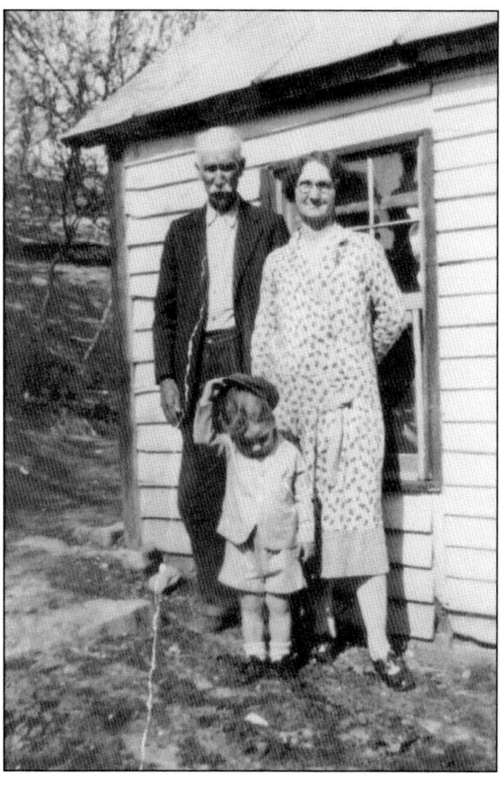

Pictured here are Edmundson Went (E. W.) Fields and his wife, Alta Cosby Ferguson Fields. The little guy with them is their grandson, Trigg Fields, who later became the sheriff of Russell County. The picture was taken on Mountain Road in Lebanon in the 1930s. (Courtesy of RCPL, provided by Alma Lester.)

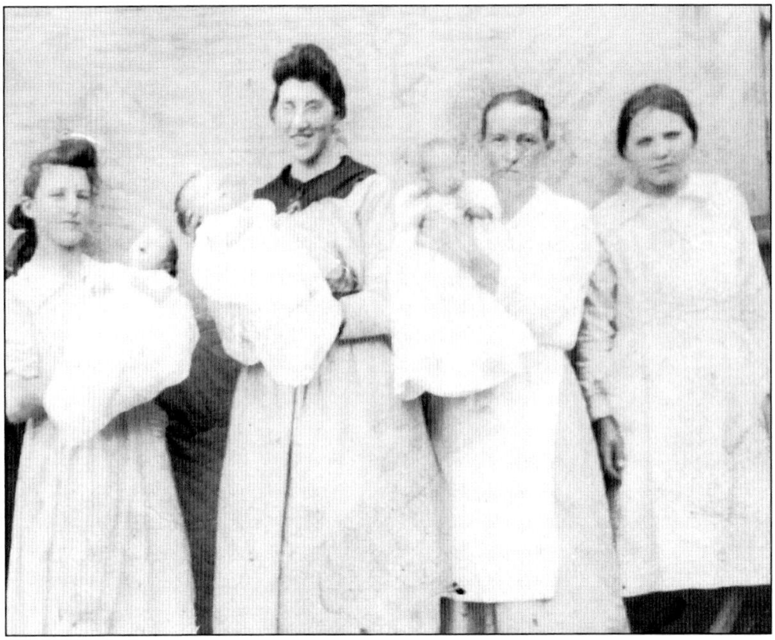

Pictured here are the Boyd triplets. There were two girls and one boy. They lived in Wysor Valley near the old Watson home place near Honaker. The boy was named Luther, one of the girls was named Lucy, and the third sibling's name is not known. They were born in the early 1920s. (Courtesy of RCPL, provided by Claude E. Griffith.)

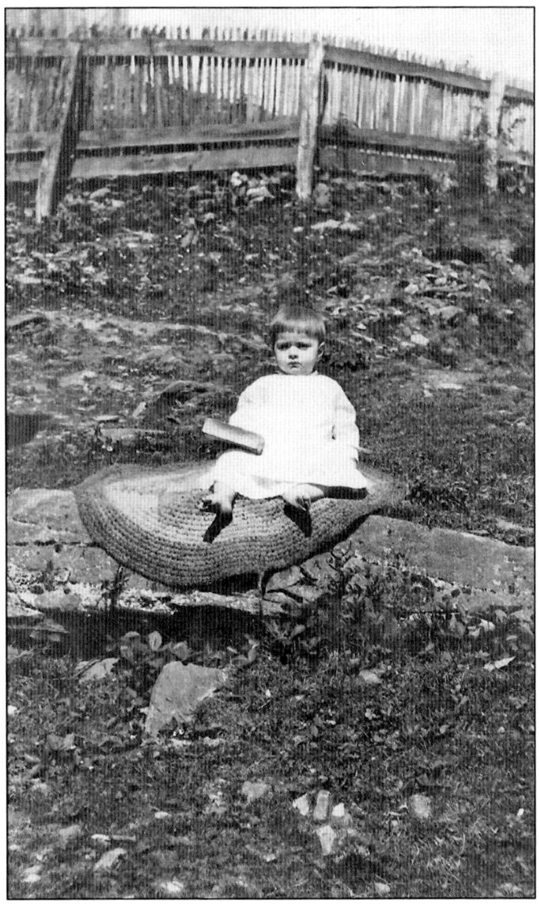

Children often played close by, as chores required the immediate attention of parents. This picture was taken in 1922. Notice the fence in the background and the rug on which the child has been lovingly placed. (Courtesy of HHM, provided by Kathleen R. Taylor.)

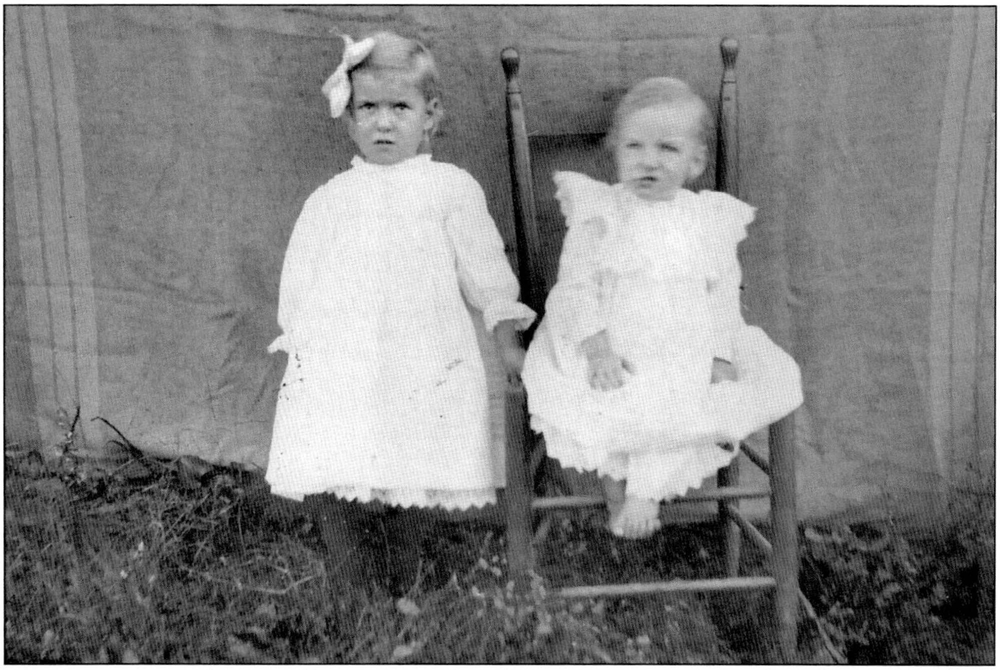

This picture is of Charlie and Mary Hale, the children of Sam and Lucy Hale. No doubt a little bit anxious about the whole ordeal, these two little ones pose all dressed up for the photograph. (Courtesy of HHM.)

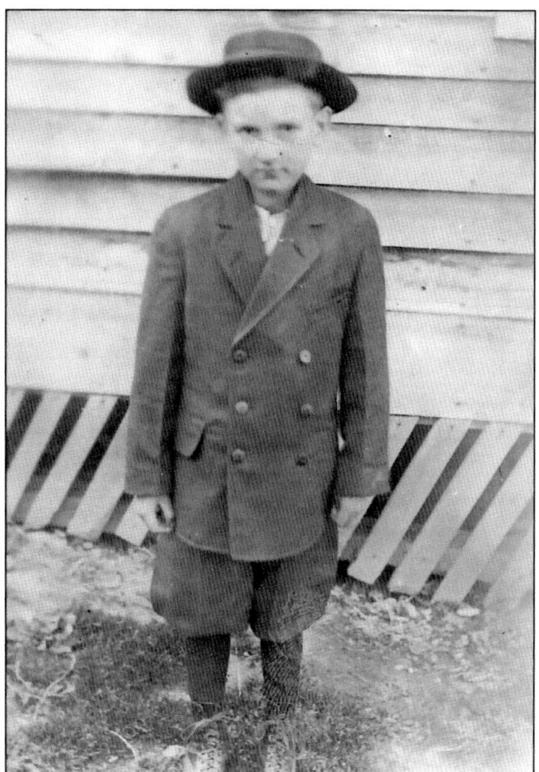

Pictured here looking a little serious yet determined and stately is Samuel Taylor. He is 12 years old in this picture. (Courtesy of HHM, provided by Kathleen R. Taylor.)

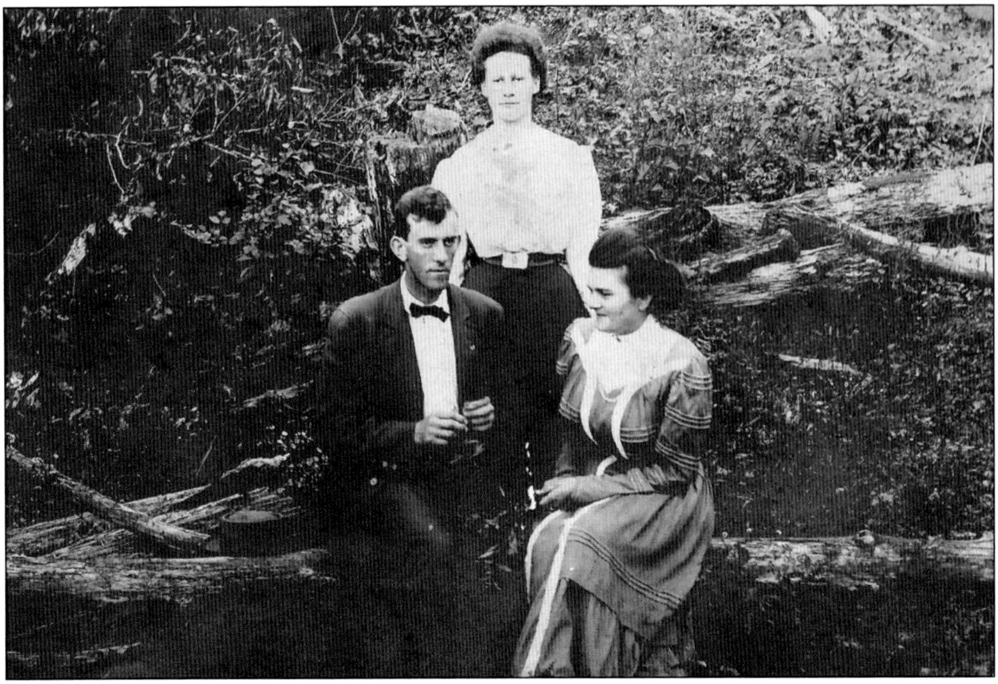

Rosa Barrett is seated with her gentleman friend. Notice the lady standing. She is the chaperone, required for young ladies of the day as they courted. (Courtesy of HHM, provided by Kathleen R. Taylor.)

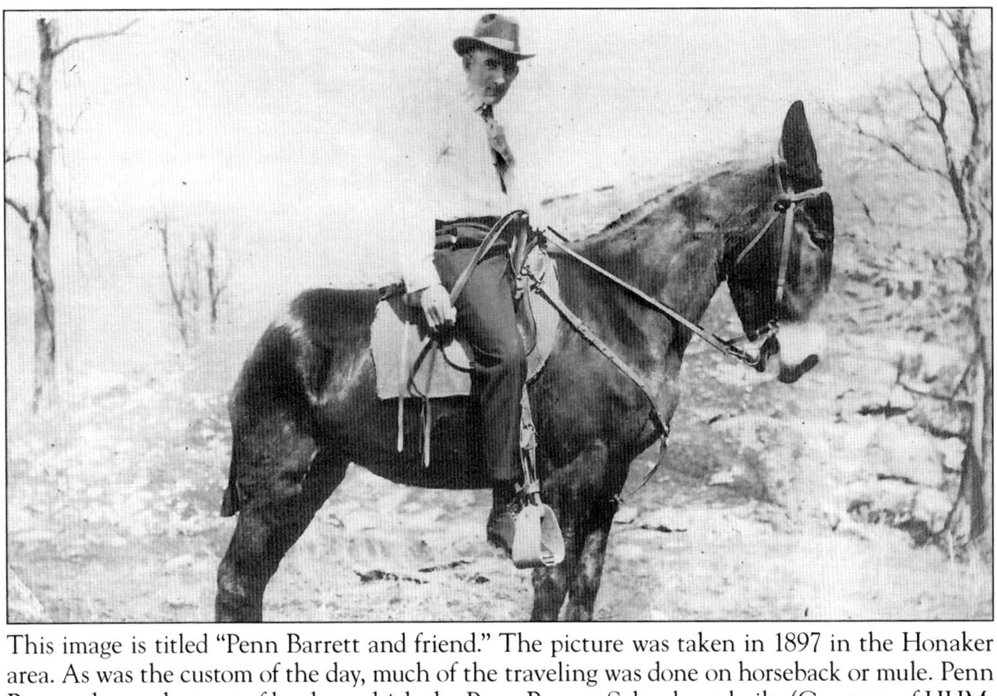

This image is titled "Penn Barrett and friend." The picture was taken in 1897 in the Honaker area. As was the custom of the day, much of the traveling was done on horseback or mule. Penn Barrett donated a tract of land on which the Penn Barrett School was built. (Courtesy of HHM, provided by Kathleen R. Taylor.)

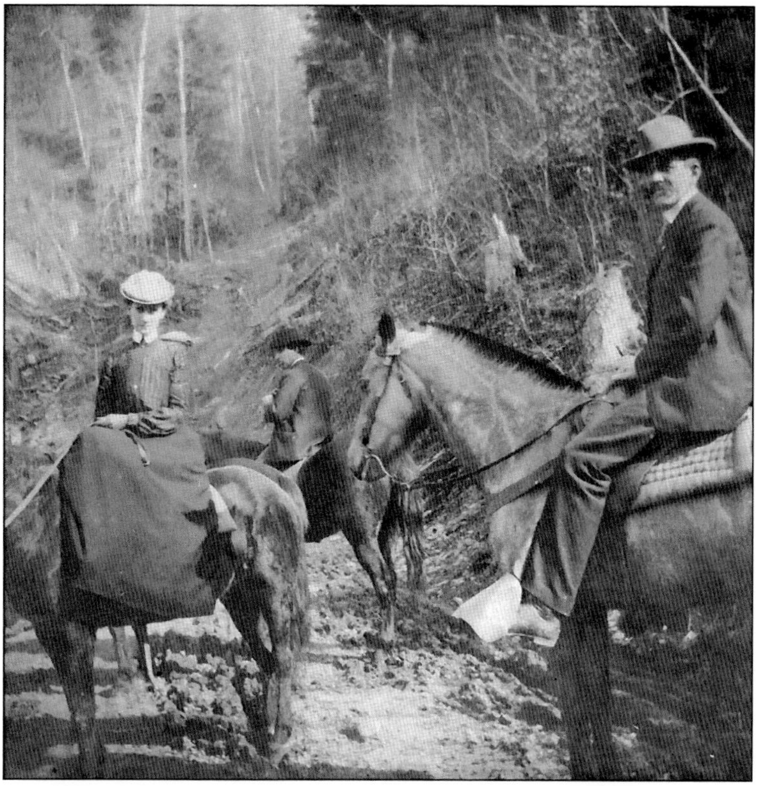

In the foreground, the two pictured in 1899 are Bud and Kate Braley. Notice the stately pose of Kate Braley as she rides as the ladies of the day often did—sidesaddle. It appears they are getting ready to proceed up the steep and rugged terrain of the area in the background of the picture. (Courtesy of HHM, provided by Kathleen R. Taylor.)

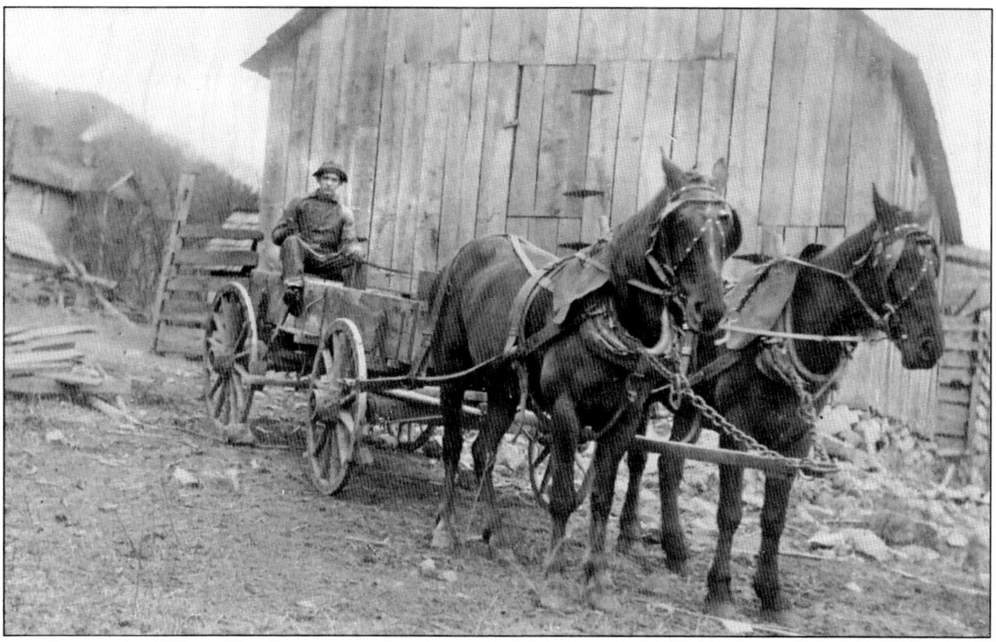

On the back of this postcard, a note states, "Grandma Barrett's—Uncle Carl." The horses and wagons played a major role in the lives of the citizens. Teams of horses were used to make trips to town for supplies or to sell items produced on the farm. The teams also plowed and readied the land for spring planting. (Courtesy of HHM, provided by Kathleen R. Taylor.)

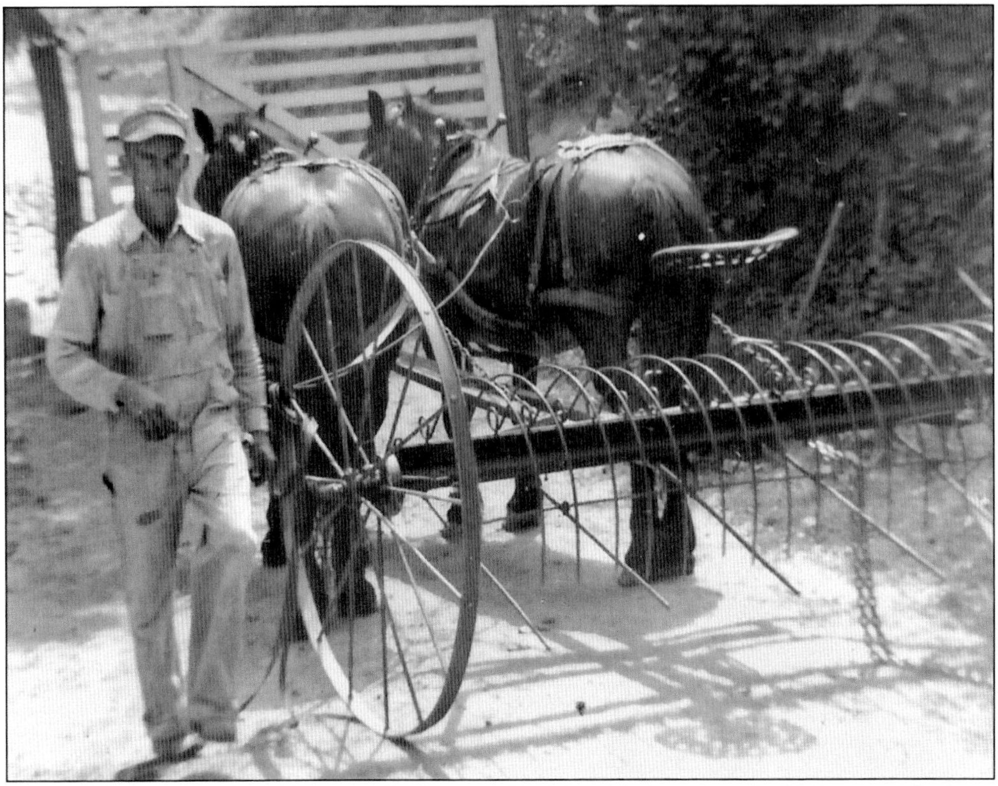

It's mowing time. Here is Cecil Robinson in a 1945 picture with his team of horses attached to a piece of farm equipment. These large pieces of machinery, simple as they were, made it possible for the farmer to tend many acres of land. (Courtesy of HHM, provided by Kathleen R. Taylor.)

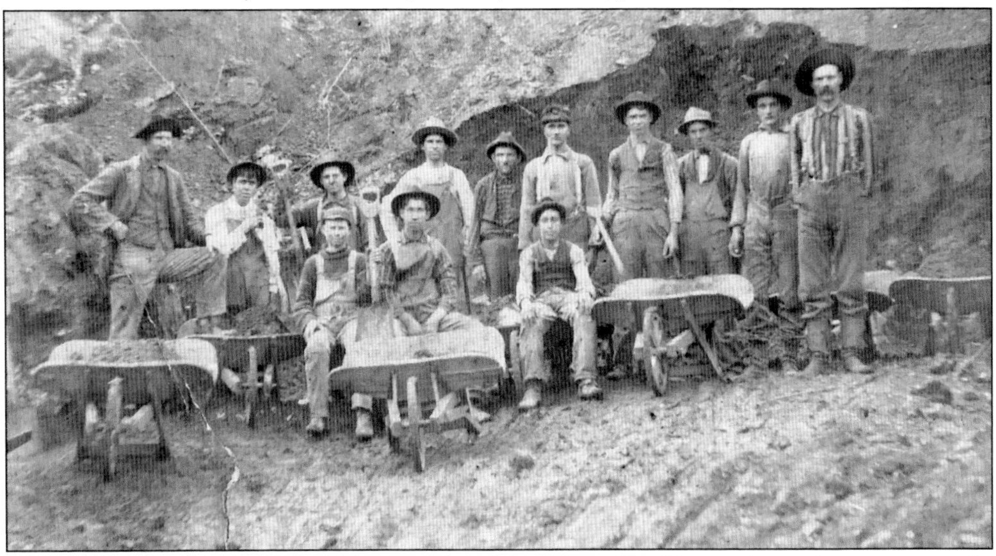

This road crew took time from their hard day's labor of road building to have this picture made. The image was taken in the Swords Creek area in the early 1900s. As can be seen from the photograph, much of the road work was done with manual labor and the use of a shovel and a wheelbarrow. (Courtesy of HHM.)

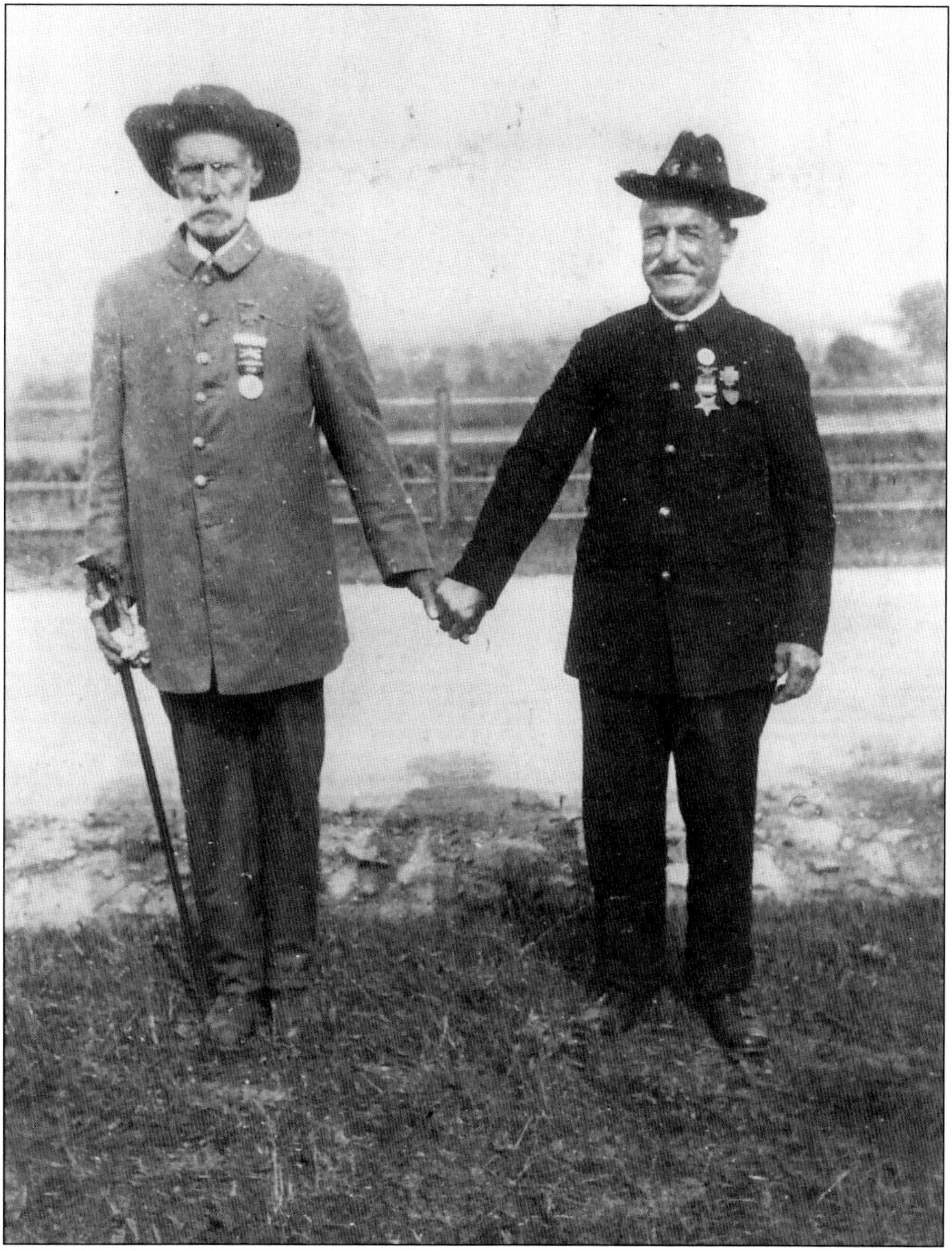

Pictured in the Confederate uniform on the left is William McGuire Hurt. He was the son of John M. Hurt, the grandson of William Darby Hurt, and the great-grandson of Garland and Martisha (Thurston) Hurt of Russell County, Virginia. He is joining hands with a soldier from the North once the Civil War was over. The Union soldier is unidentified. Hurt was born on June 30, 1843, in Russell County. During his lifetime, he was a teacher, a nurse, and a soldier. He married Mary Elizabeth Scott on November 26, 1868. She was born in 1847. They had five children who lived. William Hurt died at the Old Soldiers Home in Richmond, Virginia. (Courtesy of HHM, provided by Kathleen R. Taylor.)

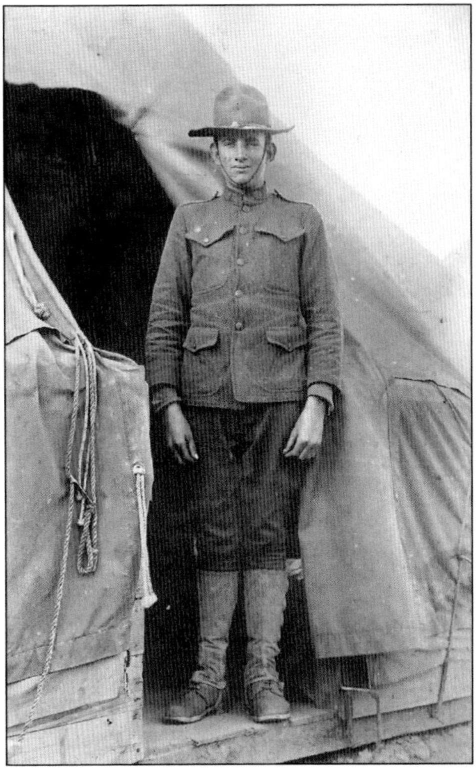

When the country went to war, so did many of the citizens of Russell County. Cecil E. Barrett is pictured here in his World War I uniform in 1918. The exact location of this picture is not known. (Courtesy of HHM, provided by Kathleen R. Taylor.)

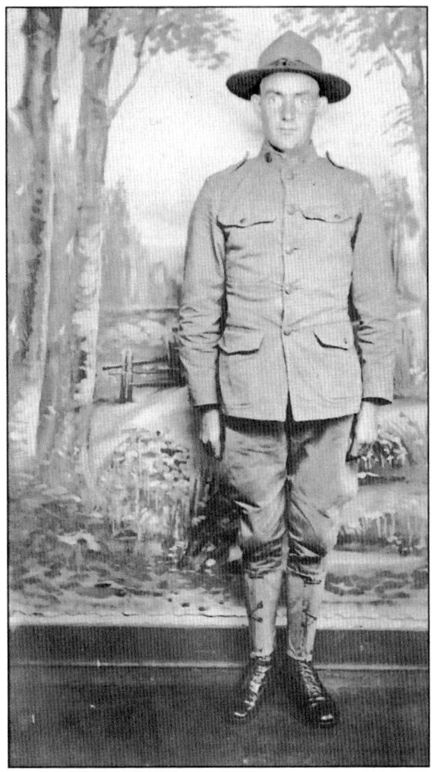

Standing in front of a backdrop of the outdoors is another of Russell County's young Americans who participated in World War I. This picture of Carl Barrett was taken in 1918. (Courtesy of HHM, provided by Kathleen R. Taylor.)

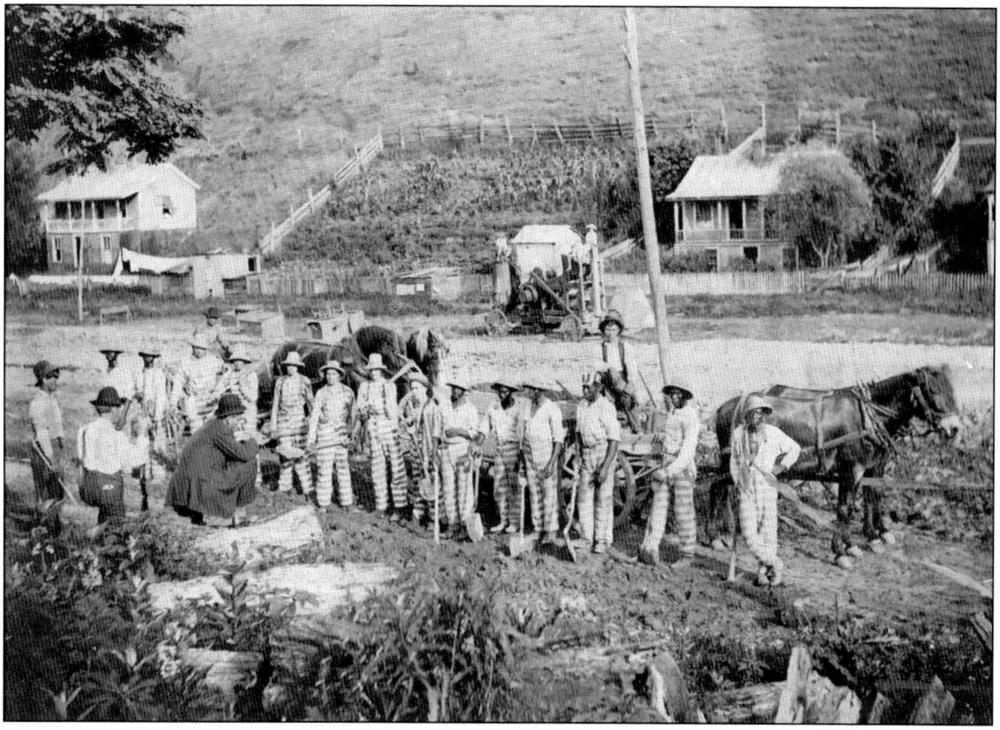

This *c.* 1910 picture was taken in Honaker at the upper end/west end of town below the depot. Sometimes called a chain gang, the workers were individuals convicted of crimes. The old road from Raven to Buchanan was built with convict labor. The donor's grandfather was one of the individuals responsible for guarding the prisoners. (Courtesy of RCPL, provided by Claude E. Griffith.)

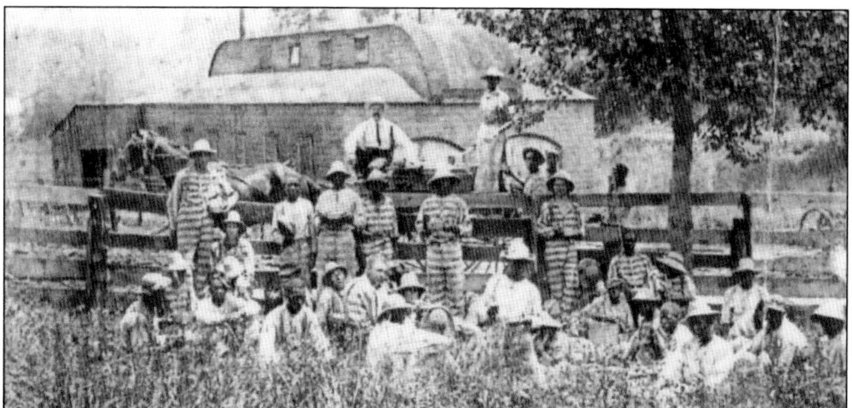

Members of Correctional Unit No. 5 around 1910 in Honaker take time for a lunch break. Notice the horse-drawn carriage behind the fence. This was the "chow" wagon, which brought the food to feed the prisoners. This picture was taken near the intersection of Balls Road and Route 80. Much work was accomplished through the use of this type of labor. (Courtesy of RCPL, provided by Janice Jessee Tiller.)

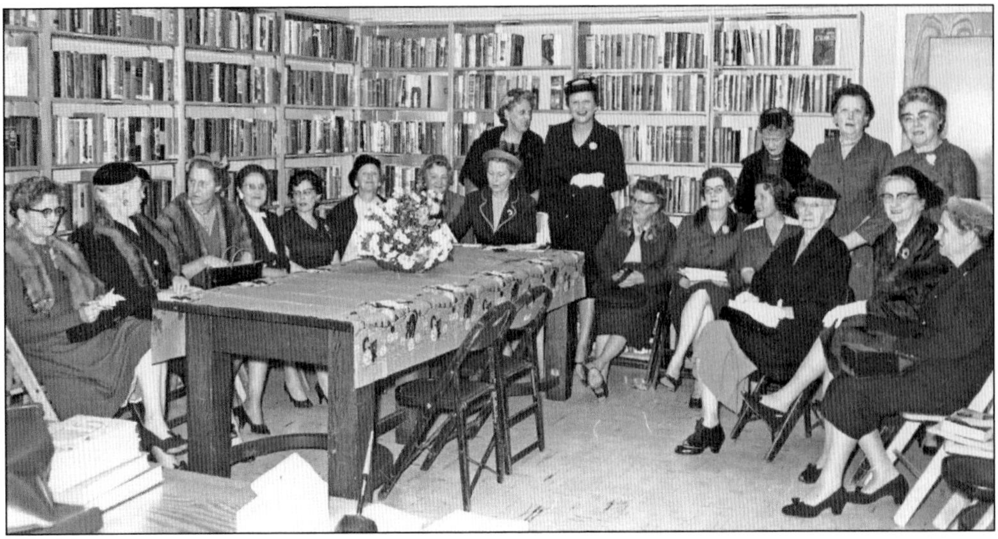

The RCPL was founded on October 22, 1959, by the Russell County Women's Club. The library was first located in the present-day courthouse, in the room occupied as the supervisors office for many years. From left to right are (seated) Mrs. Marvin Hess, Mrs. Tom Smith (Ann), Mrs. Harry Stuart (Marian Lee), Mrs. Claude Walden (Marguerita), Mrs. A. J. Lively (Mary), Eileen Kennedy, Mrs. Tucker Clay Mosby, Mrs. George Bundy Sr. (Garnette), Carolyn Gray, Mrs. Jess Hargis, two unidentified, Inez Alderson, and Mrs. Eugene Alderson; (standing) Mrs. Joe Dye (Stella Smith), unidentified, Mrs. James G. Albert (Gaynelle Lockhart), Eva Price, and Mrs. John Alderson. (Courtesy of RCPL.)

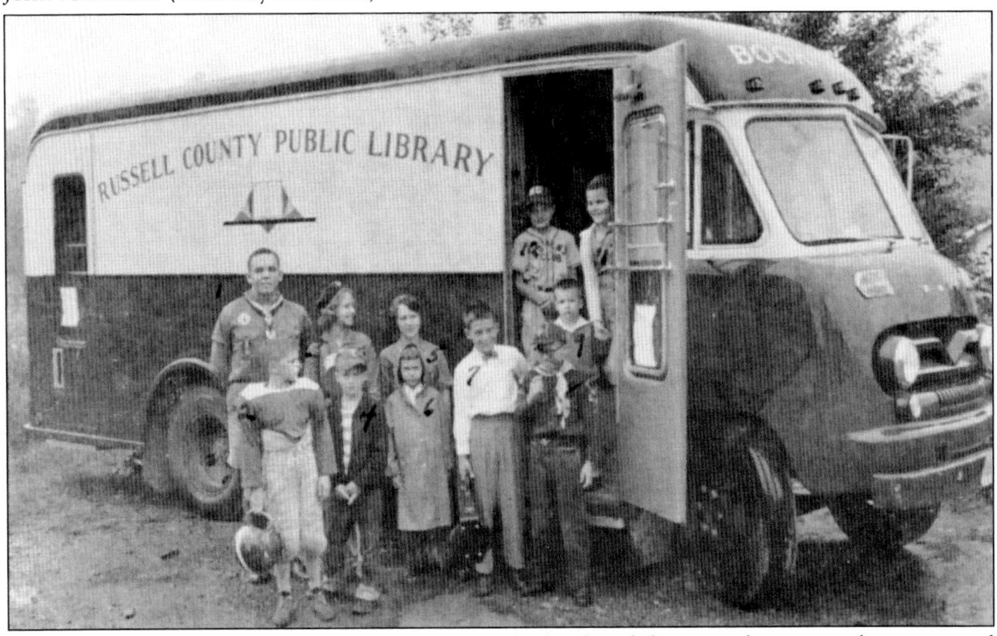

The RCPL Bookmobile is pictured here in 1961. The bookmobile's arrival was a much anticipated event for many of the county residents. These Russell County residents postponed their selection of books long enough to pose for this picture. Pictured here from left to right are Dramen Buskirk, Joe Gilmer, Gail Easterly, Buddy Gilmer, Linda Howard, Mary Sue Gilmer, Tommy Senter, Luke Houchins, John Otey Ketron, unidentified, and Sandra Norris. (Courtesy of RCPL.)

Gaynelle Albert, one of the original founders of the RCPL, loved her church, the First Baptist Church. Here she is pictured standing in front of it. Gaynelle also started the first community library in Honaker in 1932. (Courtesy of Diane Fuller.)

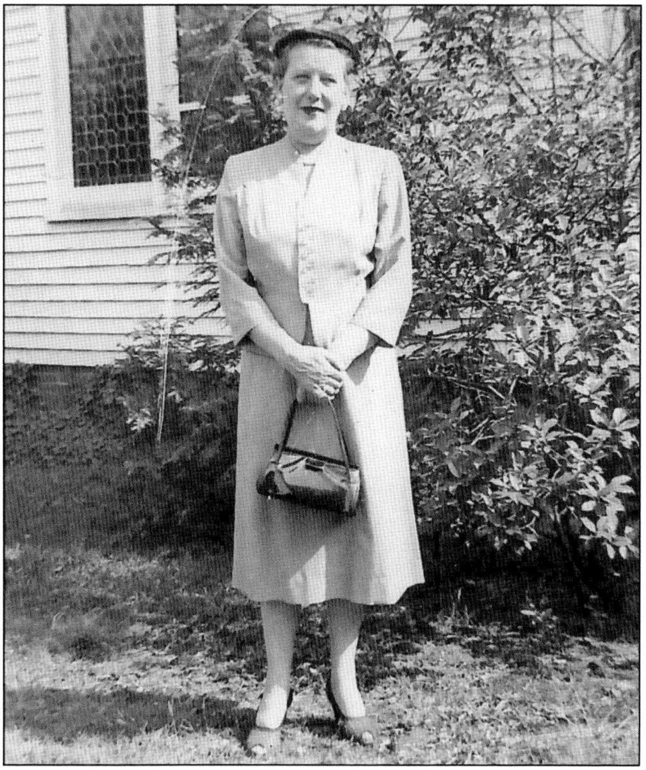

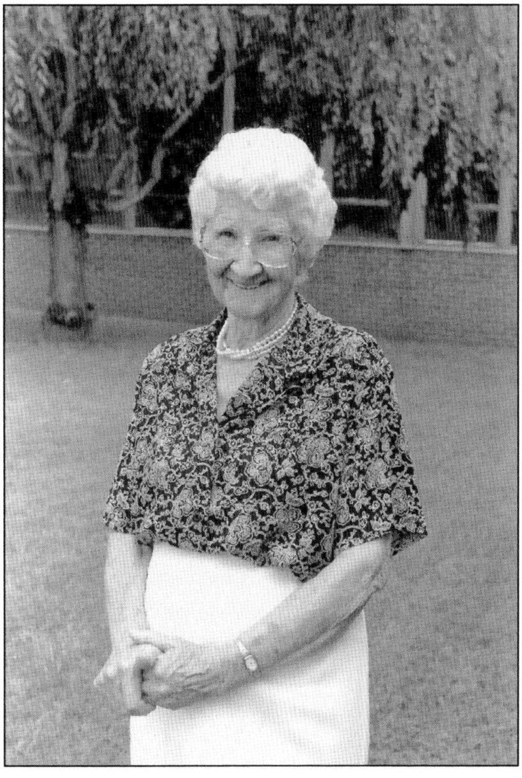

Known and loved by many, Rose Stinson (pictured here) has entertained and enthralled many with her great ability as a historian and storyteller. She has recounted, to the delight of her listeners, her stories of growing up in Russell County in the early 1900s. It has been said that she inherited her gift of storytelling from her grandmother, who also was great at telling stories. Many of the stories Rose has shared are forever etched on the minds of those to whom she told them. Others are preserved as she wrote them down, occasionally to enter into a writing contest, such as the Redbud Essay Contest. (Courtesy of HHM, provided by Kathleen R. Taylor.)

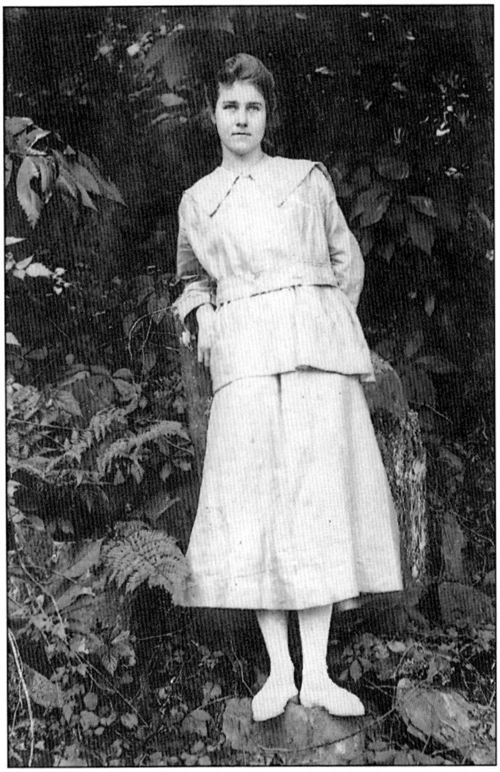

With the outdoors as a backdrop, the lovely Eva Starnes is pictured here. She was the grandmother of Steve Starnes. This picture was taken near Honaker in 1918. Eva was the wife of John Starnes. (Courtesy of Steve Starnes.)

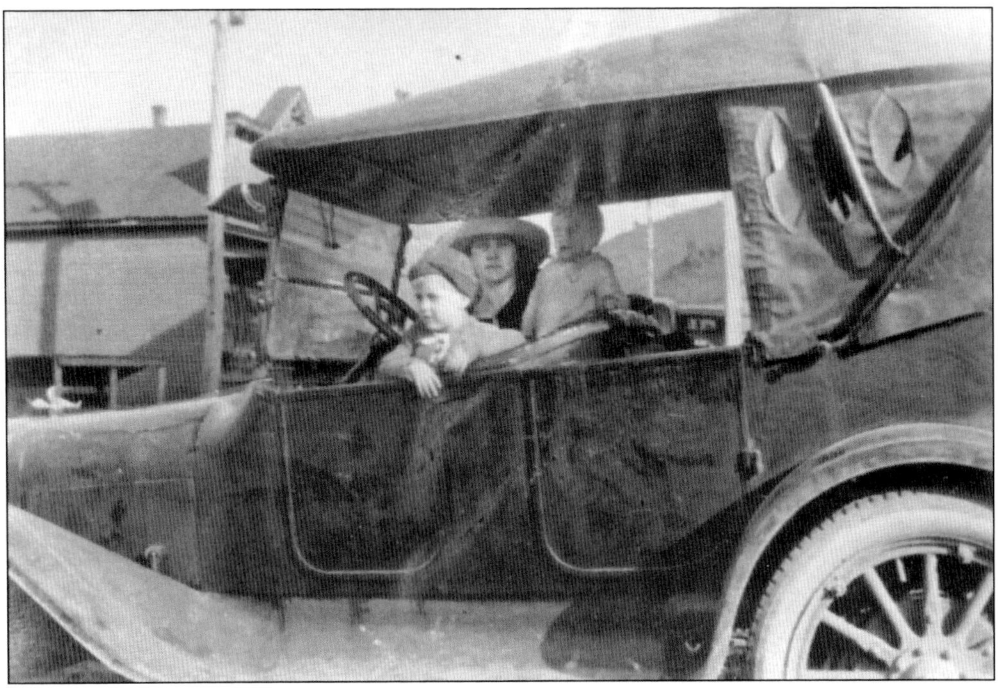

This 1924 photograph shows, from left to right, Marie Starnes Steele, Eva Starnes, and Helen Bartee Starnes. The automobile belonged to Eva Starnes and is pictured here in an alley beside Beamer's Store in Honaker. (Courtesy of Steve Starnes.)

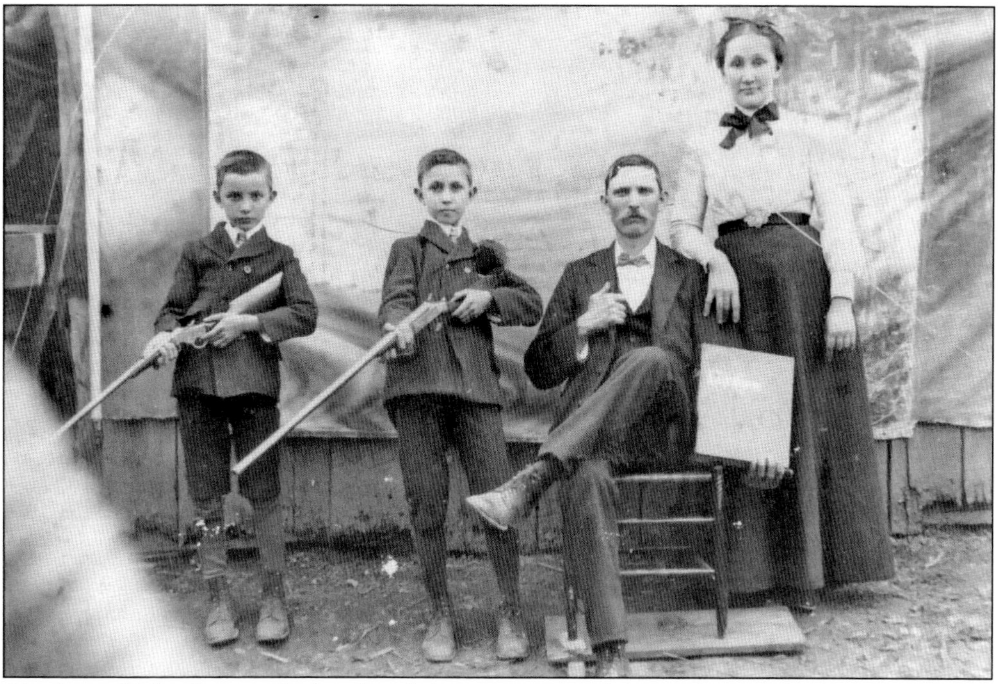

Charles and John Starnes display their father's guns. From left to right are Charles, John, Lilburn Starnes, and his wife, Virginia Starnes. This 1900 photograph was taken on Lewis Creek near the town of Honaker. (Courtesy of Steve Starnes.)

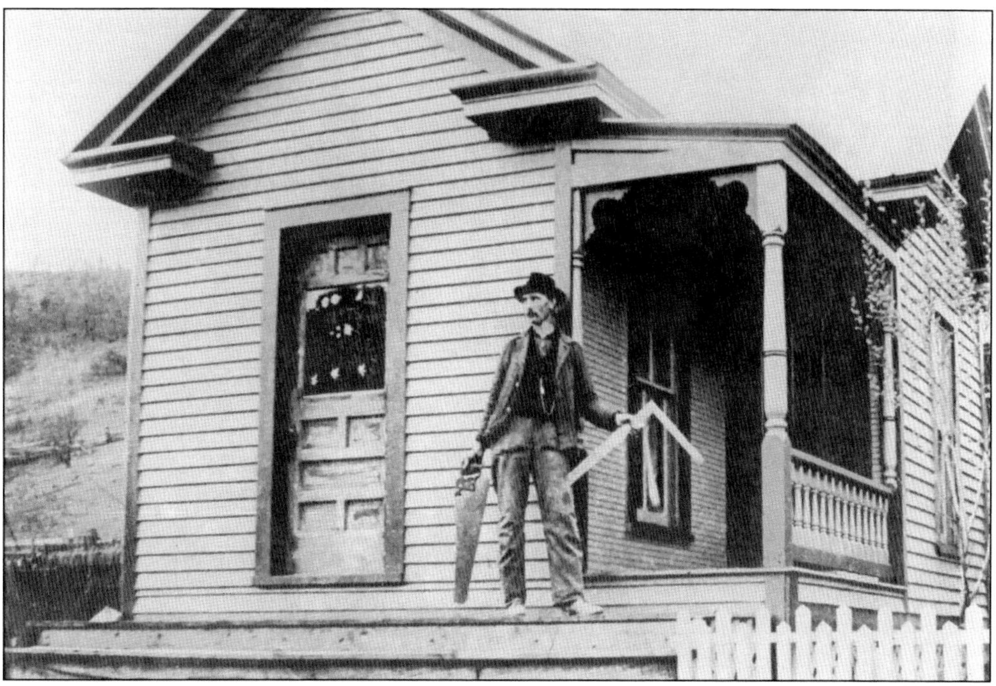

Lilburn Starnes, great-grandfather of Steve Starnes, is standing in front of Dr. Hartsock's medical office in Honaker. Lilburn Starnes constructed the building around 1900. (Courtesy of Steve Starnes.)

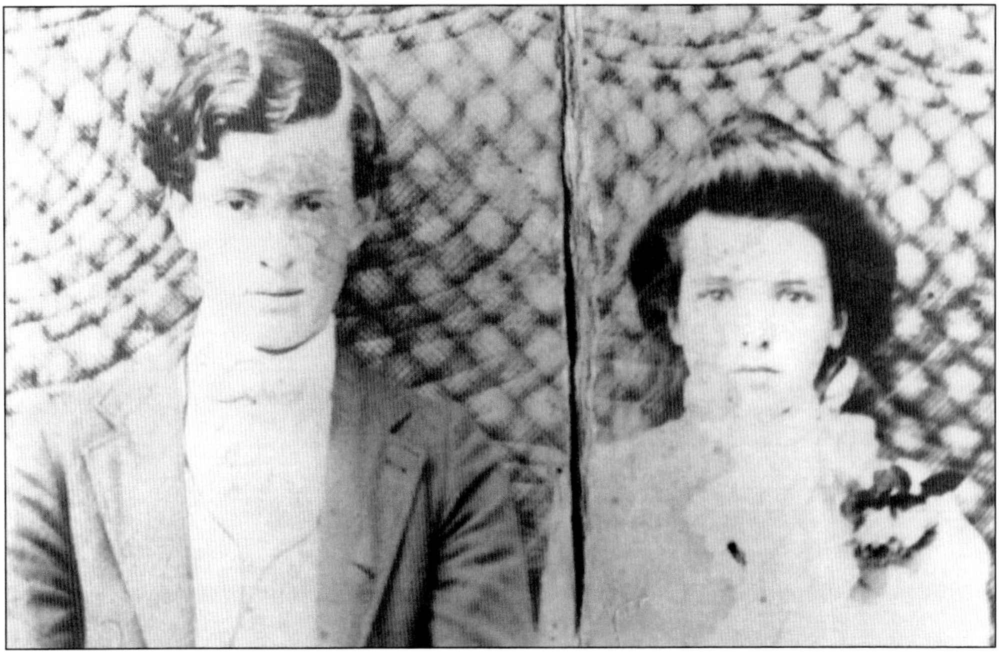

A wedding was usually memorialized with a formal photograph. Jim Meade and his lovely wife, Etta, pose for their wedding photograph in 1900. Jim Meade was a builder and resided in the Crossroads section of Russell County. He was the great-grandfather of Steve Starnes. (Courtesy of Steve Starnes.)

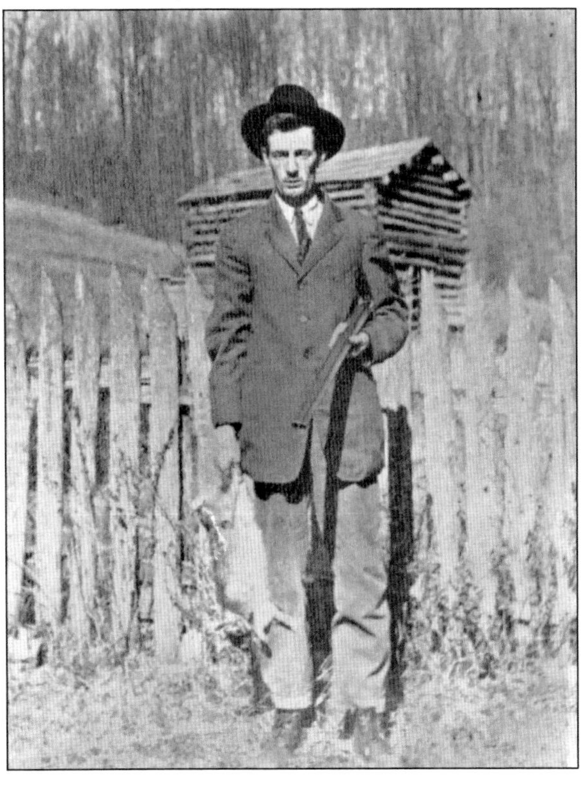

In this picture, Jim Meade, the maternal great-grandfather of Steve Starnes, is holding a rabbit as a result of a successful hunting trip in 1915. Local game was a regular part of the family meals. Notice the fence in the background and the log structure behind it. (Courtesy of Steve Starnes.)

Russell County businessman Russell Starnes was stationed at Fort Campbell, Kentucky, in 1950. He is pictured here in his uniform. Starnes was the father of Steve Starnes, who is also a Russell County businessman. (Courtesy of Steve Starnes.)

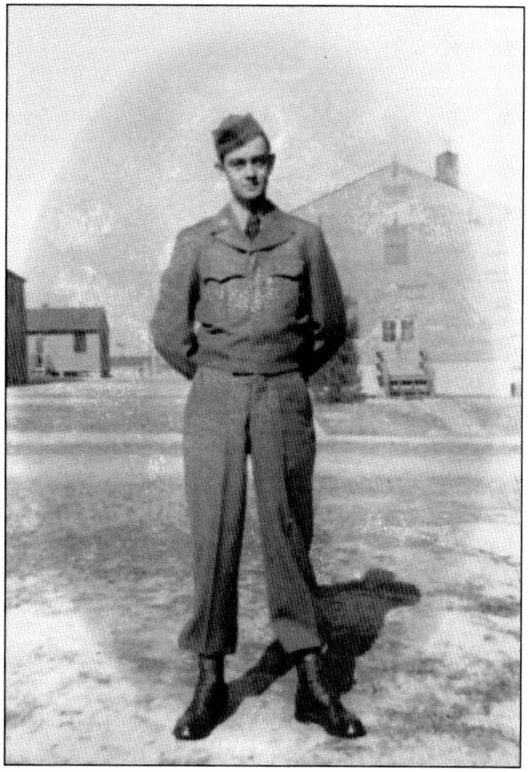

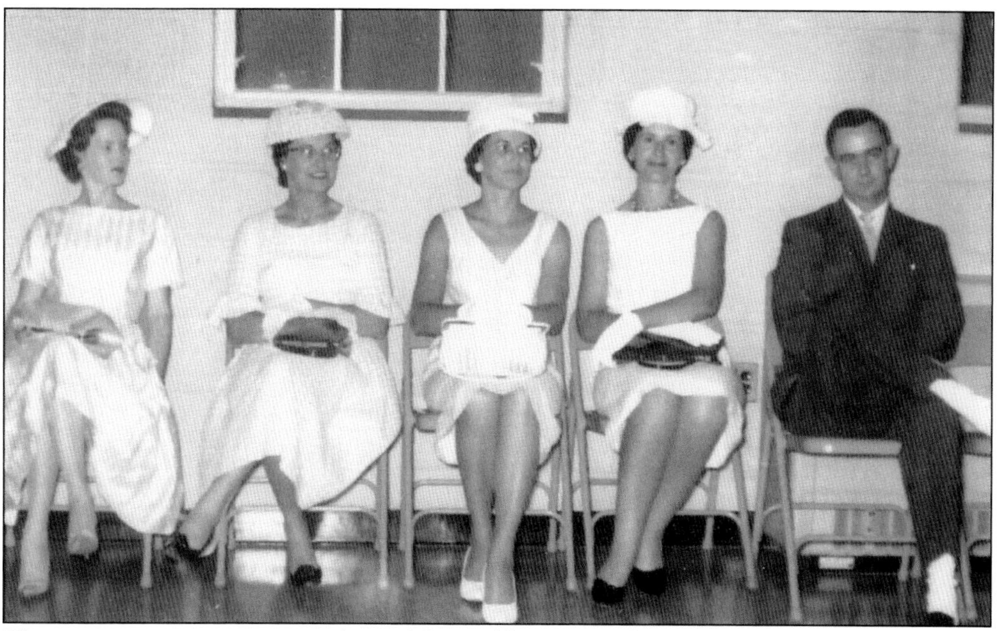

This picture captures some members of the wedding party of Joann Starnes. Seen in 1960 from left to right are Peggy Starnes, Helen Starnes Barter, Eula Starnes Smith, Rheba Starnes, and Russell Starnes. Rheba and Russell Starnes are the parents of Lebanon businessman Steve Starnes. Notice the stylish dressing of the day, including the lovely hats and gloves. (Courtesy of Steve Starnes.)

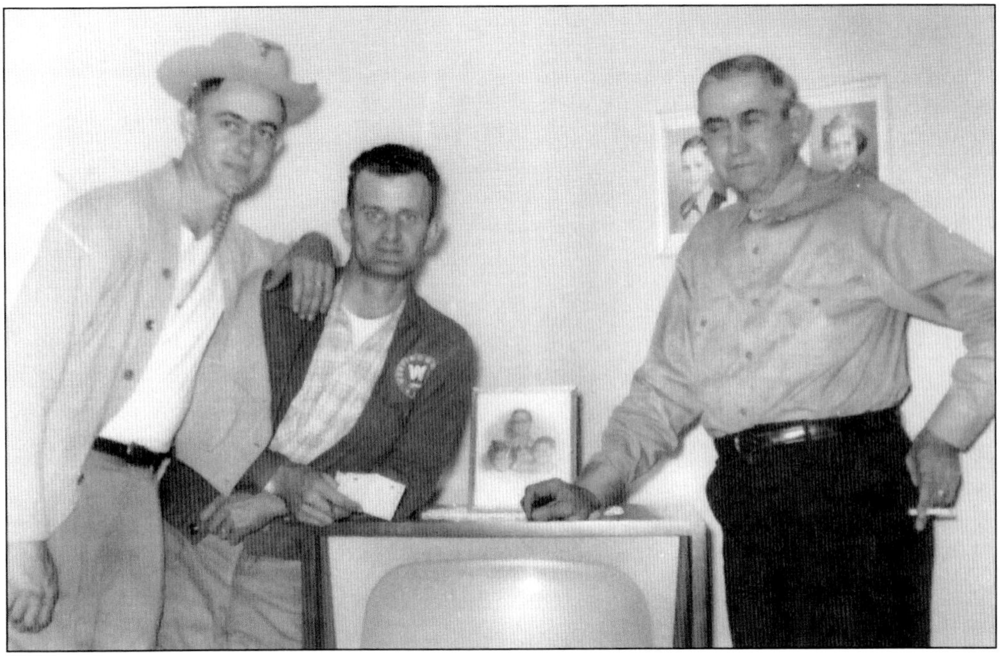

From left to right are Russell Starnes, Elmer Steele, and John Starnes. It appears they are inspecting a new television set. The Starnes family were builders in the Russell County area for many years. This picture was taken in 1956 as the nation embraced the new technologies and inventions designed to meet the growing needs of the consumer. (Courtesy of Steve Starnes.)

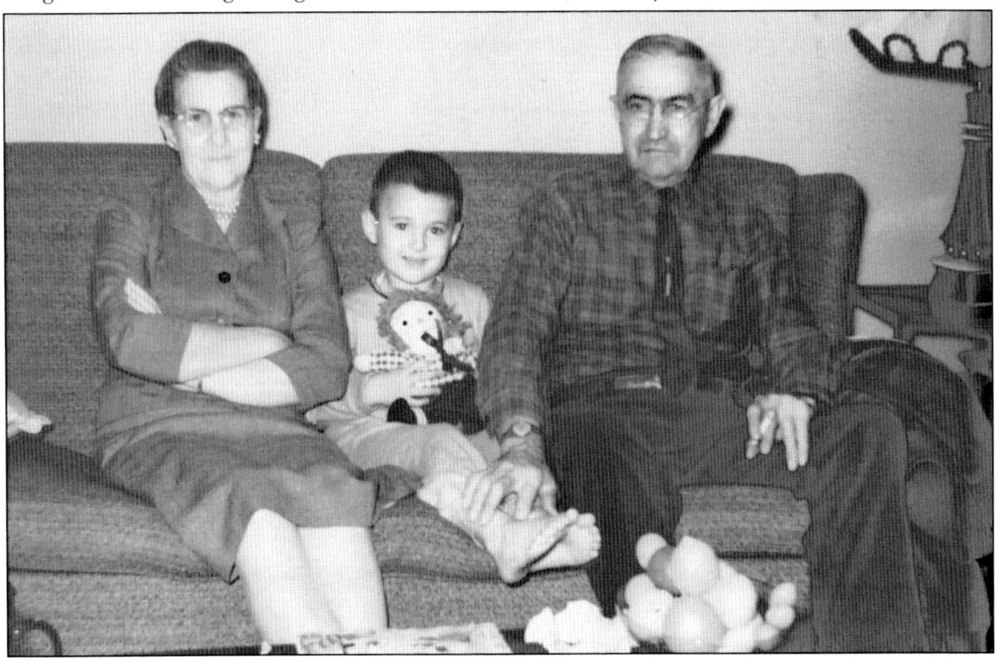

A barefooted, four-year-old Steve Starnes sits here between his grandparents, Eva and John Starnes. Everyone looks happy and content. Maybe they are watching their new television set. Notice the modern furnishings and the *Better Homes and Garden* magazine on the coffee table. (Courtesy of Steve Starnes.)

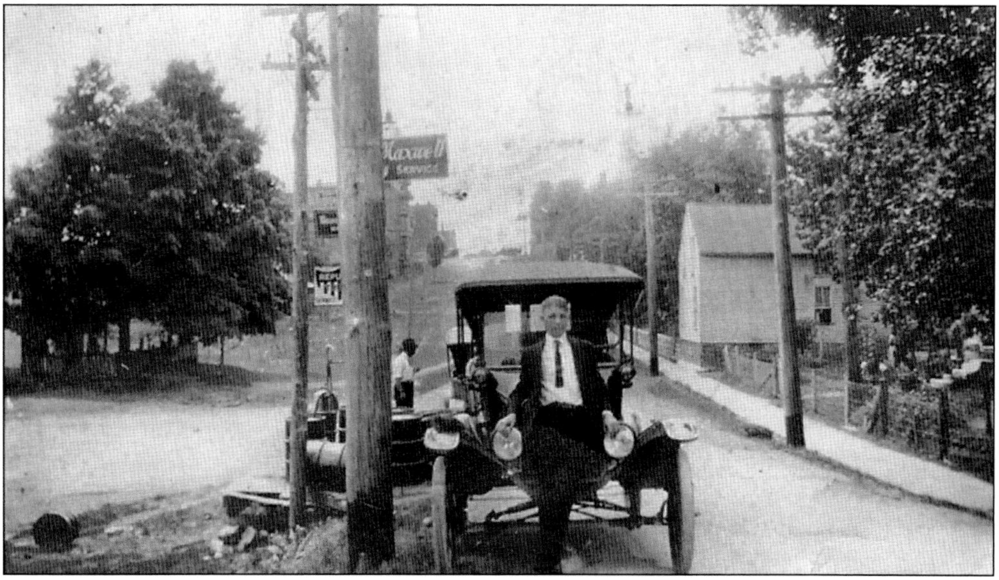

James S. Easterly proudly poses in front of his 1920s Ford automobile. Increased automobiles on the roads also meant the need for road improvements, gasoline stations, and generally increased mobility. The lives of folks began to change in ways they never imagined. (Courtesy of Jim Easterly.)

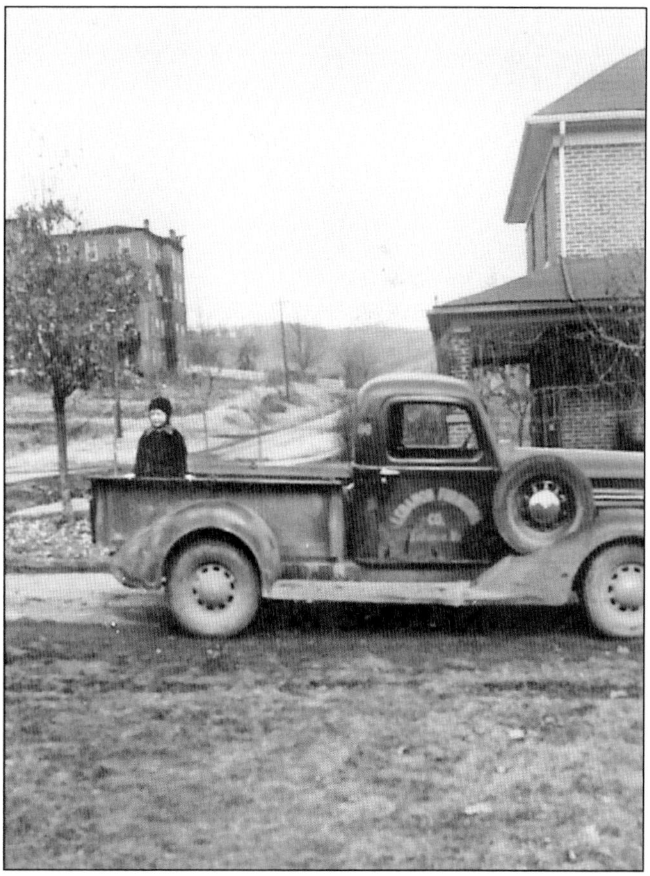

James S. Easterly Jr. is shown here sitting in the back of his father's truck, used as a delivery truck for his father's furniture business. This picture was taken in the early 1940s; local businessmen paid careful attention to the needs of their customers and strove to meet those needs. (Courtesy of Jim Easterly.)

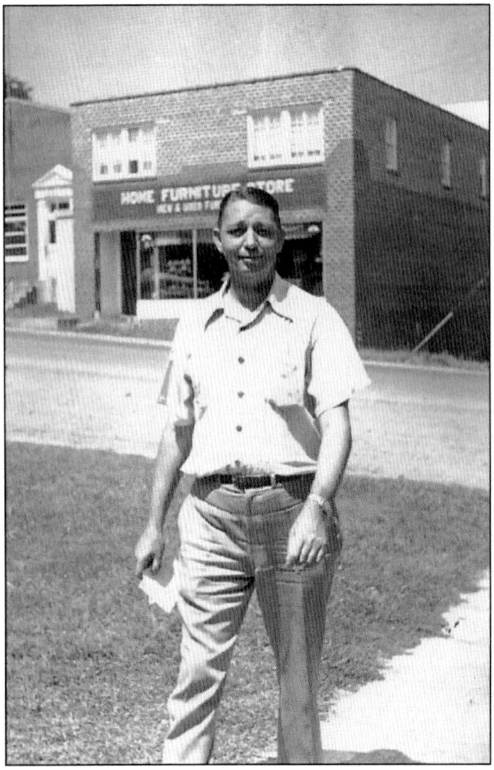

Taken in the early 1940s, this picture shows James Sutton Easterly taking a brisk walk down a street in Lebanon. Easterly founded the Lebanon Furniture Company. His business can be seen in the background. (Courtesy of Jim Easterly.)

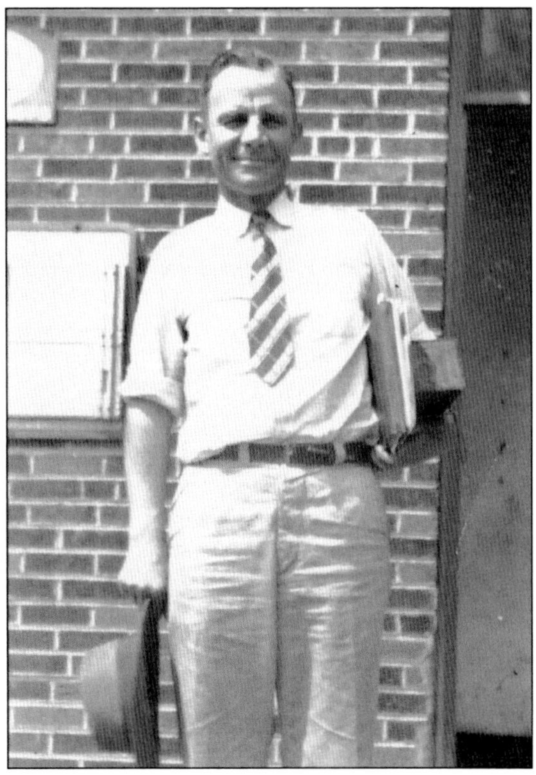

In the early 1940s, Branch Connelly started the Russell County Cooperative. Connelly, pictured here, was the uncle of Jim Easterly. Easterly is a retired Russell County businessman. (Courtesy of Jim Easterly.)

Dr. Walton Carlton Elliott (1903–1984), or Dr. W. C., as he was affectionately known, left his footprints in the medical history of Russell County. He began his medical career in Wilder, Virginia, a coal-mining town in northwestern Russell County. Riding a horse or mule much of the time, he made house calls over a radius of many miles of the rugged hollows and ridges. In 1939, Dr. W. C. and his brother, James W. Elliott, opened the Lebanon General Hospital with 25 beds. In 1930, Dr. W. C. married Margaret Elizabeth Jenks. The couple's children were Nancy Jones, Fred Carlton, and Margaret Ann. After the death of his wife Margaret, Dr. W. C. married Estella Helton Graham. His wide range of professional activities included his service in the Virginia General Assembly as a delegate from 1952 until 1964. (Courtesy of Stella Elliott.)

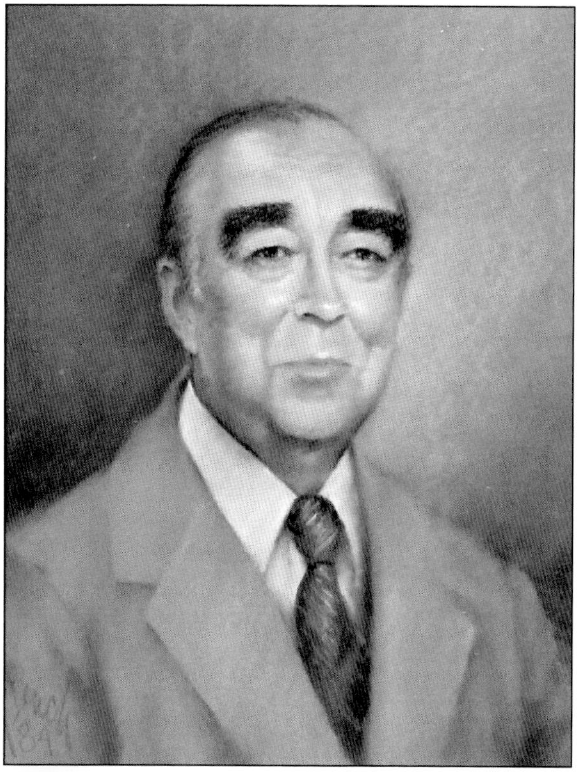

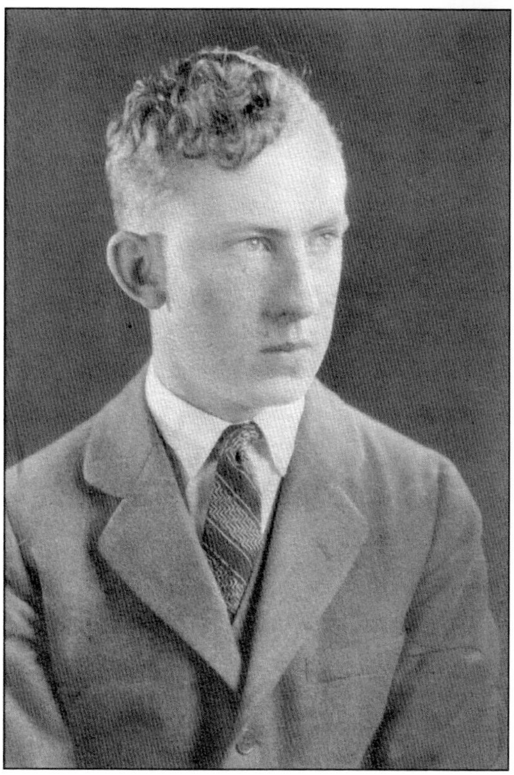

Well known and respected as an entrepreneur, Bill Hendricks founded many businesses in Russell County. In addition to being a successful businessman, Hendricks was the owner of substantial amounts of property in the Lebanon area. He is pictured here as a young man. (Courtesy of Ginny Fuller.)

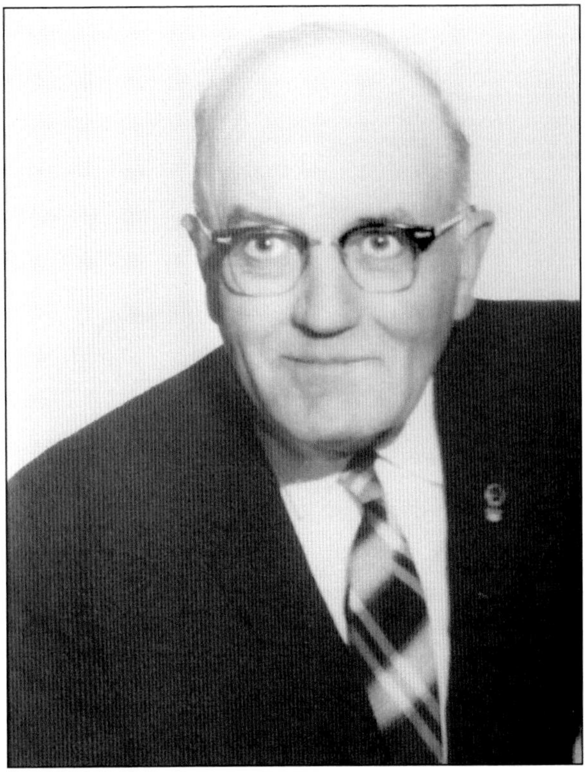

Sherman Wallace (1910–1987) was a member of the Russell County Board of Supervisors for 20 years. He played a major role in bringing many industries to the county and was the primary founder of the Cumberland Plateau Planning District, a four-county economic development agency formulated in 1967. Wallace served on the executive boards of the Virginia Association of Counties, the Lonesome Pine District for Boy Scouts, RCPL, Russell County Cooperative, and the Cumberland Plateau Planning District. He spent his life on a tobacco and cattle farm in Reed's Valley, one mile south of the town of Cleveland. Here he lived with his wife, Ethel, and children, Janette Wagoner, Amelia Flora, Gene Morgan Dean, and Sherman Jr., a prominent Russell County businessman and farmer. (Courtesy of Sherman Wallace Jr.)

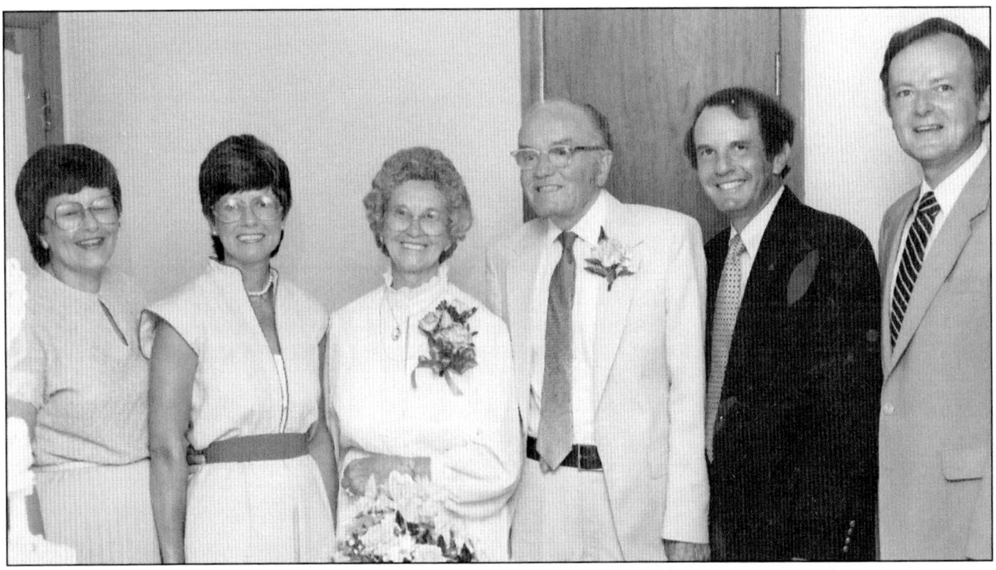

Pictured here are Sherman and Ethel Wallace at the celebration of their 50th wedding anniversary in 1983 with their children. From left to right are Janette Wagoner, Amelia Flora, Ethel, Sherman, Sherman Jr., and Dean. Sherman Wallace was appointed by two Virginia governors to serve two four-year terms on the Conservation and Economic Development Commission representing Virginia's Ninth District. He was also appointed by Gov. John Dalton to serve on the Agriculture and Consumer Affairs Commission. Wallace is well known for his many contributions to Russell County. (Courtesy of Sherman Wallace Jr.)

This 1938 picture reflects a row of Virginia State Police trooper vehicles. Each of the cars is a Ford Roadster except the first, which is a Plymouth. The home in the background is the home of Virginia state trooper Sgt. Charles William Puckett. These vehicles are lined up for the funeral procession of Sergeant Puckett as he is taken to his final resting place. Sergeant Puckett, stationed in Lebanon, died on March 28, 1938, from pneumonia, which he contracted from exposure while performing his duty. He was successful in apprehending the murder suspect but paid the ultimate price to protect the lives of others. Sergeant Puckett was the father of Lewis Puckett of Lebanon. (Courtesy of Ginny Fuller.)

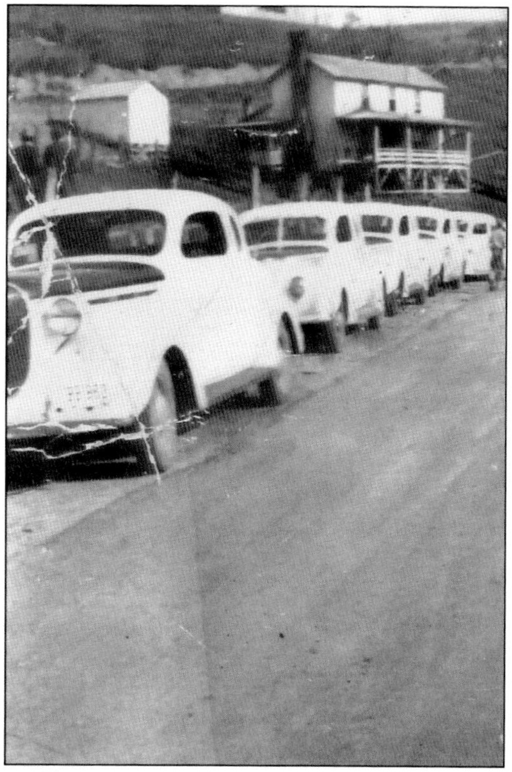

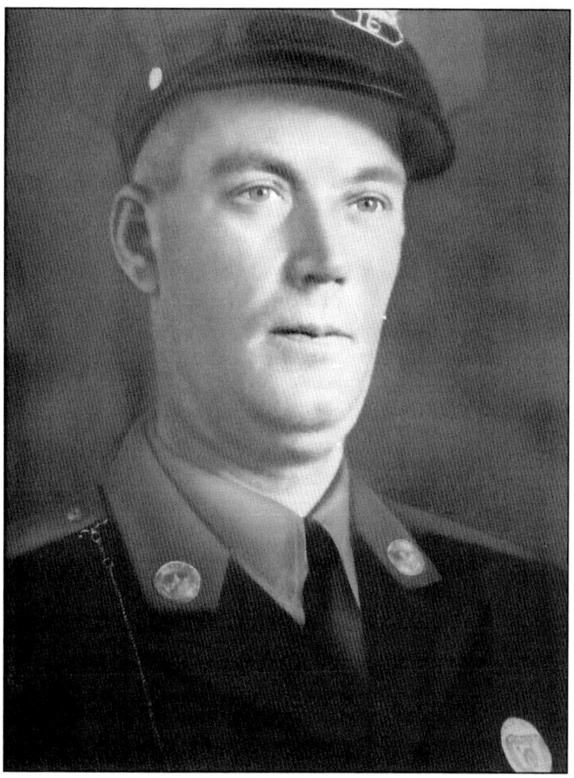

Virginia state trooper Sgt. Charles William Puckett was born in 1892 and died in 1938. (Courtesy of Ginny Fuller.)

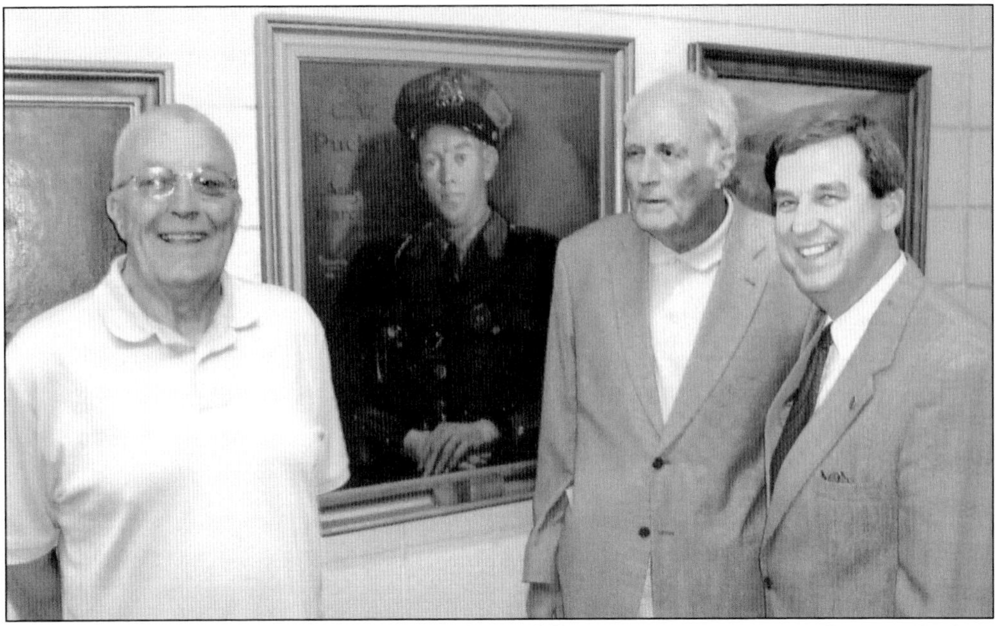

The Pucketts honor Sgt. Charles William Puckett, a fallen Virginia state trooper. Sergeant Puckett died as a result of pneumonia contracted from exposure while apprehending a murder suspect. This picture was taken at the Virginia State Police Academy in Richmond, Virginia. From left to right are L. R. Mack Puckett, the photograph of Sergeant Puckett displayed at the academy, Lewis Puckett, and Virginia State senator Phillip Puckett. (Courtesy of Ginny Fuller.)

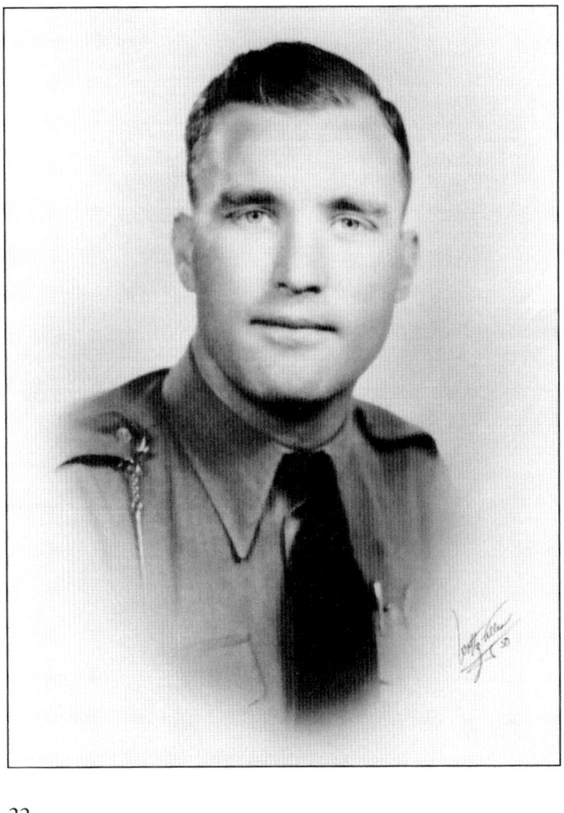

Herman Puckett (1922–1981) entered the U.S. Army in 1944 and served in the European theater until the end of World War II. Herman and his wife, Lillian Kiser Puckett, were married on August 18, 1943, and were the parents of three children: Michael, Phillip, and Ellen. He served as deacon and Sunday school director of the Lebanon Baptist Church and was active in local politics. He served on the Lebanon Town Council for 10 years, served two terms as mayor, and was twice elected to the Russell County Board of Supervisors. He also served several years on the executive board of the Cumberland Plateau Planning District Commission. Herman's son Phillip serves as a state senator for Virginia's 38th District, and his other son, Mike, serves as vice chairman of the Russell County Board of Supervisors. (Courtesy of Ginny Fuller.)

Lebanon resident R. Lewis Puckett served in the U.S. Army during the Korean Conflict from 1951 until 1953. He was one of the eight children of Charles William (the fallen Virginia state trooper) and Callie Breeding Puckett. Lewis had five brothers—Paul, Bill, Lester, Herman, and Mack—and two sisters, Bess and Grace. (Courtesy of Ginny Fuller.)

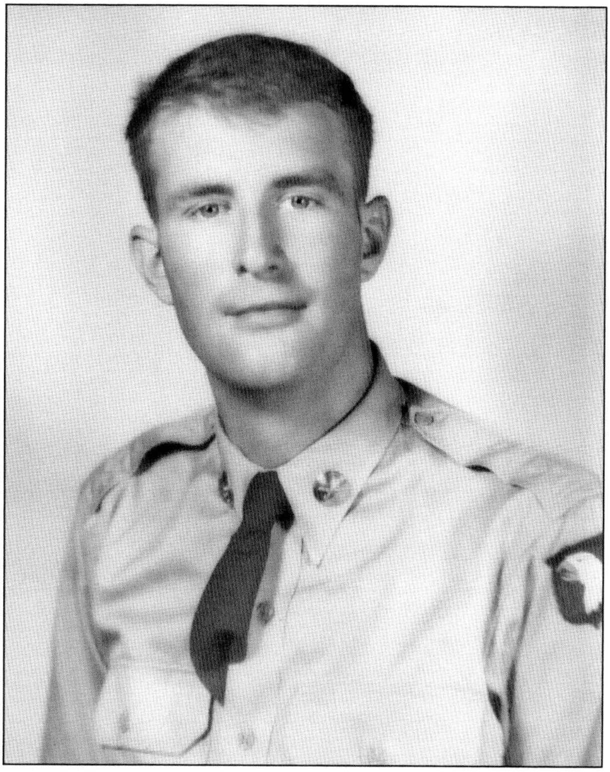

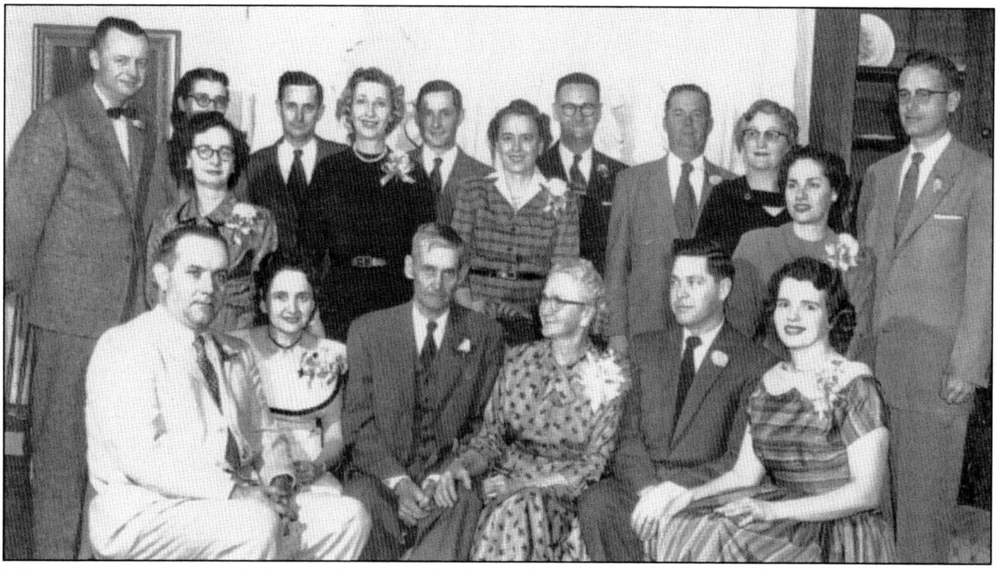

The happy occasion of the celebration of a long, happy marriage was often chronicled with a picture to capture the moment. Here in the center are the anniversary couple—William Robert Howard and Ollie Pearl Taylor, his bride. Also pictured are all of their children and their spouses, including Robert G. Howard, Claude Robert, Margarite Ann Boyd, Eugene Lee, Margaret Stephenson, Ralph Taylor, Dorothy Nell Boyd, Irene Belle, Harold Eugene Taylor, Mary Lucille, James Taylor Skeens, William Sunday, Jeanne Miller, Helen Ruth, Frank R. Finney, Jack Donald, and Joan Wysor. (Courtesy of James C. and Nellie R. Jessee.)

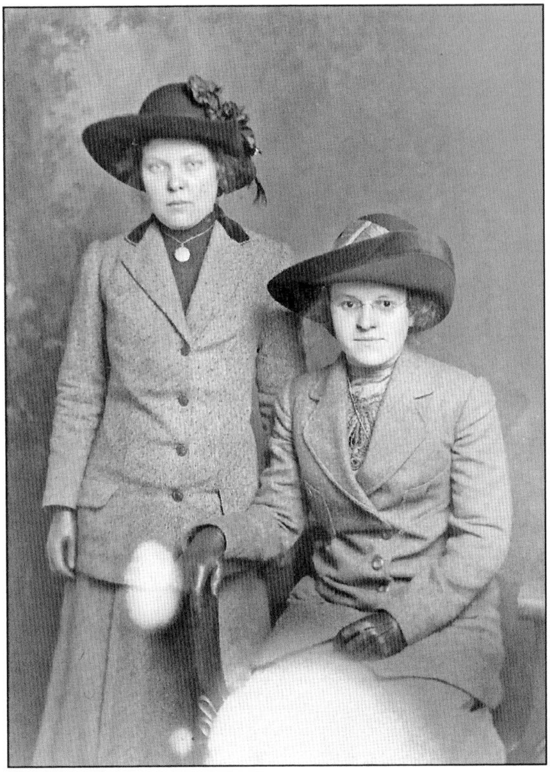

Pictured here are Mabel (left) and Roxie Barrett. This picture is from an old postcard dated 1905. On the back of the postcard is a handwritten note that states these two sisters are the daughters of "Uncle Reese." (Courtesy of HHM, provided by Kathleen R. Taylor.)

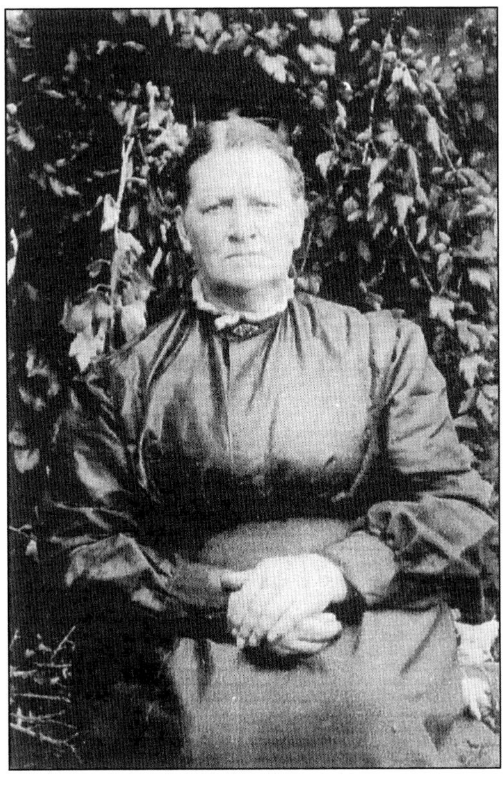

Nancy Catherine Taylor Barrett was born in 1855 and passed away in 1939. In this picture, she wears a dress with lace around the collar and a decorative pin. She was the mother of 13 children. (Courtesy of HHM.)

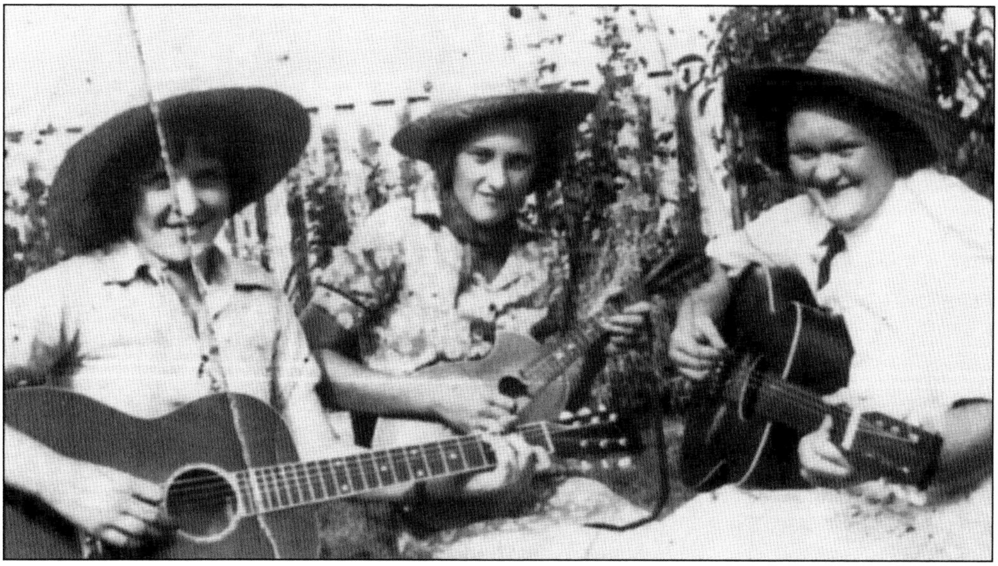

Irene Jessee (left) played the guitar. Anna Jackson (center) played the mandolin and sang tenor. Gladys Jackson (right) played the guitar and was the lead singer. They were known as the Jackson String Band. One band member, Harold Hensley, started playing with "Tennessee" Ernie Ford, moved to Hollywood, and was in the movies. The Jackson String Band played at theaters, conventions, reunions, churches, and broadcasts. Some of their songs most often requested by listeners were "Wildwood Flower," "Davey Crockett," "When the Roll is Called up Yonder," and "Canaan's Land," to name a few. (Courtesy of HHM.)

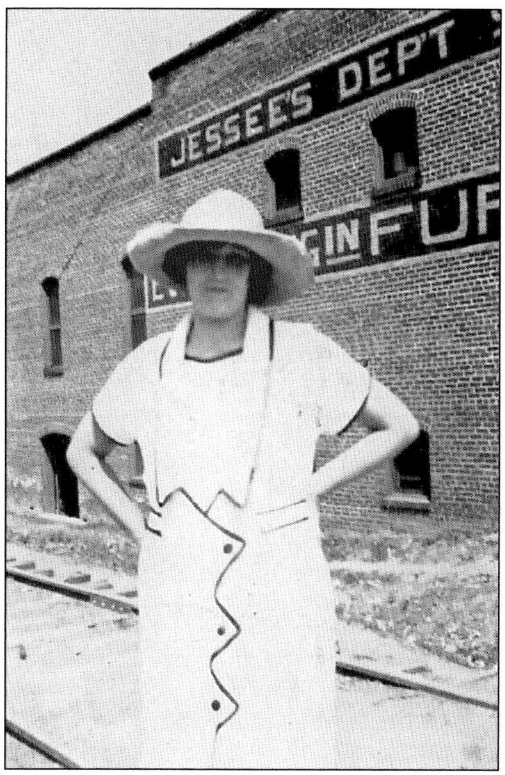

In front of the Claude Jessee Department Store in 1935 is Grace Fleenor. Grace is dressed up and looking pretty. Going to town was an event. Folks dressed up for the occasion. It was an opportunity to catch up on the events of the day. (Courtesy of Mrs. Ralph Owen.)

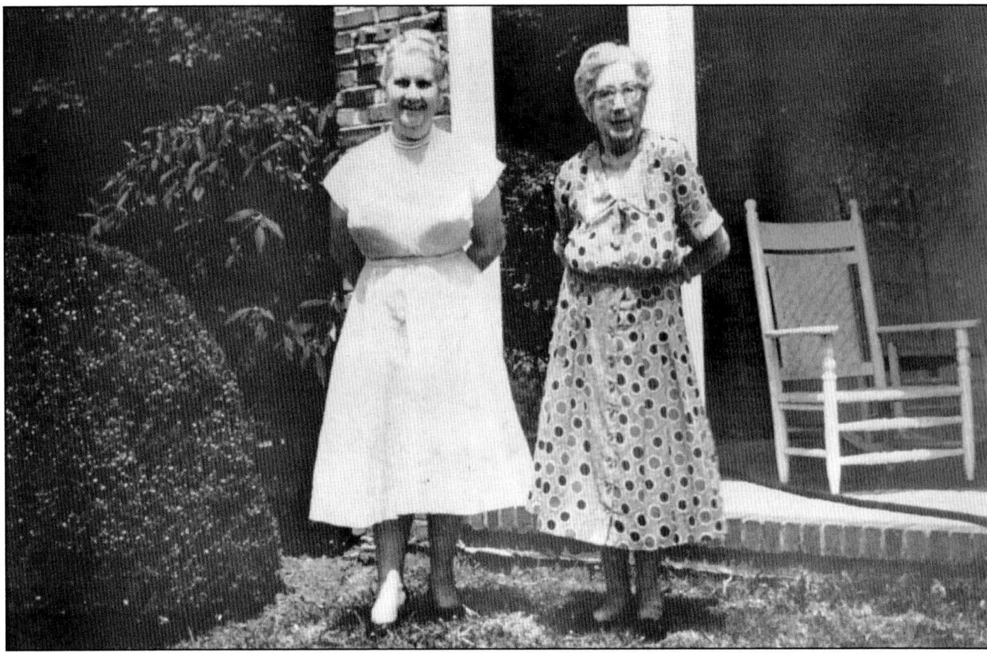

Verna Routh (left) and Rose Smith pose for this picture on a bright, warm day in the late 1920s. Behind them and just steps away are the front porch and that great invention—the rocking chair. At a time when the pace was slower and folks stopped to pass the time of day, many an hour was spent rocking on the front porches of homes across Russell County. (Courtesy of Jim Easterly.)

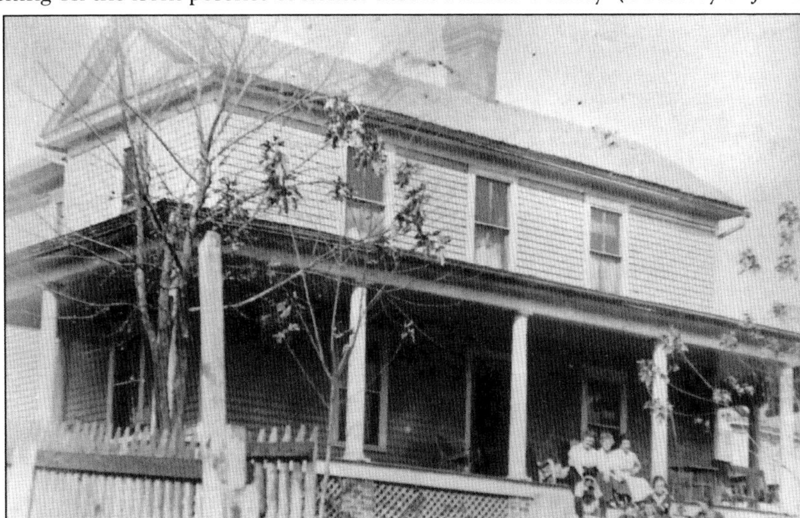

This home was built for Charles W. Hurt in 1904 by Dow Fletcher and is pictured on November 11, 1918. The house is still standing near the Honaker High School. This home was sold to the Russell County School Board in 1954 for use as a home for the principal of the Honaker High School, A. P. Baldwin. The well-known and loved principal Baldwin lived there from 1954 until 1976. It had by then become known as the Baldwin House. It is currently known as the Redbud House, in honor of Honaker, which is acclaimed as the Redbud Capital of the World. (Courtesy of HHM, provided by Kathleen R. Taylor.)

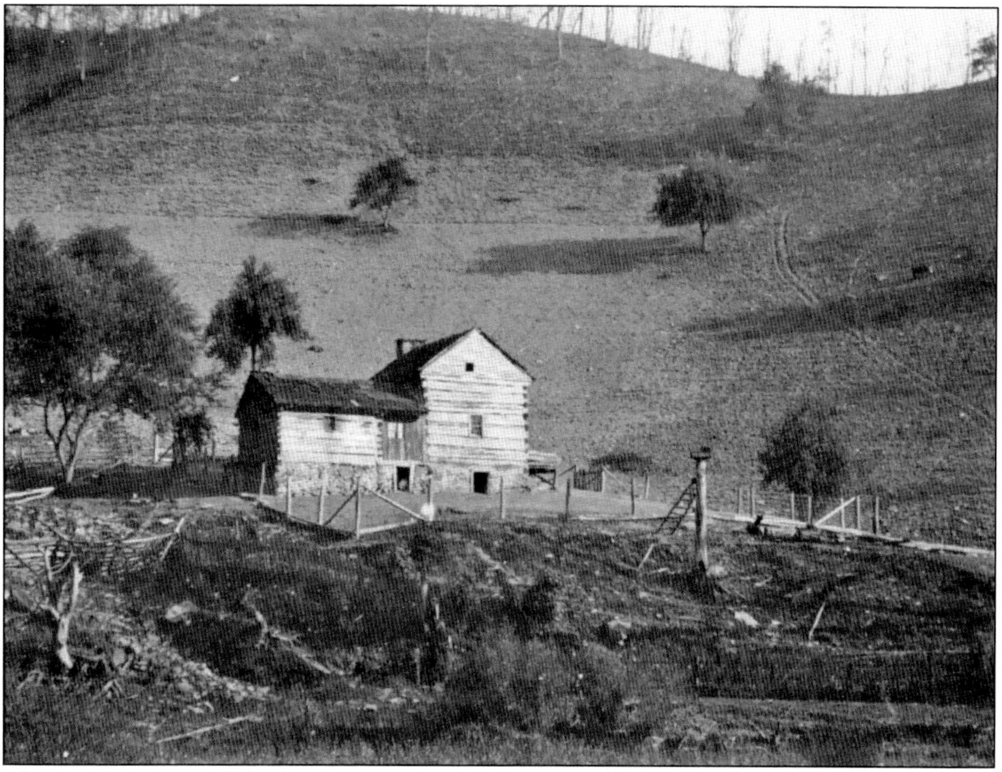

This 1957 picture is of the Noah Counts home, which was built on Lick Creek in Russell County in 1813. With the many county boundary line changes since it was first built in 1813, it was first located in Russell County, then in Buchanan County, and is now located in Dickenson County. (Courtesy of RCPL, provided by Bill and Toy Sutherland.)

The home of James Jasper Bays was located in Elk Garden, Russell County, Virginia. This home is typical of the log construction of the day. Notice the white horse in the foreground, indicative of the primary method of transportation of the day. (Courtesy of RCPL, provided by Barry Hess.)

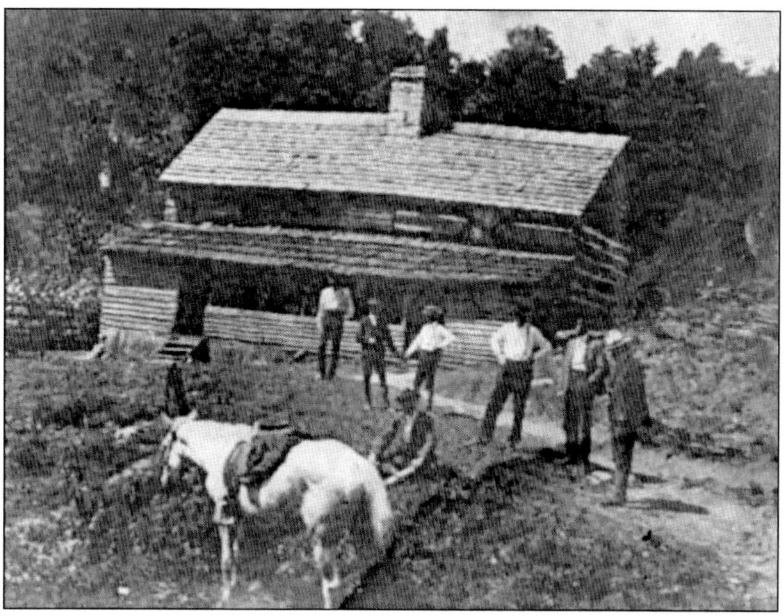

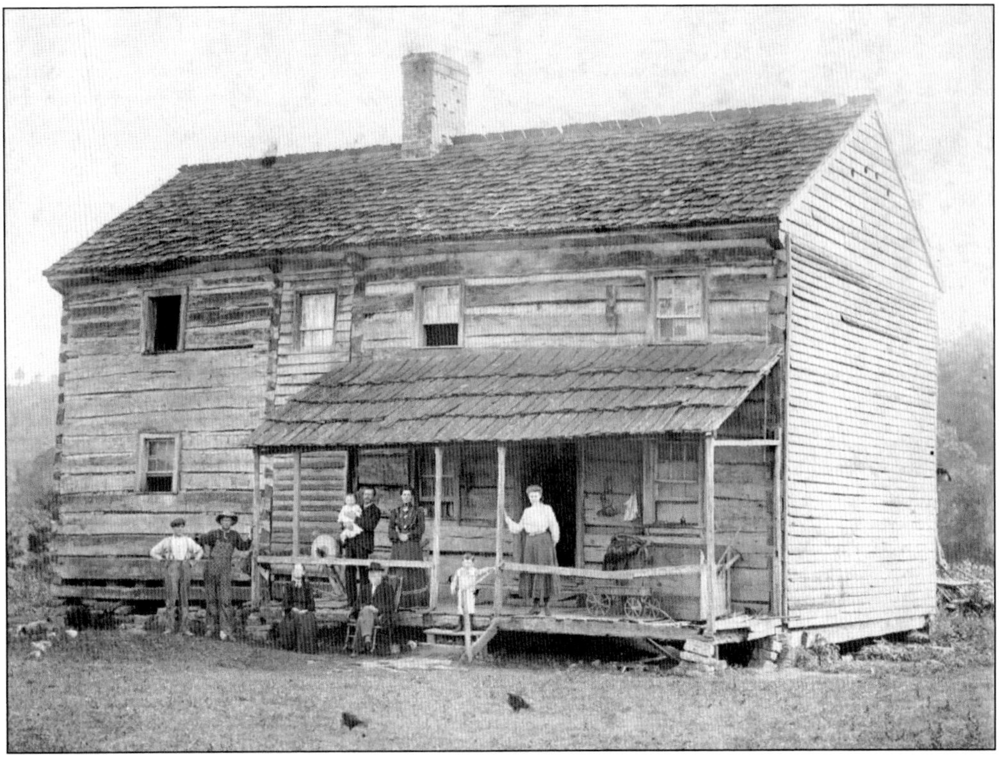

The historic Dickenson house was built on the Clinch River in 1771 by Henry Dickenson, the first clerk of Russell County. From left to right in 1905 are (first row, seated) Elizabeth Gibson and Henry Patton Dickenson; (second row) probably a Mr. Campbell; Jim Jessee; Frank and Lula Dickenson and their sons, Randolph (in arms) and Franklin (on steps); and Eliza Gibson Perry (on porch). Notice the wood box on the front porch and the child's wagon. This was the first and only home of Henry Dickenson, who lived to be 93 years old and left his home only when driven away by the Native Americans who forced him and his family to take refuge for a brief time at the fort of Castle's Wood (now Castlewood). (Courtesy of RCPL, provided by Hope Dickenson.)

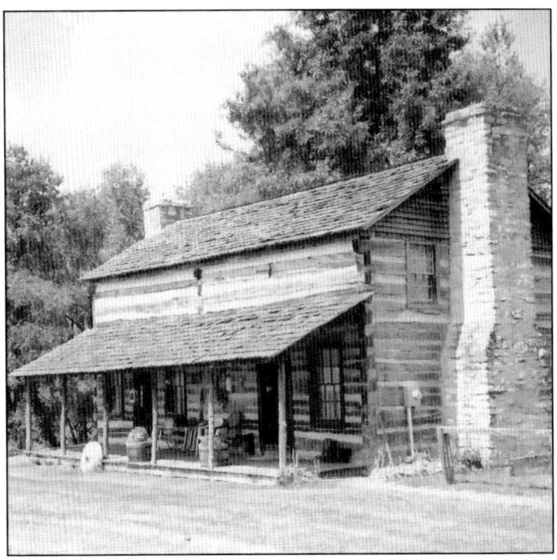

The Dickenson Log House was donated to Russell County by Donald and Virginia Gray, owners of the old Henry Dickenson farm on Clinch River. As part of a bicentennial project, this log cabin was moved to its present-day location on the grounds of the old courthouse property at Dickensonville. More than 90 percent of the logs were considered to be sound. Some of the logs were as much as 30 or more feet long. The heirs of James ("Jim Frosty") Dickenson provided the Bundy Log House to be made a part of the project. The logs from both homes were then utilized to reconstruct the Dickenson-Bundy Log House. (Courtesy of Andrew Chafin.)

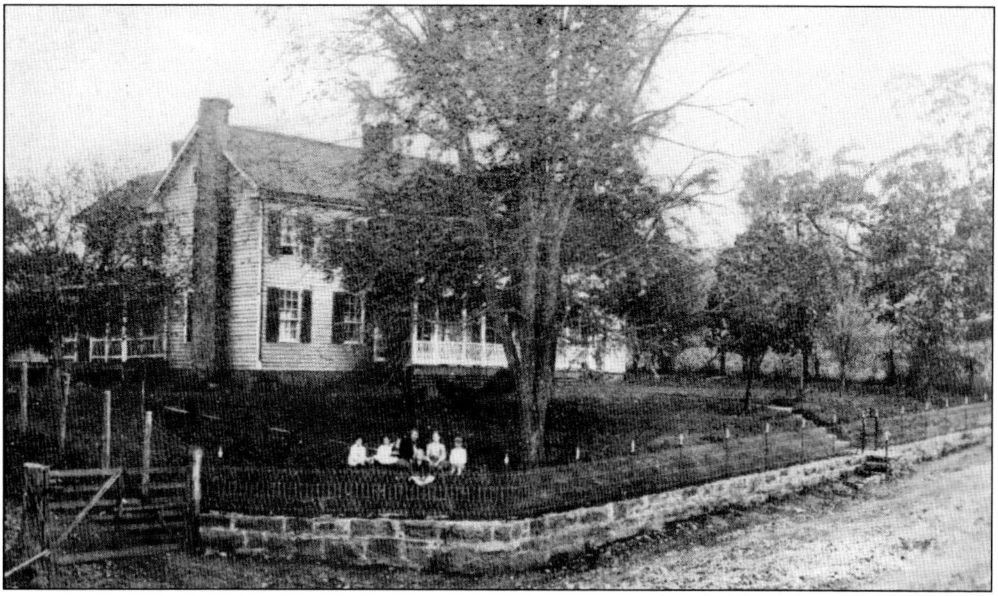

The Wayside creates an inviting picture around 1890. The Wayside was the ancestral home of Rosalind Dickenson and Emily Dickenson Lyttle. It was the original home of John Bickley. John Bickley was the great-great-grandfather of these two ladies. The Wayside was located at Bickley Mills. The house had 12 rooms and was more than 100 years old when it burned in the 1920s. Pictured on the front lawn are some of the family children. (Courtesy of RCPL, provided by Eugenia D. and Ed Dorton.)

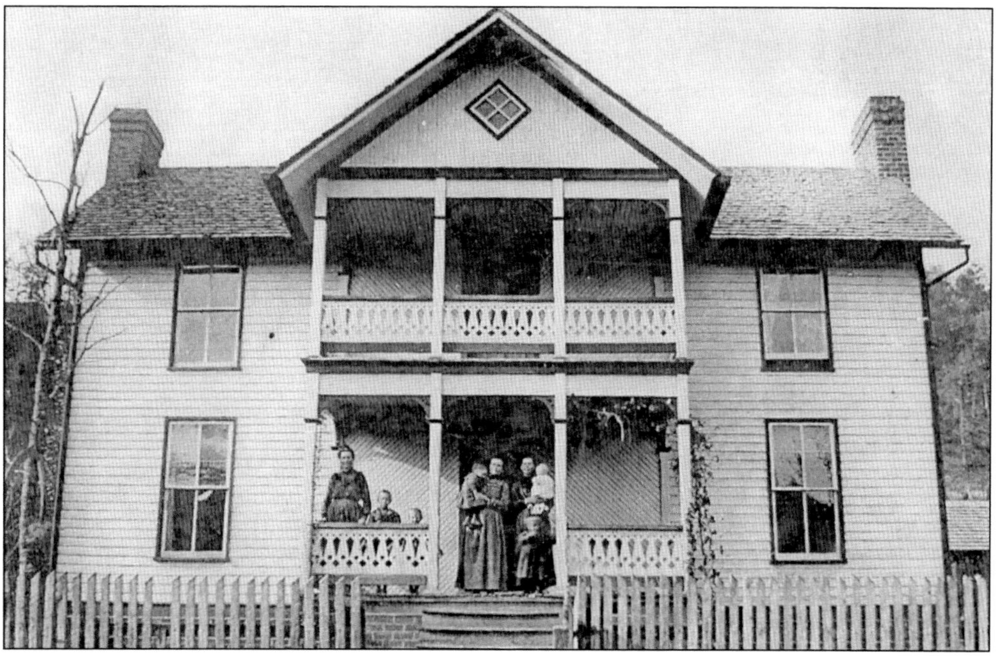

This photograph was taken sometime between 1885 and 1895. It shows the home of Elijah Beauregard "Gard" and Winnie (Kiser) Sutherland. The home place was located in Carbo, Virginia. Notice the additional porch on the second story and the fence in the front. (Courtesy of RCPL, provided by Evelyn Meyer.)

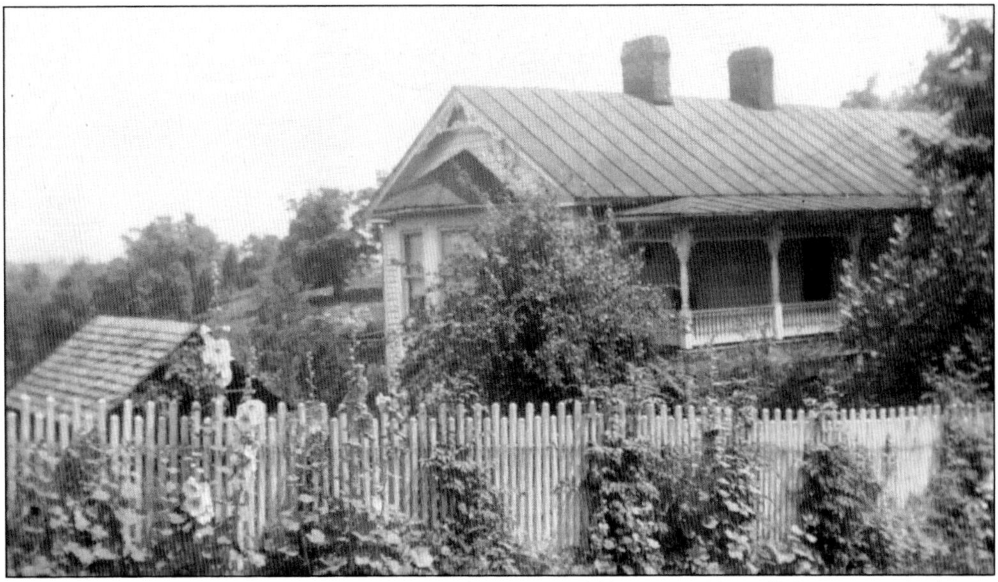

Photographed in 1939 as part of a project to document old homes in Russell County is the home of Wade and Grace Dickenson, located in Castlewood. Notice the smokehouse on the front and to the left, as well as the lovely design on the porch and fence railing. (Courtesy of RCPL, provided by Hope Dickenson.)

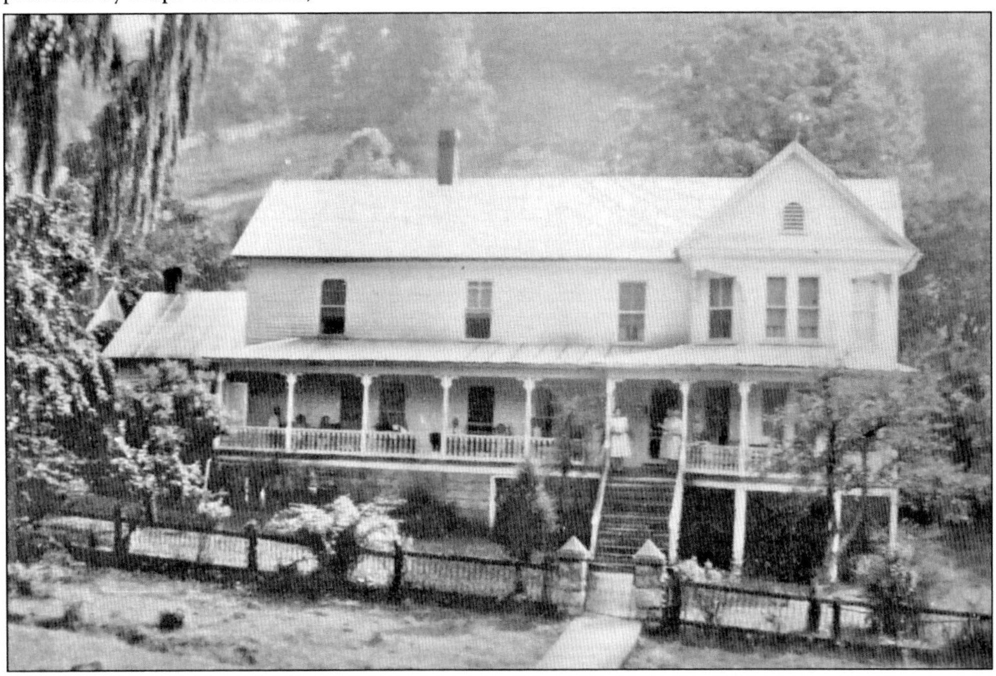

Pictured is the Purcell House in Cleveland, Virginia. Cleveland was located on the north side of the Clinchfield Coal Corporation, which had mines at Wilder and Dante. On August 1, 1890, the first passenger train to "run over" the Clinch Valley Division of the Norfolk and Western passed through the town. J. P. Purcell and Boyce and Hendricks were some of the first stores to open about 1890. This lovely home with its spacious wraparound porch surely provided a pleasant and inviting place to enjoy time with family and friends. (Courtesy of James C. and Nellie R. Jessee.)

In 1912, Dr. Claborn Baker Greear began to build this home in East Honaker. Though it was located away from the downtown businesses, he felt the town as it expanded would do so in that direction. He was accurate in this belief. Each block that was used in the house was made by Dr. Greear and another man by the name of Honaker using an iron mold. Twenty blocks at a time were made and then spread out on the adjoining church property as they dried. Dr. Greear's home had the first residential heating system in town. Notice the watering trough in the foreground. (Courtesy of HHM, provided by Kathleen R. Taylor.)

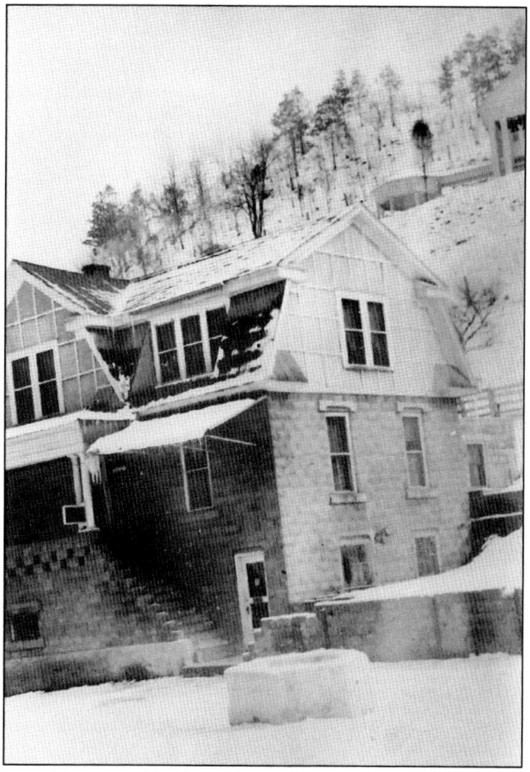

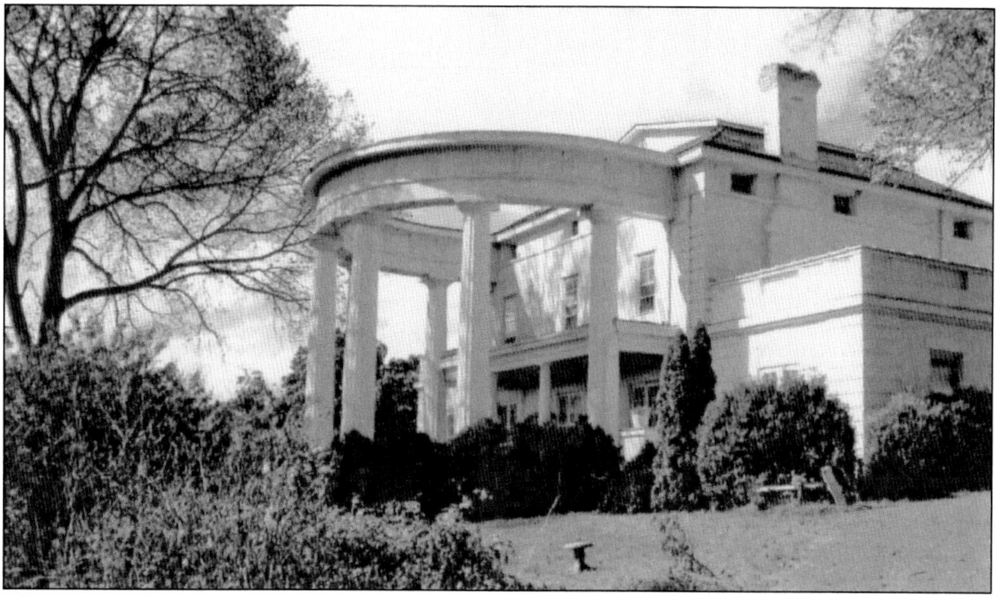

The Stuart Residence in Elk Garden, shown in 1950, was the home of Gov. Henry C. Stuart, a renowned farmer and cattleman. He was governor of Virginia from 1914 until 1918. The original estate contained over 60,000 acres at the time. The landholdings were so vast the land was actually in parts of four different counties—Russell, Tazewell, Smyth, and Dickenson. The bricks for the home were made on the property. The foundation was 18 inches and was made from local limestone. (Courtesy of Barry Hess.)

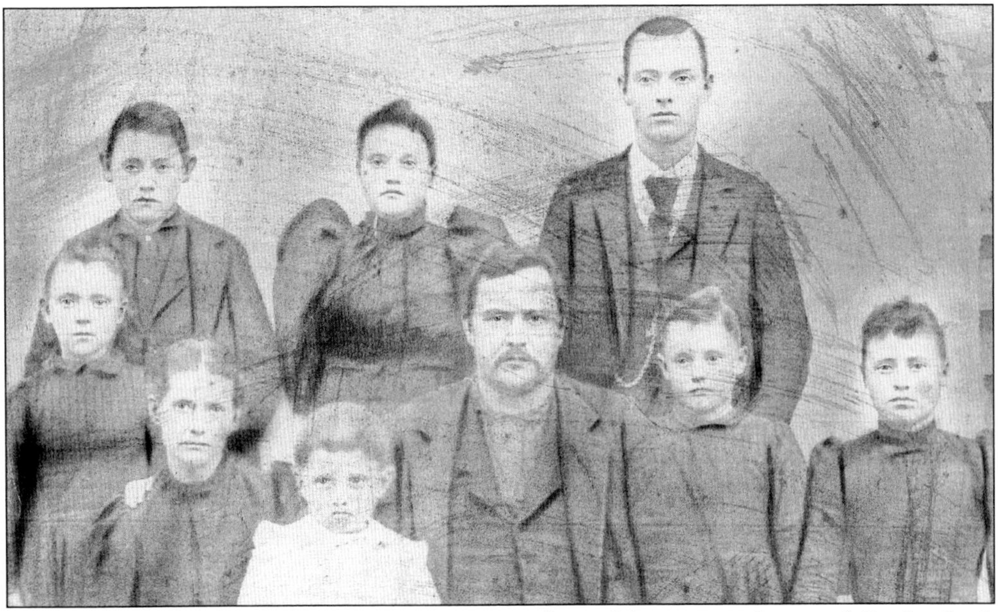

Issac V. Cook Hart (known as "Big Ike") was a grandson of the pioneers Issac and Cecilia Cook Hart, who settled on what became known as Hart's Creek in Russell County. They originally owned nearly 800 acres of land in that area. Many descendants of Big Ike still live in the Russell County area. From left to right are (first row) Edna Mae McGlothlin, Phoebe Ann Musick Hart, Frank Hart, Issac V. Cook Hart, Emma McGlothlin, and Nannie Bell Smith; (second row) Della Hart, Ada Wilson, and Charlie Hart. (Courtesy of RCPL.)

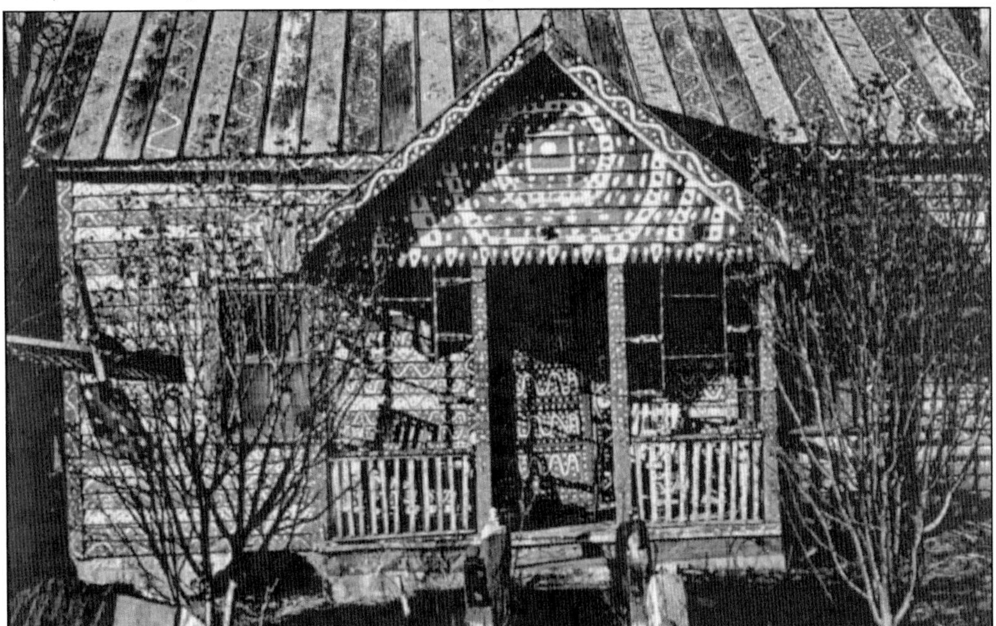

Affectionately known by his friends as "Creek Charlie," Charlie Fields spent the 83 years of his life on Big Cedar Creek. Here he built (with logs over 100 years old) and decorated his home. Literally thousands of people came each year to see his unique home, and each year for as long as he was able to hold a paintbrush, he would redecorate. (Courtesy of RCPL, provided by Barry Hess.)

One year, Charlie Fields's house was red, white, and blue. He loved his country and proudly displayed its colors. Another year, the house was painted with red and white stripes. Still another year, his selection was a polka-dot pattern. "Creek Charlie" also painted the furniture and the inside of his home. (Courtesy of RCPL, provided by Barry Hess.)

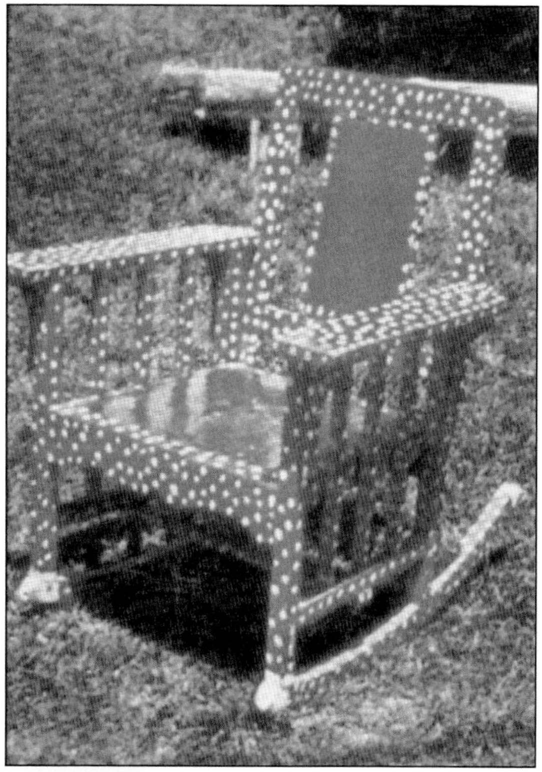

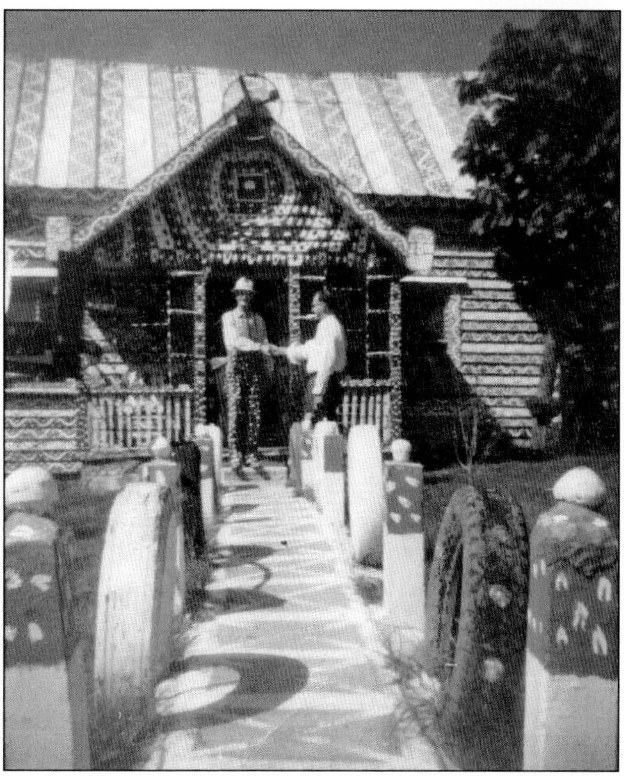

The Charlie Fields house had dozens of wind chimes and gadgets that surrounded his home and made a distinct sound. These items added sound to the wonderful visual that was his home. (Courtesy of James C. and Nellie R. Jessee.)

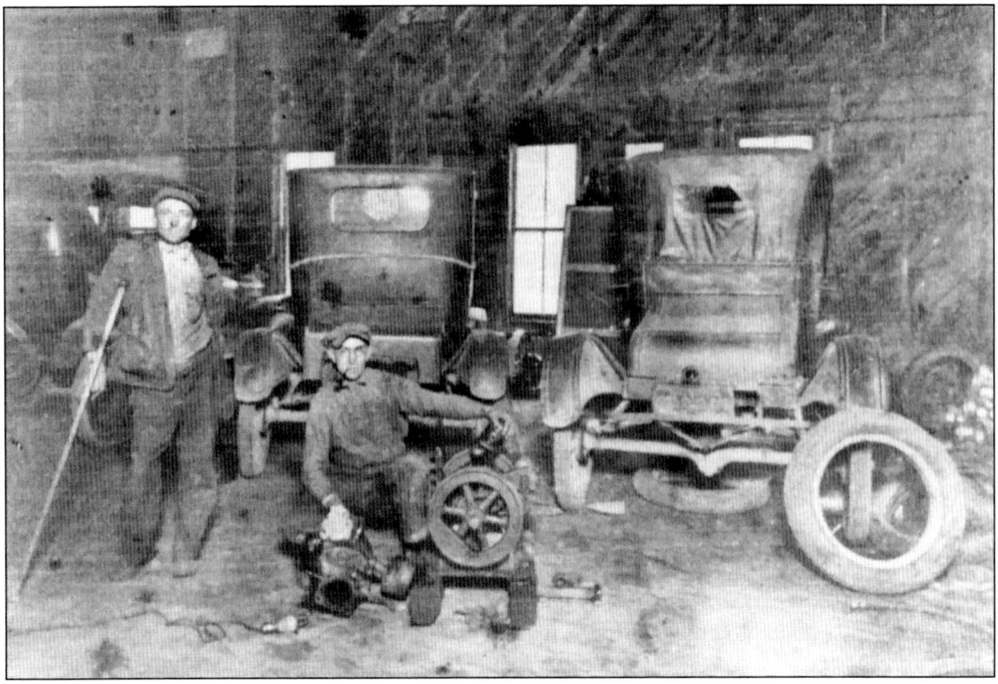

This 1920 photograph shows John Starnes's garage in Honaker, where Starnes worked on Model Ts. Few garages were available, and Starnes always had a steady business keeping the Model Ts running. The gentleman using the crutch is Dewey Harrison. (Courtesy of Steve Starnes.)

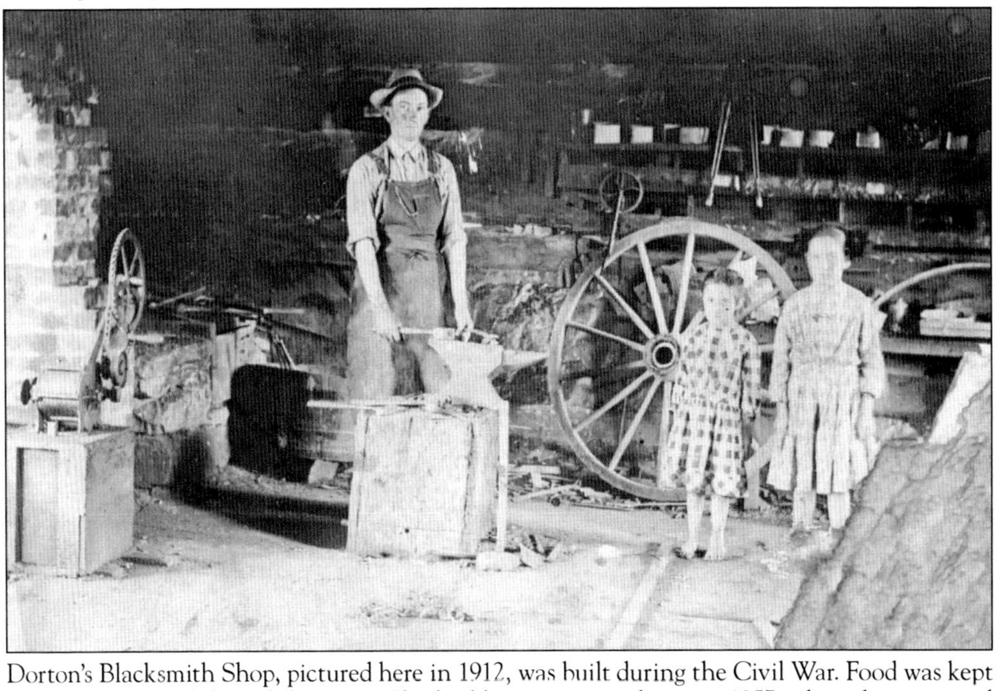

Dorton's Blacksmith Shop, pictured here in 1912, was built during the Civil War. Food was kept hidden under coal for safe keeping. The building was torn down in 1957, when the new road came through on Route 71 between Dogtown and Nickelsville. (Courtesy of RCPL, provided by Eugenia D. and Ed Dorton.)

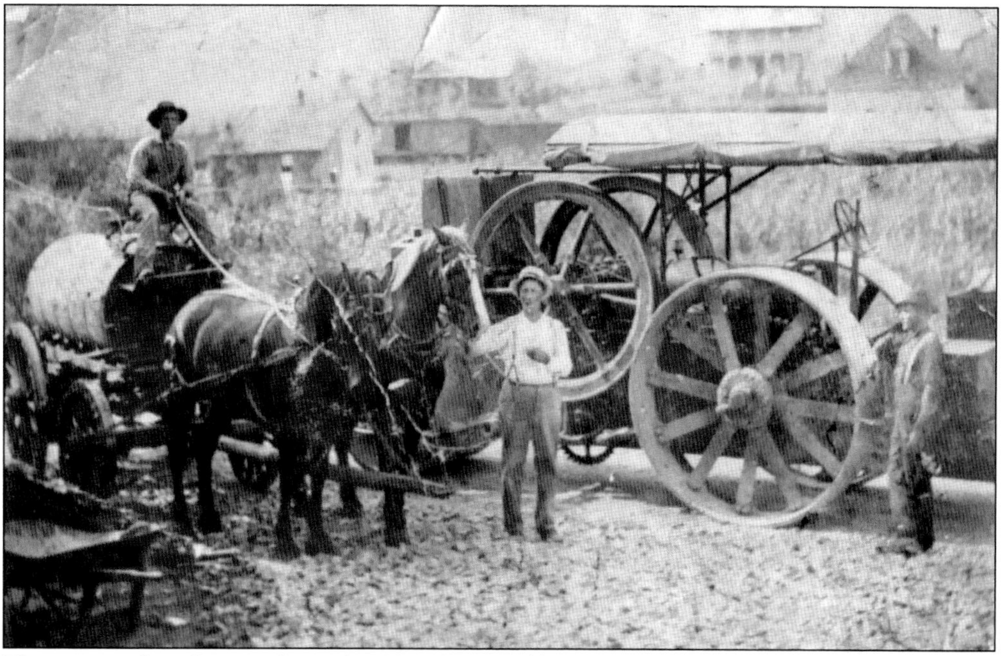

This scene takes place in the early 1920s. Depicted here is a road paving crew. Notice the water wagon to the left. The piece of equipment to the right is the steamroller. The ever-more-popular automobiles and the desire of folks to be more mobile created a demand for better roads. (Courtesy of RCPL, provided by Claude E. Griffith.)

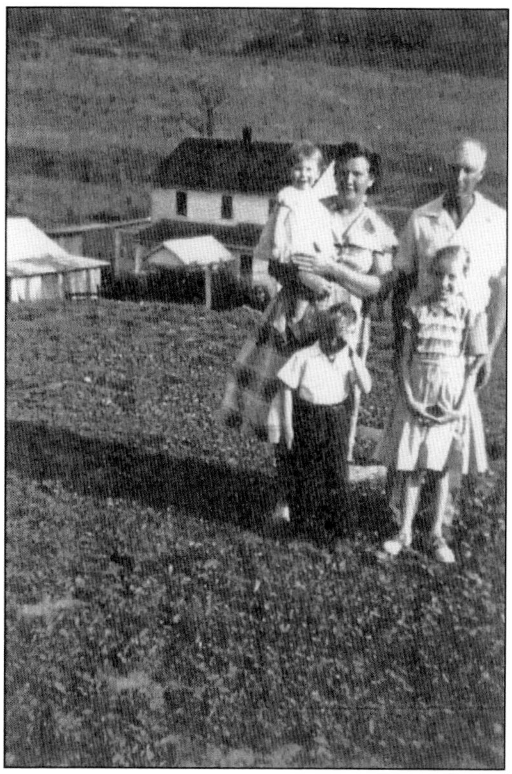

The Poor Farm located in Russell County, as its name implies, was a place of sanctuary for those with no other means to meet their needs for food, clothing, and shelter. Residents worked on the farm to earn their keep. The last overseer of the farm was Lon Hess. He is pictured here with his wife, Ethel, and their grandchildren, from left to right, Velma Breeding, Richard Breeding, and Shirley Breeding. When the farm closed in 1957, Hess purchased it at auction. (Courtesy of RCPL.)

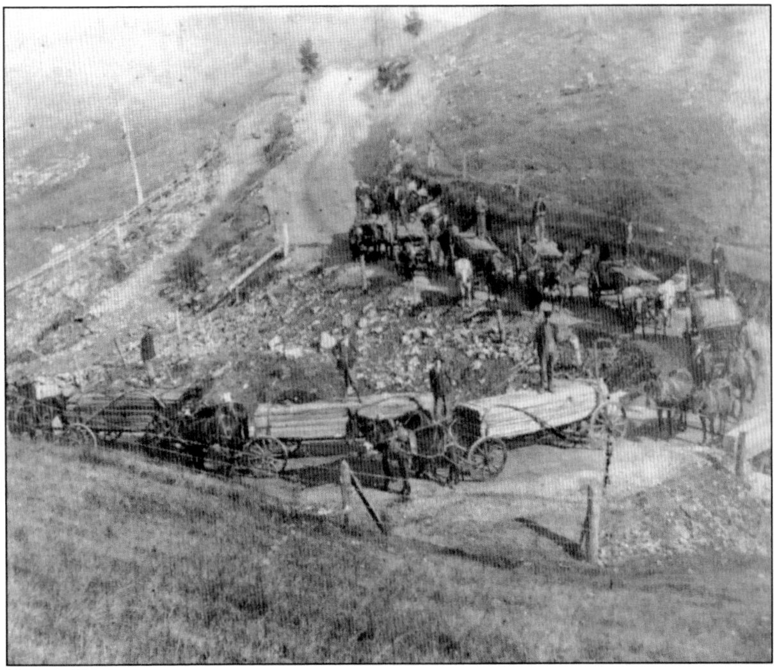

This scene in Cleveland in the 1920s or 1930s shows a lumber crew traveling down the dirt road with a load of lumber. The lumber had to be transported by horse to get to the lumber mill or the railroad for shipment. Present in the picture are Sam Campbell, Bill Campbell, Elihue Campbell, Jim Price, and Vic Taylor. (Courtesy of RCPL, provided by Alma Lester.)

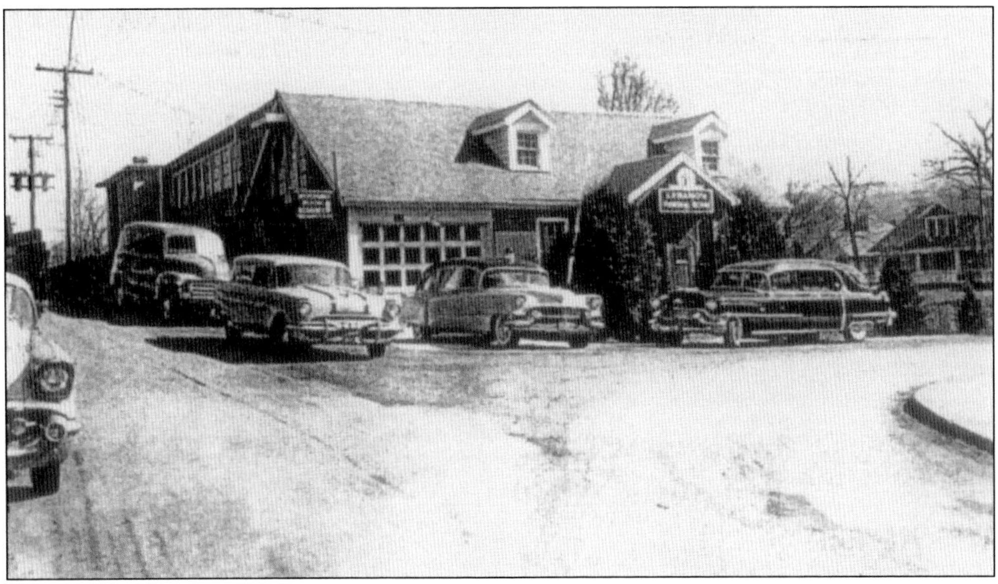

The Finney-Easterly Funeral Home is pictured here around 1950, a modern funeral home meeting the needs of the community. Prior to the establishment of funeral homes, bodies were kept at home until burial services. Family members came from all around to the home of the deceased, bringing food and comfort to the family. Someone in the family, out of respect, would sit up with the body during the night. Oftentimes family and friends would have traveled long distances to pay their last respects and would stay for a number of days. Many tell stories of the excitement of seeing seldom-seen family and remembering happier times; it would sometimes get the best of folks, and the event would take on the appearance of a reunion—meaning no disrespect, just that everyone was so happy to see one another and spend time together. (Courtesy of RCPL, provided by J. C. Jessee.)

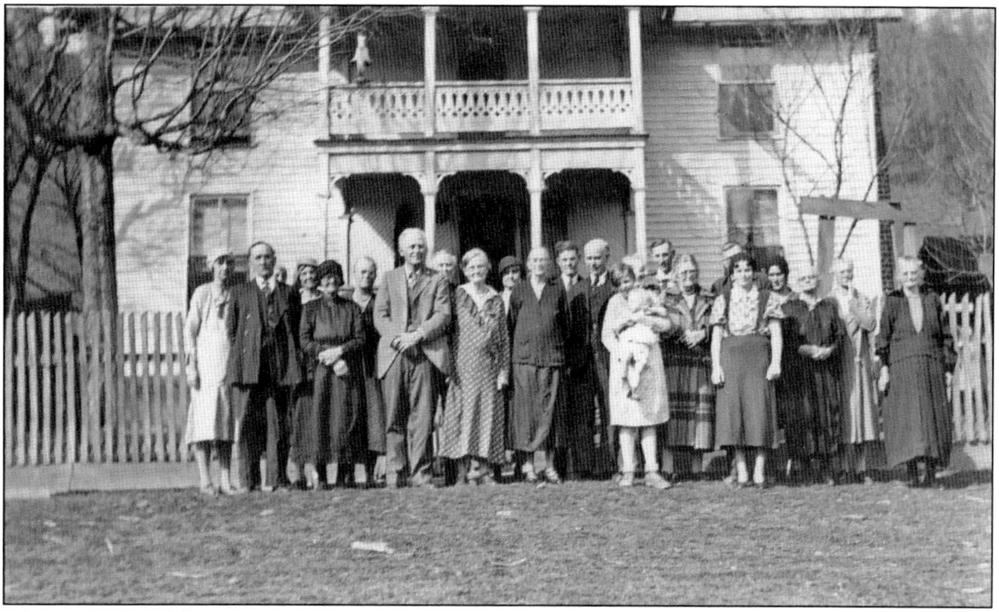

The Sutherland home place, located in Carbo, is seen on the occasion of the 50th wedding anniversary of E. B. "Gard" and Winnie (Kiser) Sutherland. The couple was married on January 31, 1883. (Courtesy of RCPL, provided by Evelyn Meyer.)

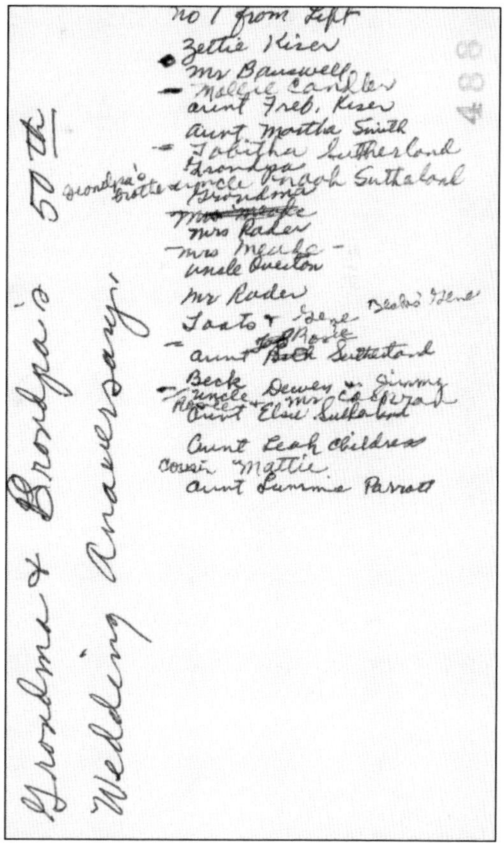

Grandma & Grandpa's 50th Wedding Anniversary

no 1 from Left
Zettie Kiser
Mr Barnswell
Mollie Candler
aunt Freb. Kiser
aunt Martha Smith
Tabitha Sutherland
Grandpa
grandpa's brother uncle Noah Sutherland
Grandma
mrs Rader
mrs Meade
uncle Overton
mr Rader
Toots & Gene
aunt Rosie Sutherland
Beck Dewey & Jimmy
uncle mr C. C. Grant
aunt Elsie Sutherland
aunt Leah Childress
Cousin Mattie
aunt Summie Parrott

This note, lovingly written, includes for all times the names of those attending the 50th wedding anniversary of E. B. "Gard" and Winnie (Kiser) Sutherland. (Courtesy of RCPL, provided by Evelyn Meyer.)

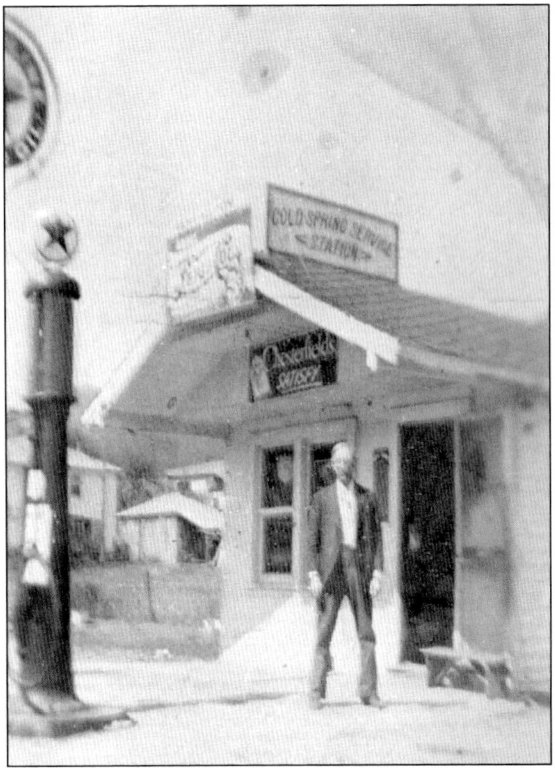

Near Elk Garden School, this classic yesteryear service station beckons to all who pass it, with its huge gas pump reaching high into the sky to announce its existence. This station was known as the Smithfield Service Station and the Cold Springs Service Station. (Courtesy of RCPL, provided by Dave Leonard.)

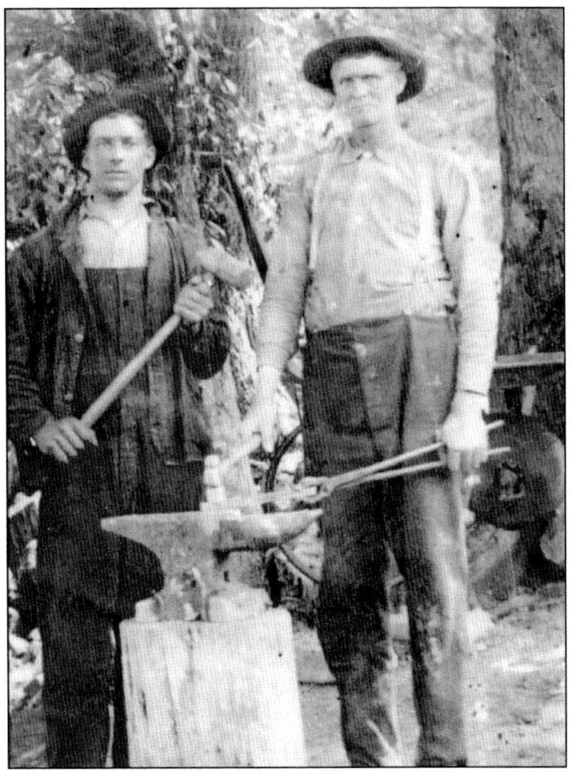

Pictured here are James Henry Campbell (left) and George W. Campbell on the day they began their blacksmith shop in August 1873 in Castlewood. (Courtesy of Beulah H. and George J. Campbell, provided by Patricia Garrett.)

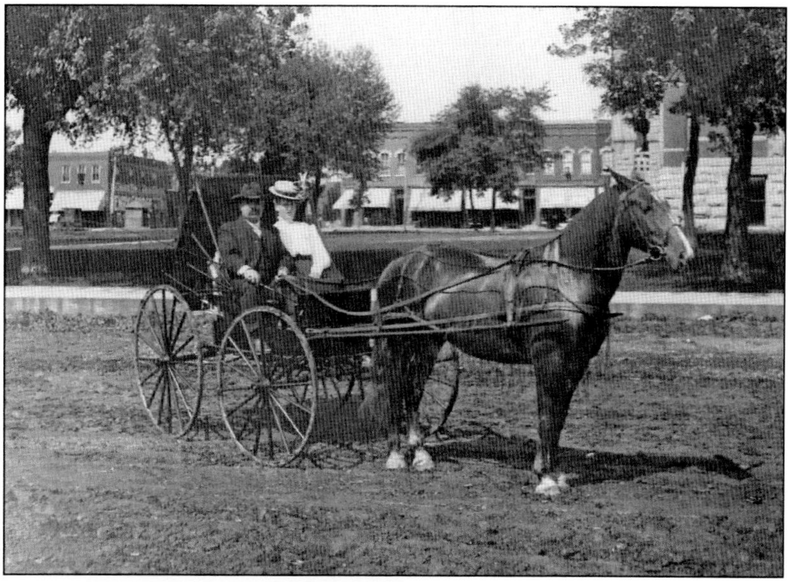

This picture is of Louise Sternberg. Notes on the reverse of the picture indicate that Mr. and Mrs. Sternberg traveled in their new horse and buggy to Dundee from Hampton, Iowa, and that it took 10 days to make the trip. (Courtesy of HHM.)

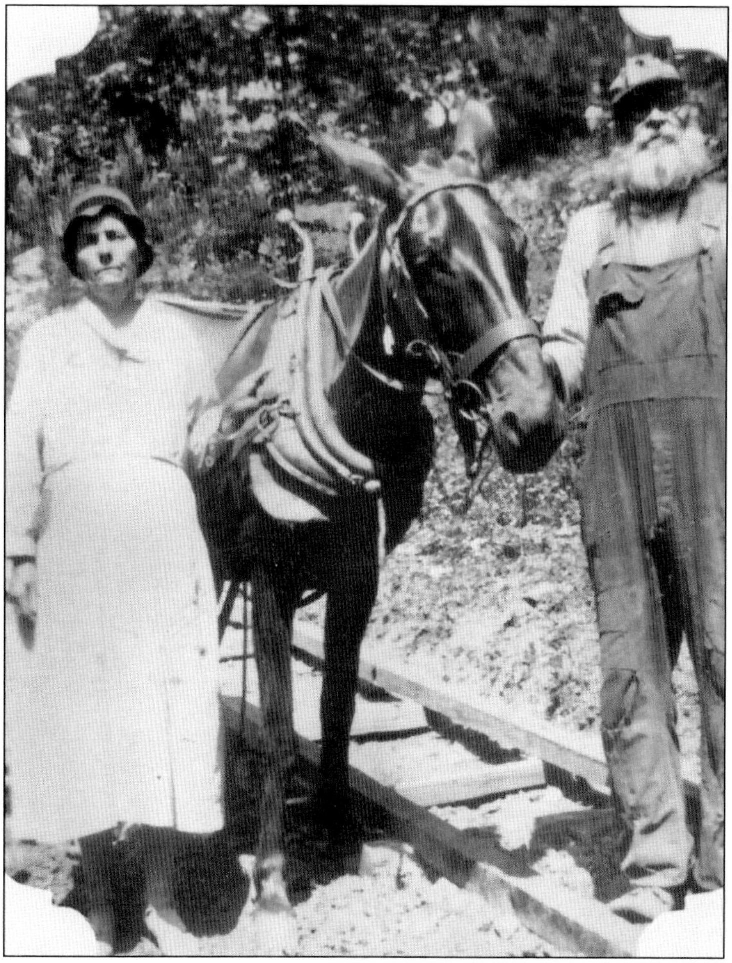

Jane Dishman Ramsey and Buck Ramsey are using a mule to help pull a cart filled with coal from a small truck mine. Sometimes on a farm, there would be a coal seam big enough to supply the needs of the family and even enough to sell to nearby friends and neighbors. This was known as truck mining. This picture was taken in the 1940s in Gravel Lick. (Courtesy of Beulah H. and George J. Campbell, provided by Patricia Garrett.)

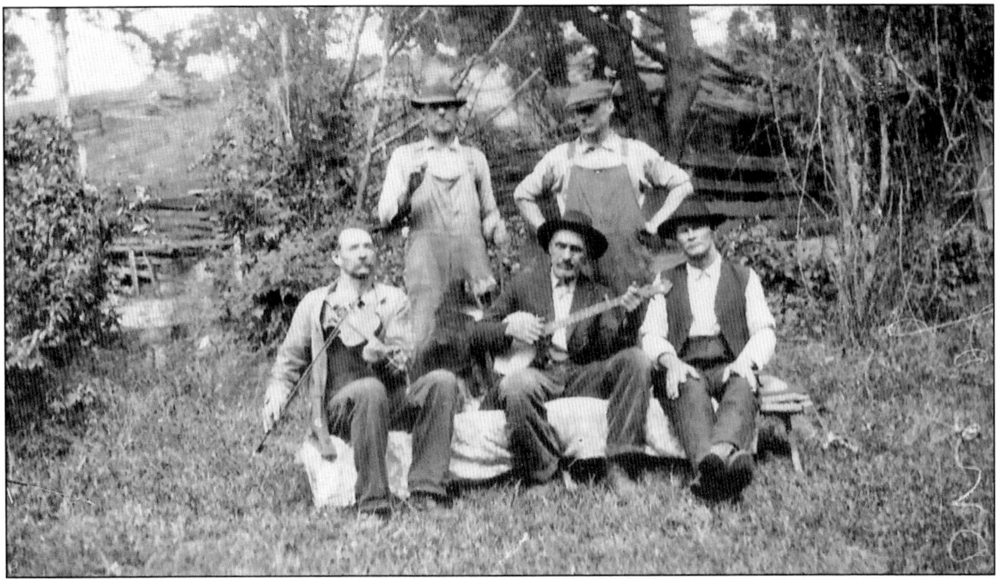

Enjoying the outdoors and some music making are, from left to right, (seated) George Cowan Campbell on the fiddle, George W. Campbell on the banjo, and possibly Jeremiah Couch. It is not known who those standing are. It was not uncommon for people to play instruments to entertain themselves and their family and friends. Music was an important part of any festive occasion. (Courtesy of Beulah H. and George J. Campbell, provided by Patricia Garrett.)

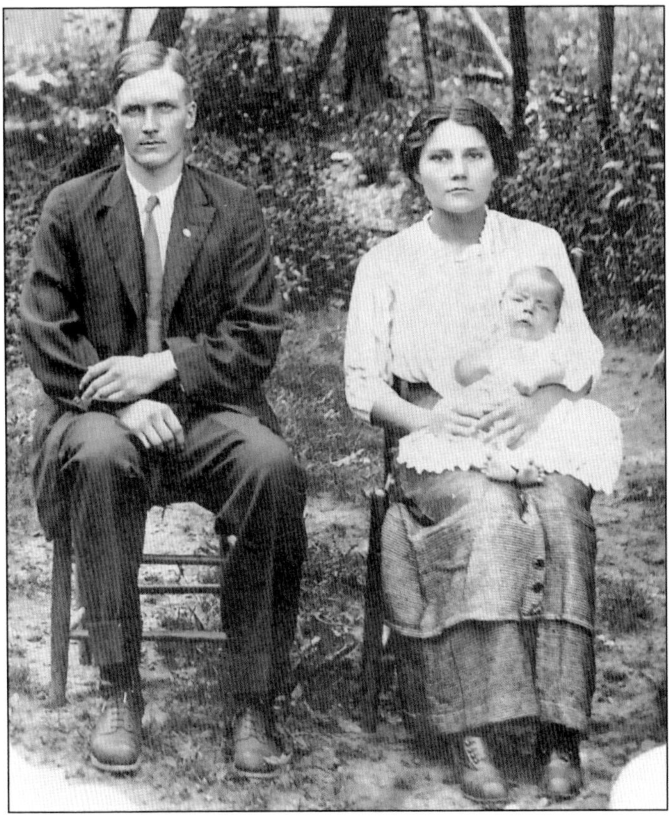

The baby happily seated in his mother's lap is Early Hobbs. Lakie Dishman Hobbs is the mother, and the father is George R. Hobbs. This picture was taken in 1915 near Castlewood. (Courtesy of Beulah H. and George J. Campbell.)

Molly Reedy Couch stands here with her husband, James. He is holding the baby, Everett. This picture was taken in the early 1900s near the Clinch River. (Courtesy of Beulah H. and George J. Campbell.)

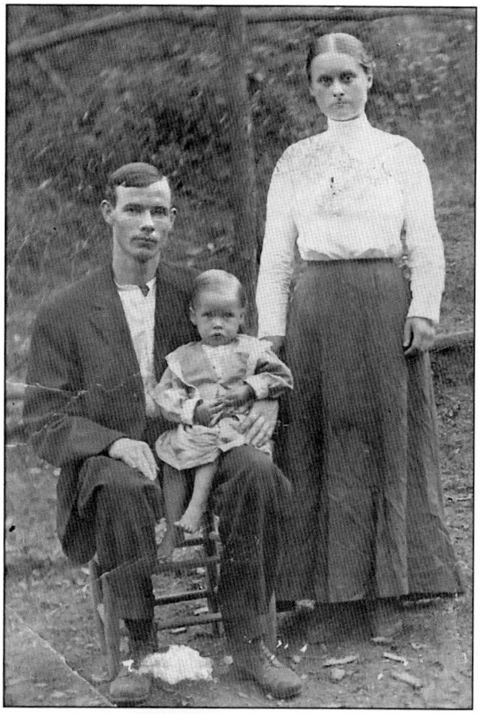

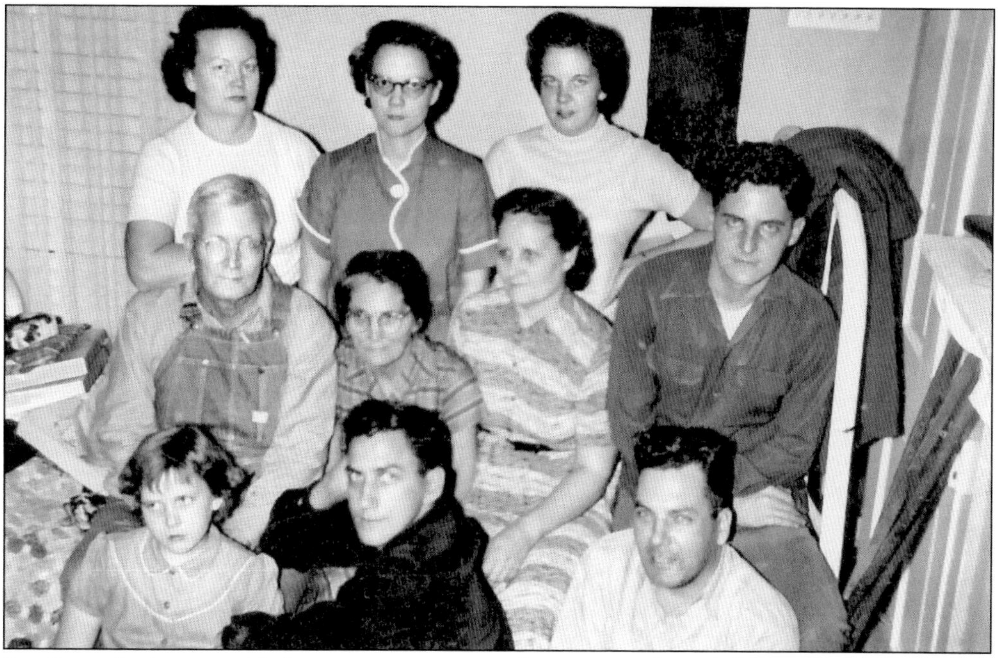

Family gatherings provided a great opportunity for picture taking. This picture was taken in Dante in 1950–1951. From left to right are (first row) Shirley Hobbs Linkous, Clarence Hobbs, and Early Hobbs; (second row) George Hobbs, Lakie Dishman Hobbs, Bertha H. Brooks, and James Hobbs; (third row) Gladys Hobbs Williams, Buena H. Evans, and Beulah H. Campbell. Not pictured are family members Bob Hobbs and Marvin Hobbs (killed in service). (Courtesy of Beulah H. and George J. Campbell, provided by Patricia Garrett.)

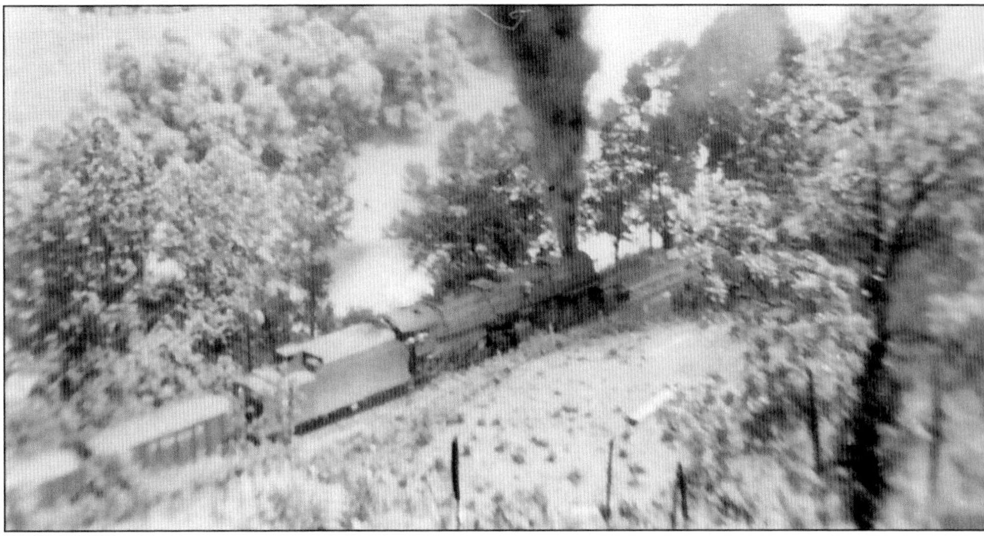

This photograph shows the head end brakeman tapping on sand pipes to help release clogged pipe from the sand dome. This put sand on the track. The engineer is leaning out the window, and the fireman is standing in the gangway to grab the order at the Castlewood Train Station. The station used a type of stick to hold the orders, which allowed for the end to be removed as it was grabbed while the train remained in motion. The fireman would take the orders off it as quickly as possible and then toss the end down by the side of the tracks. This is the first photograph taken by a 12-year-old George Campbell in 1939. George would run and pick up the stick for the station master. (Courtesy of Beulah H. and George J. Campbell, provided by Patricia Garrett.)

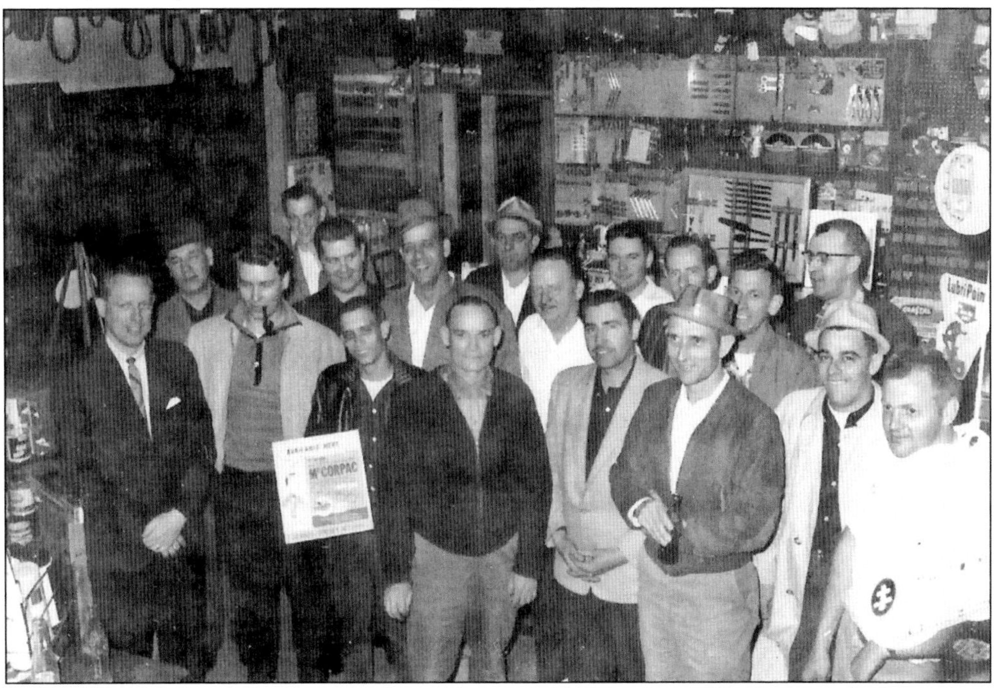

Pictured here in the early 1960s are the employees of Phillips Auto Warehouse in Sun, Virginia, located in Russell County. George J. Campbell is in front of the picture on the right, holding the bottle of Coca-Cola. (Courtesy of Beulah H. and George J. Campbell.)

Martha Jane Hobbs, lovingly known as Grandma Hobbs by her grandson George R. Hobbs, smiles as her picture is being taken around 1915 near Mendota. (Courtesy of Beulah H. and George J. Campbell.)

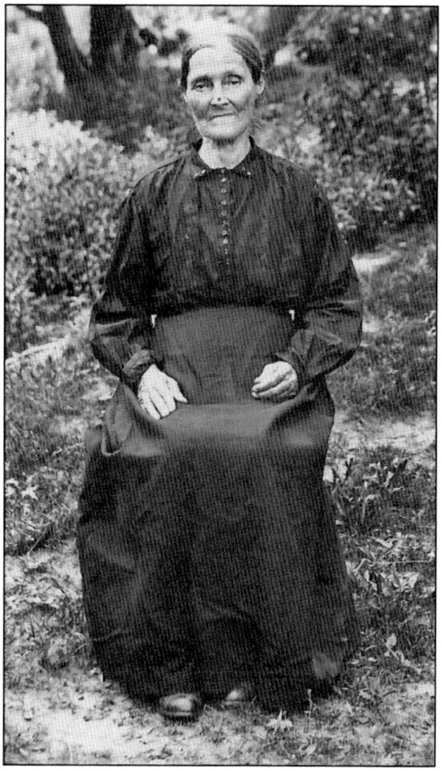

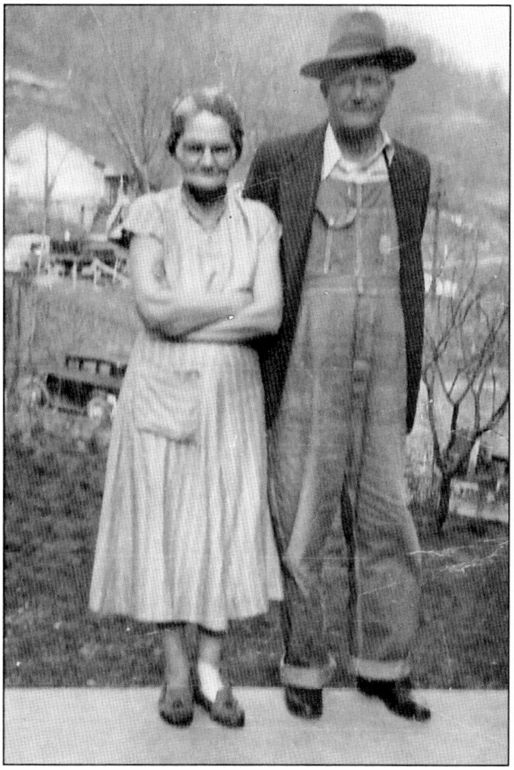

George Hobbs and Lakie Dishman Hobbs are pictured here near their home in the Bear Wallow section of Dante in the 1940s. (Courtesy of Beulah H. and George J. Campbell, provided by Patricia Garrett.)

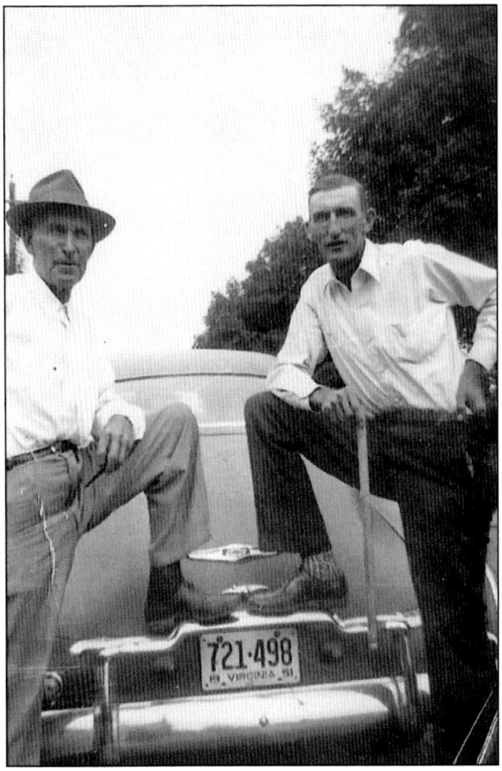

On the left is Henry Bascom Garrett, and on the right is his son, Woodrow Garrett. This picture was taken in Lebanon in 1951. Henry Bascom Garrett worked for Governor Stuart in Elk Garden. Notice the Chevrolet automobile and the license plate in the picture. (Provided by Patricia and Gary Garrett.)

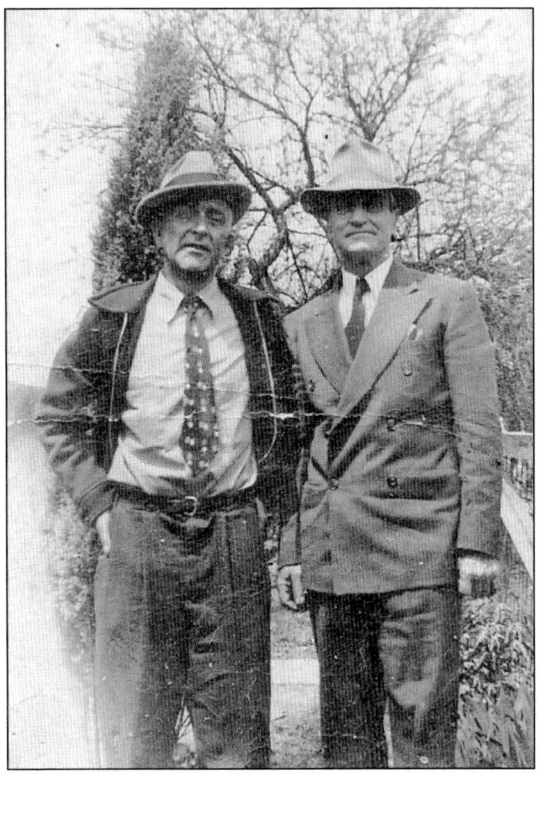

George Duff Campbell, left, is the father of James C. Campbell. He is pictured here in the late 1930s. He operated a steam shovel in Castlewood and worked for the Clinch Railroad in Dickinson County and in Kentucky. On the right is his brother, Charlie Campbell, who was in town for a visit. (Courtesy of Beulah H. and George J. Campbell, provided by Patricia Garrett.)

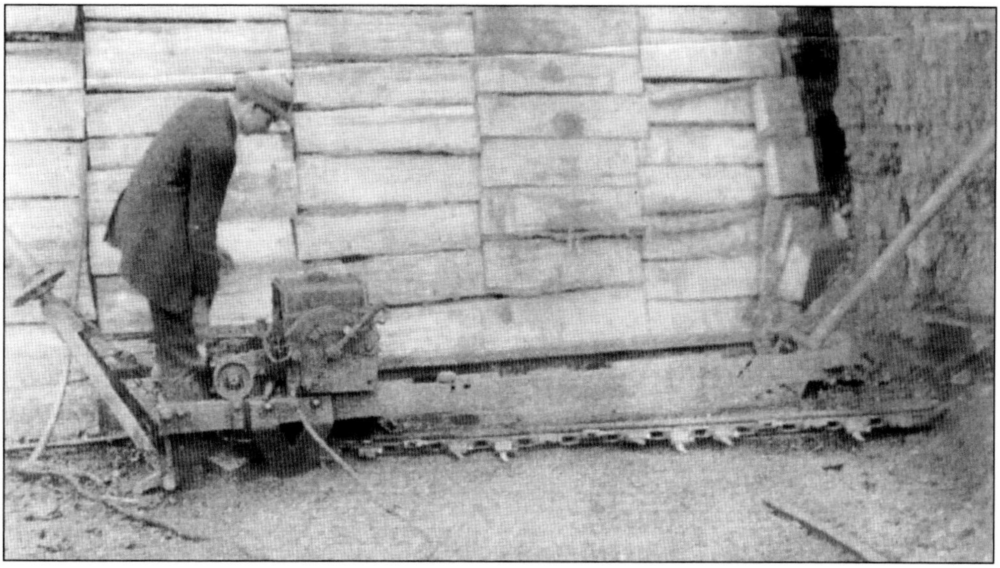

Coal mining provided jobs and income for families in the early days. Many men left the farms for the first time to seek work outside the rural farm setting. Coal mining was hard work, and the dangers were many. Though safety was not taken lightly, accidents did occur. Here is a picture taken of an accident scene on January 10, 1913. (Courtesy of RCPL, provided by Barry Hess.)

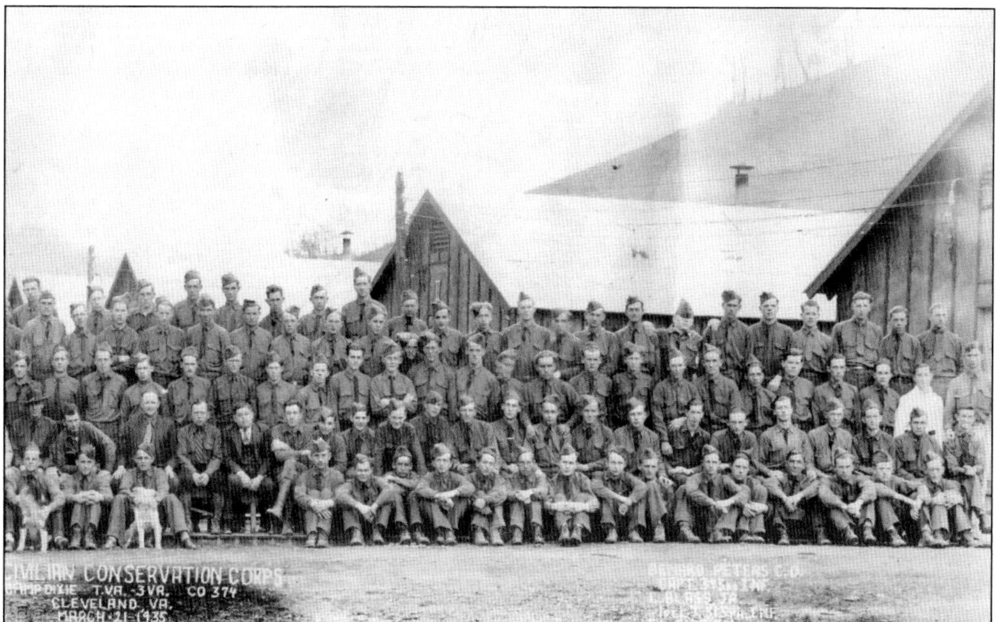

Pictured here is the Civilian Conservation Corps, Company 374 stationed in Cleveland on March 21, 1935. The Civilian Conservation Corps put to work unemployed youth across the country. These young men came from everywhere. During a time of much unemployment, the corps provided jobs. These young people built roads and fire trails, planted trees, combated erosion, and helped develop parks across the United States. (Courtesy of RCPL.)

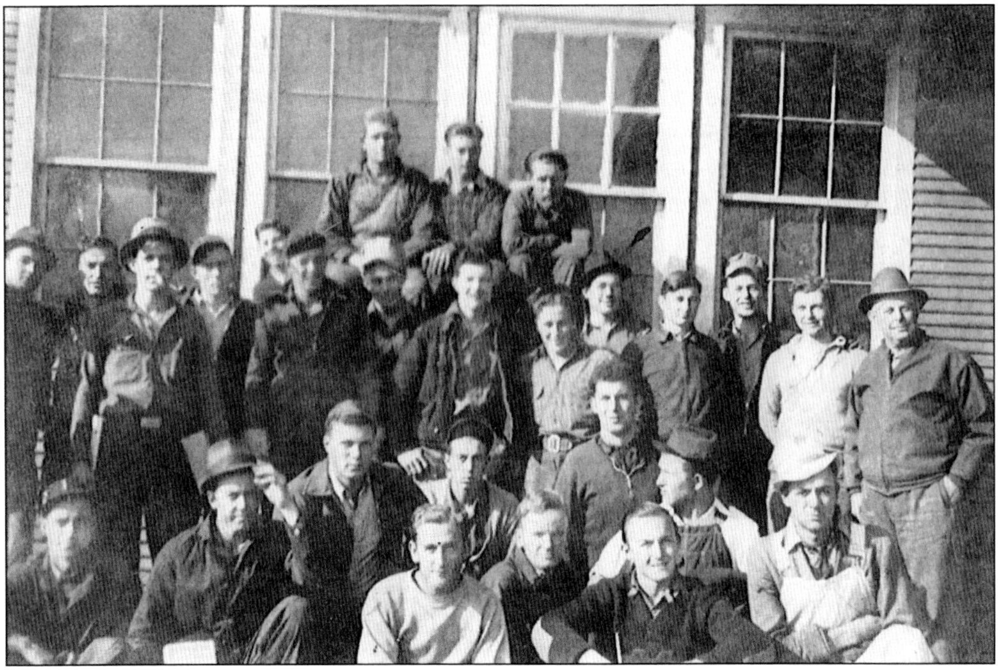

Taking time out for a photograph is the Honaker High School carpentry class. The exact year of the picture is not known, but it is believed to be in the 1940s. (Courtesy of RCPL.)

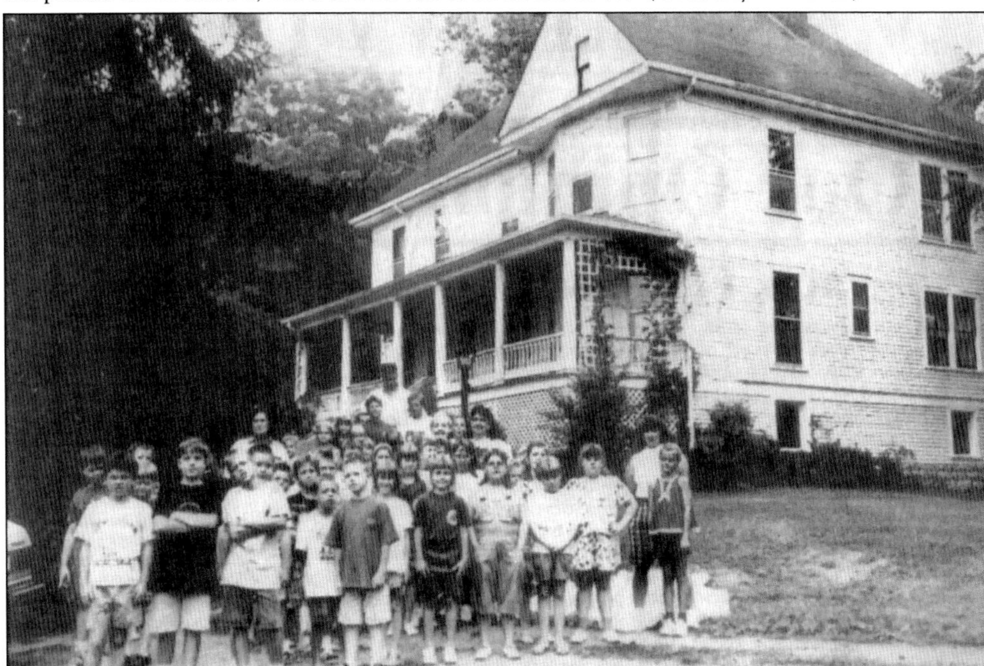

James P. Carrell, the second clerk of court of Russell County, built this home. The plantation slave quarters were located on the property, as was the cemetery. The owners as well as the slaves were buried there. It later became known as the Combs Plantation. In this picture, the Lebanon Elementary summer school class visits this historical landmark. (Courtesy of RCPL.)

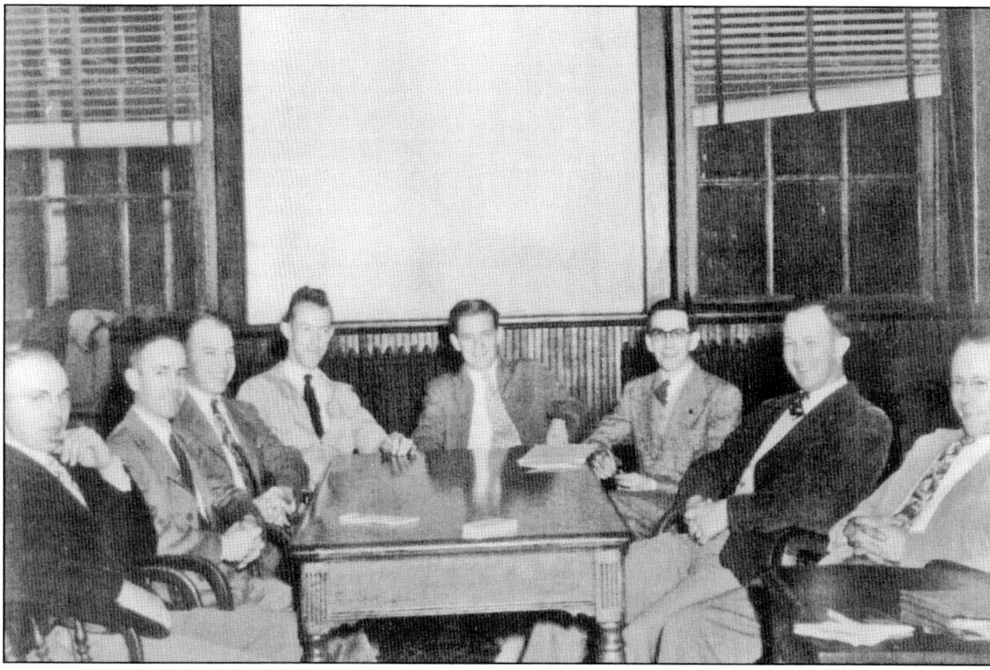

Pictured here is the organizational meeting in the Russell County Courtroom of the Lebanon Jaycees in March 1950. From left to right are Warren Jessee, Herman Jessee, Bill Jessee, Ralph Snead, Bob Weisfield, Elwood Bausell, Roy Smith, and John Gilmer. Ralph Snead is the only survivor. (Courtesy of Ralph Snead.)

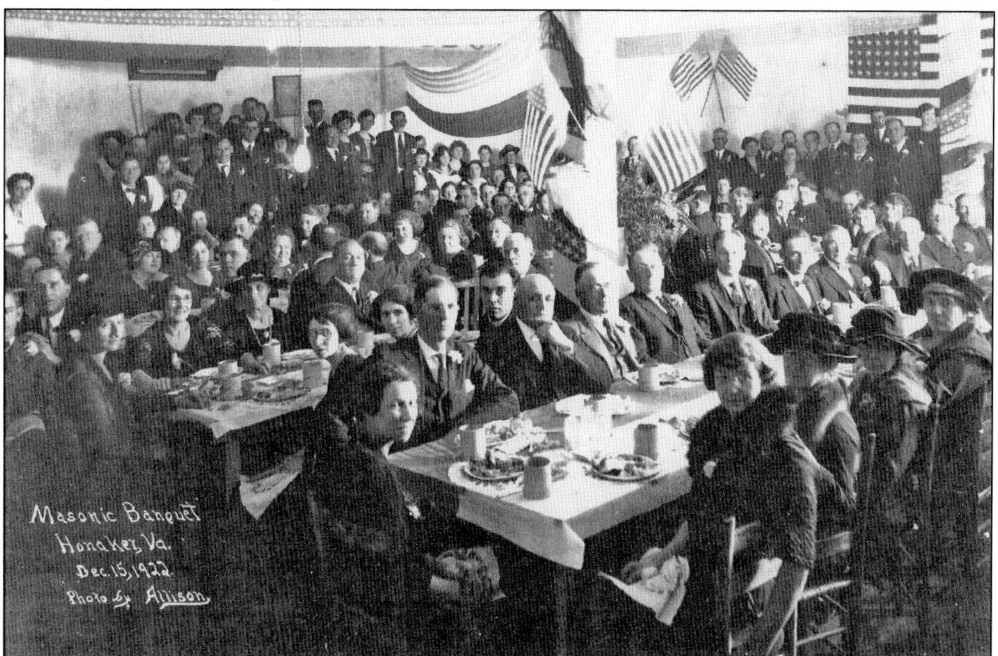

This Masonic banquet held in Honaker on December 15, 1922, reflected a festive occasion and the great pride these folks had for their country. (Courtesy of New Peoples Bank, Honaker Branch.)

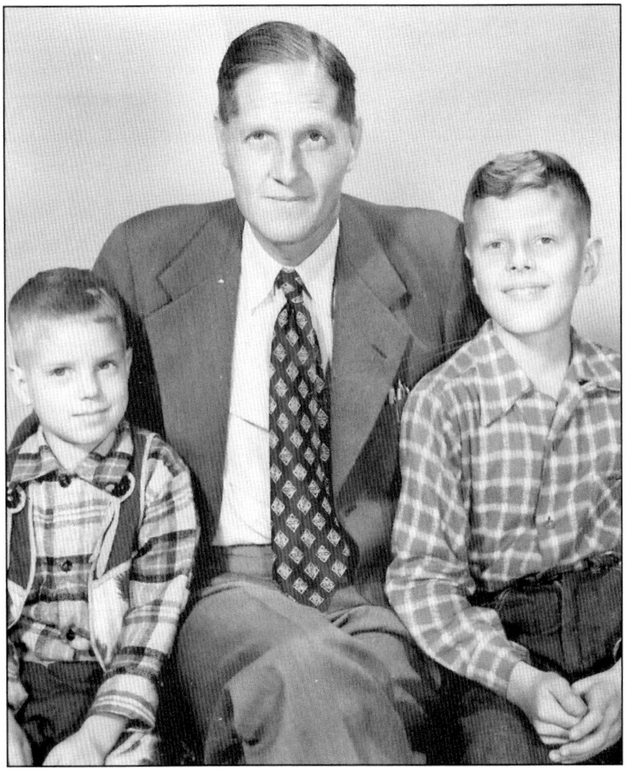

This picture is of A. P. Baldwin and his two young sons, Jim on the left and Bill on the right. Baldwin was a well-loved and respected educator in Russell County. He served as principal of Cleveland and Honaker High Schools before becoming superintendent of Russell County schools. An avid supporter of high school athletics, he was active in the formation of the Clinch Valley District. The A. P. Baldwin Gymnasium at Honaker High School was named in his honor. Though he passed away in 1981, local folklore has it that he can still be seen late at night roaming the gymnasium. (Courtesy of Jim Baldwin.)

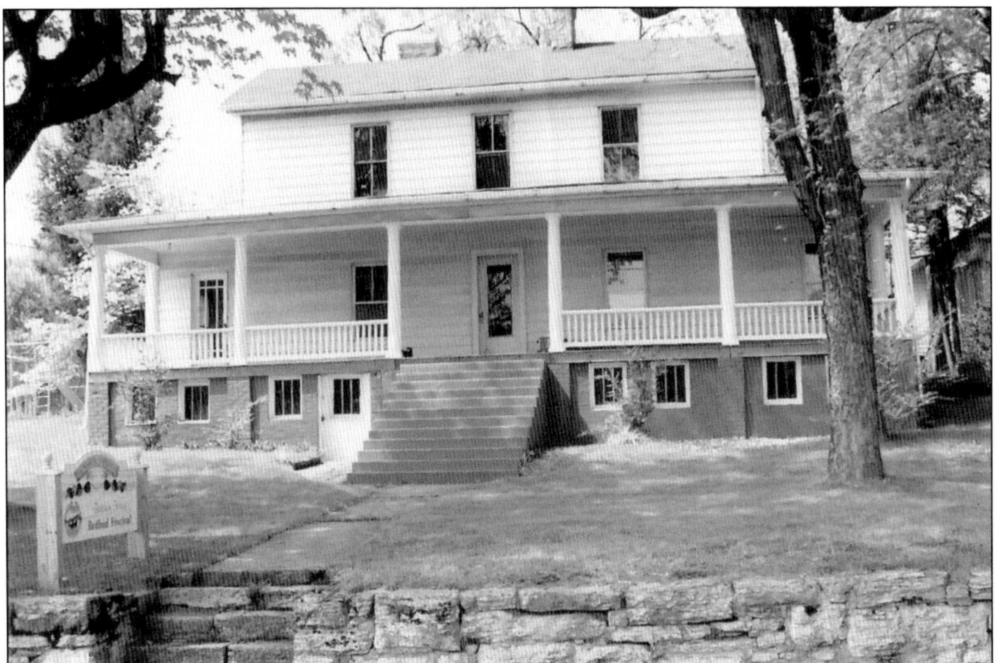

The town of Honaker is called the "Redbud Capital of the World." The former home of the A. P. Baldwin family, built in 1911, is now known as the Redbud House and serves as the headquarters of the Redbud Festival. (Courtesy of Jim Baldwin.)

Two

Street Scenes and Landscapes

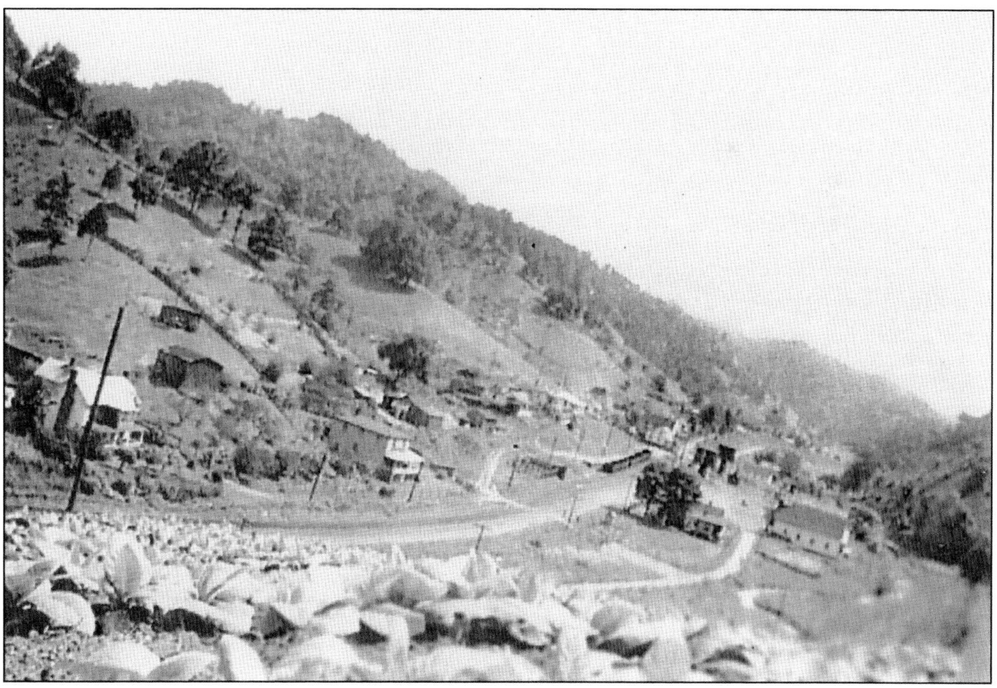

Taken from Lum Sykes's tobacco field is this view of Finney as it appeared in 1930. From left to right are Frank and Laura Sykes's house and Jim and Susan Sykes's house. The Finney Baptist Church is on the right. (Courtesy of James C. and Nellie R. Jessee.)

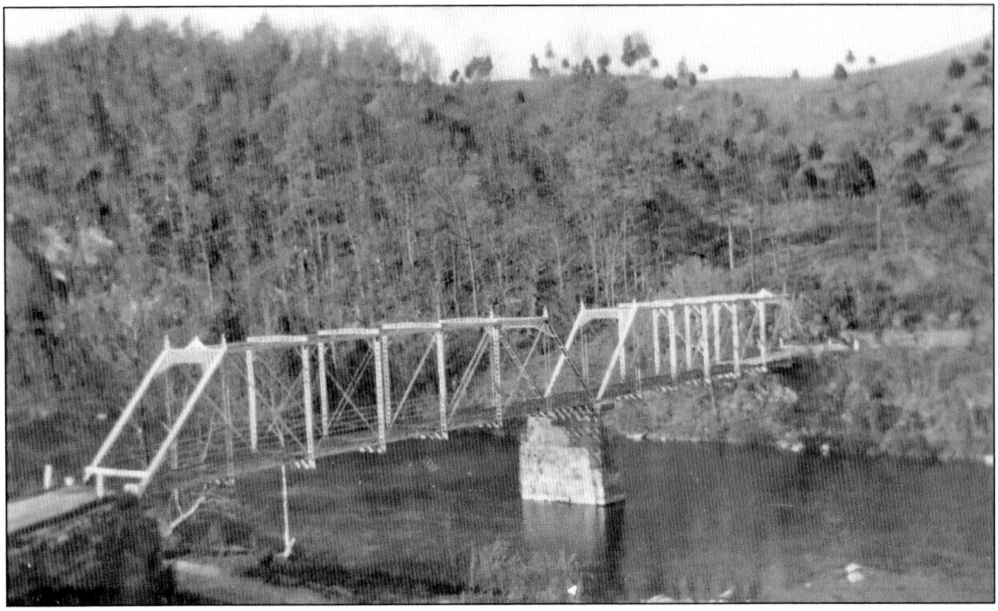

Pictured is a one-way bridge across Clinch River at Blackford. This bridge was built in 1889. It was later moved to Puckett's Hole in 1945. (Courtesy of HHM, provided by Kathleen R. Taylor.)

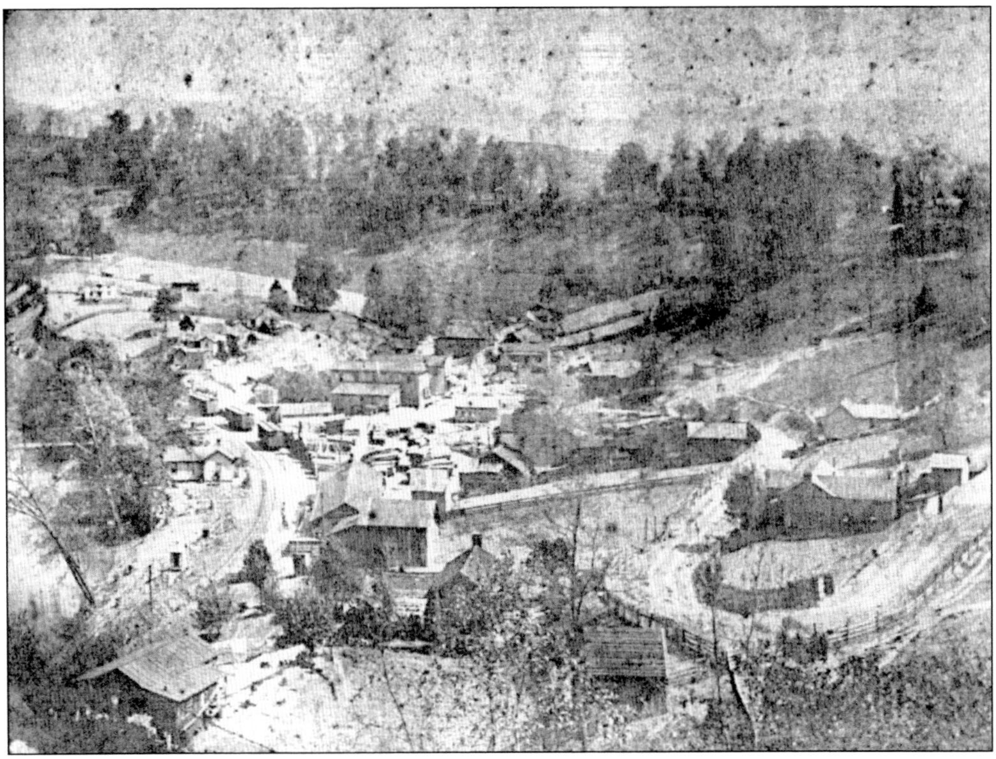

Shown here is a 1906 aerial view of Old Castlewood. This picture reflects Old Castlewood at a time when it was a shipping point for sheep, cattle, and vast amounts of lumber. Notice that the pens for the sheep and cattle and also the lumberyard are located near the depot and the railroad tracks. (Courtesy of RCPL, provided by Eugenia D. and Ed Dorton.)

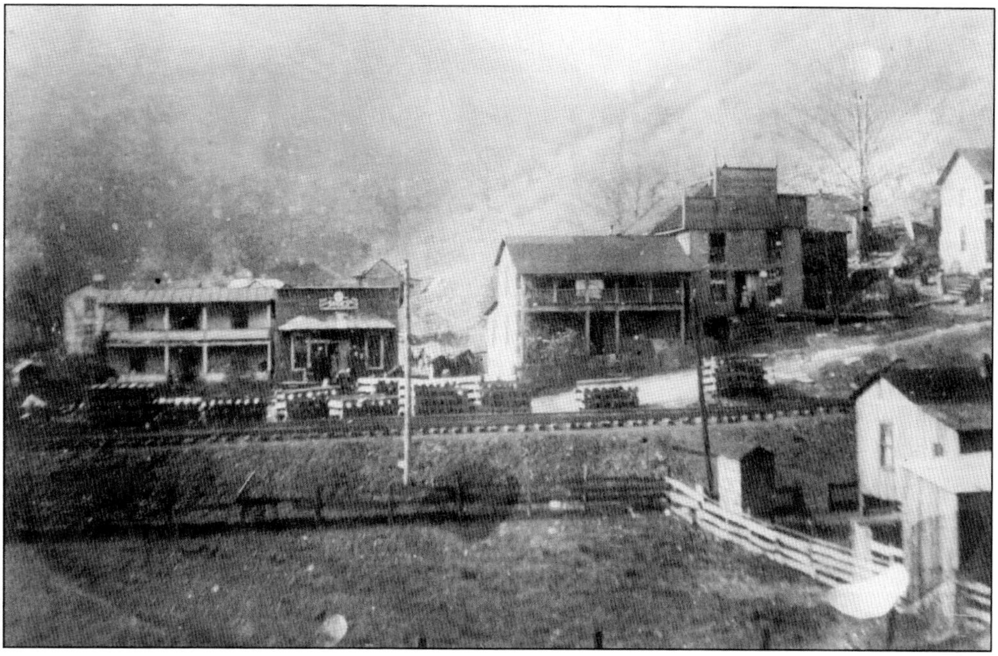

Finney in the 1890s, at the time this picture was taken, was a busy town. Left of center is the Banner Hardware Store. To the right of center is the Finney Hotel. The road now runs at the left of the photograph, then behind the buildings. (Courtesy of RCPL, provided by R. C. Sykes.)

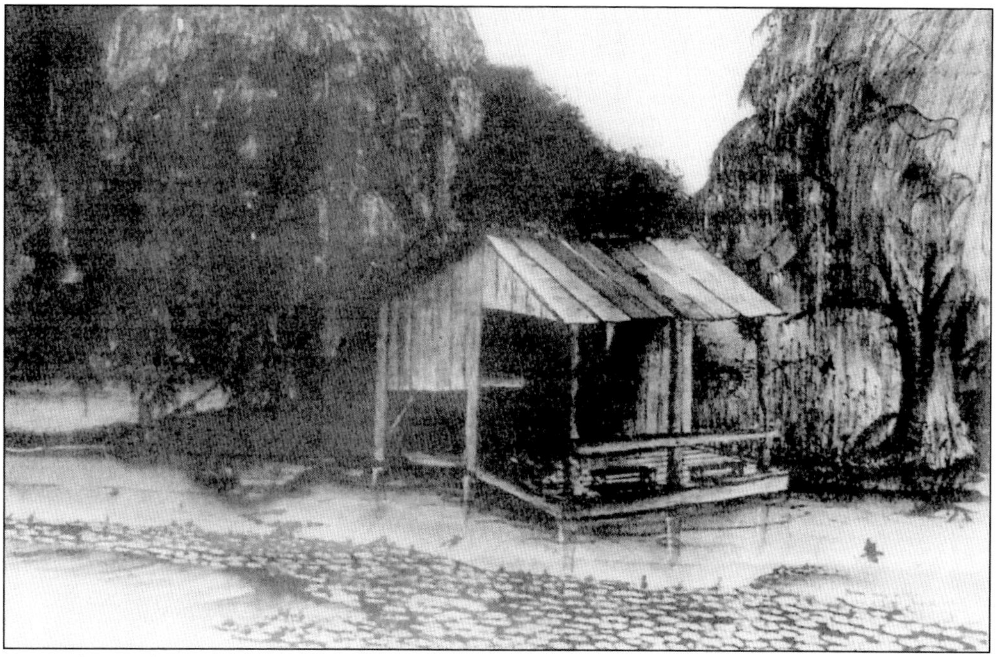

Howard's Pond in Rosedale, Virginia, is sketched here to look much as it did in the mid-1950s. A favorite destination to swim, fish, and have picnics has many happy memories for residents of Russell County. Many remember sitting on the front porch of this little building and dangling their feet into the water below. There was also a small restaurant for those who did not wish to bring a picnic lunch. (Courtesy of James C. and Nellie R. Jessee.)

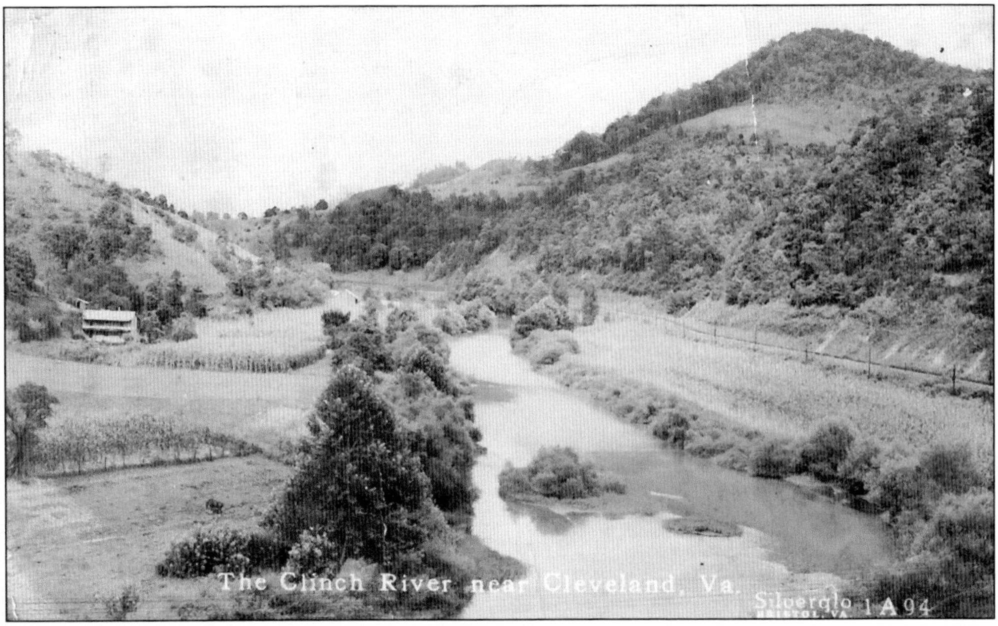

This is one of two postcards, each sent to two brothers stationed in the navy during World War II. They were sent from a family member encouraging the new recruits with mention of the dreaded illness known as being "homesick" and hoping that they were not suffering from it. Both of these postcards began their very separate journey with a 1¢ stamp, only to be joined together again much later. The beauty of the Clinch River Valley is forever captured in these cards and a reminder of what was waiting at home for these young men once they returned. (Courtesy of Pauline Salyers and Brian Kiser.)

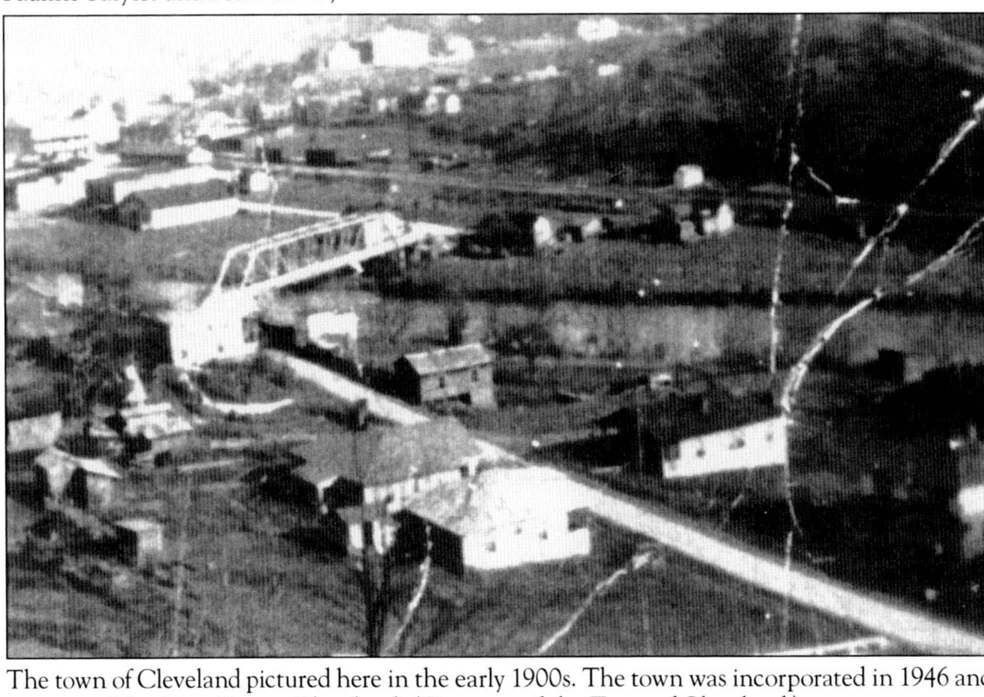

The town of Cleveland pictured here in the early 1900s. The town was incorporated in 1946 and was named for Pres. Grover Cleveland. (Courtesy of the Town of Cleveland.)

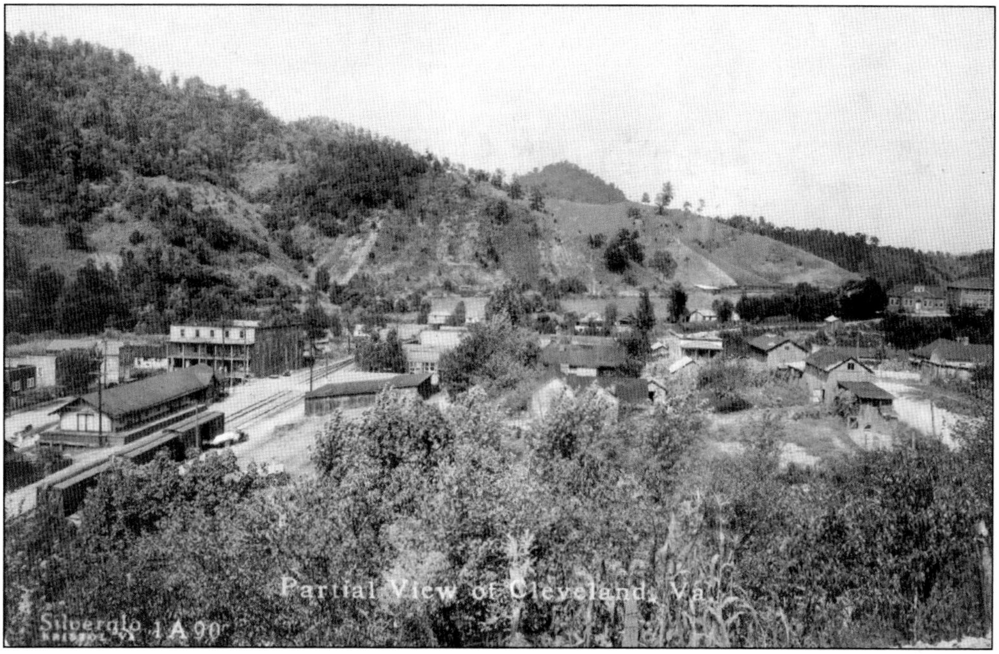

The town of Cleveland is depicted on a 1935 postcard. Notice the railroad tracks on the left of the picture, the depot, and the various businesses located along the railroad tracks. (Courtesy of RCPL, provided by Polly Salyers, Vernon Salyers, and Brian Kiser.)

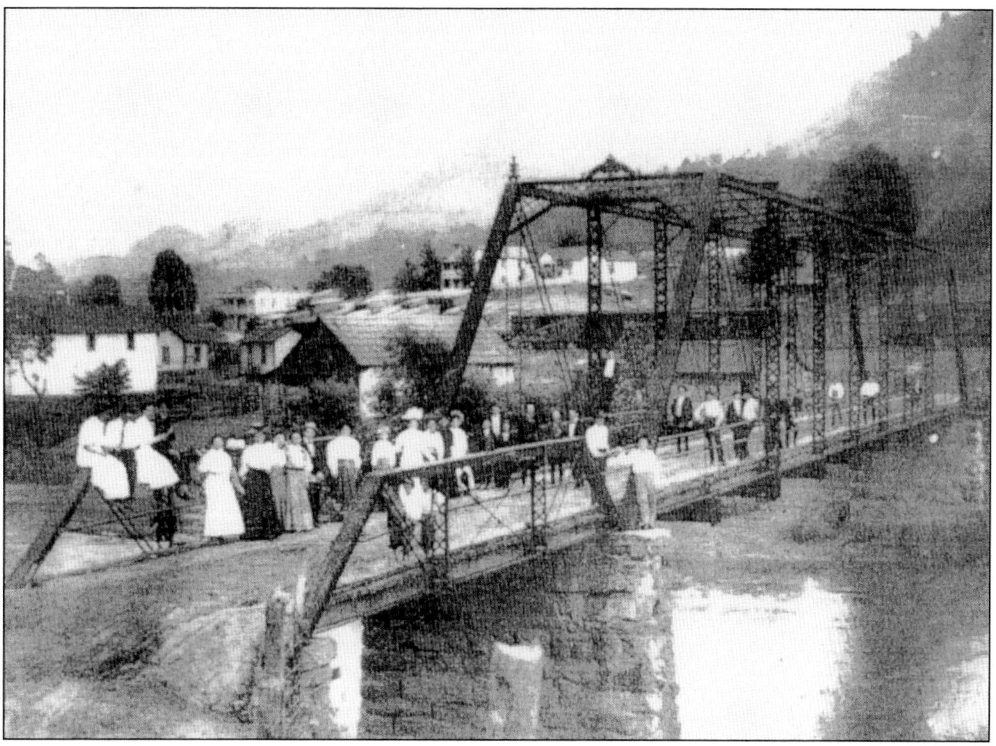
The first bridge across the Clinch River at Cleveland was built in 1891. The bridge stood until it was torn down in 1953. (Courtesy of the Town of Cleveland.)

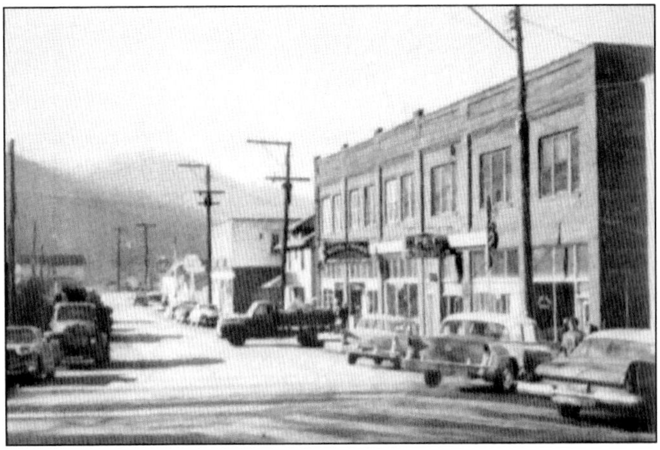

This Cleveland street scene picture was taken between 1955 and 1958. Automobiles filled the streets. This new form of transportation was one of the reasons for the lack of need for passenger trains and ultimately resulted in a number of depot closings as folks preferred this more convenient means of travel. (Courtesy of James C. Jessee.)

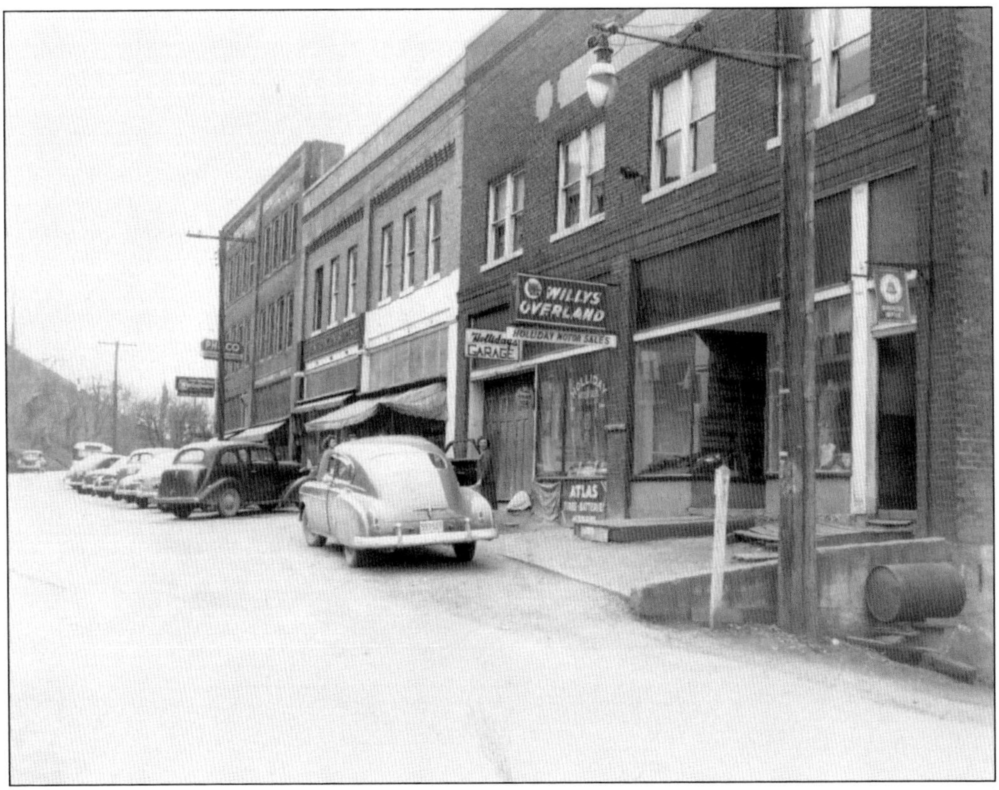

Downtown Honaker in the 1940s was a busy place. The signs reflect Holliday's Garage and Holliday Motor Sales. The telephone operator was located upstairs above Holliday's Garage. Notice the large number of automobiles parked on the street. (Courtesy of RCPL, provided by Claude E. Griffith.)

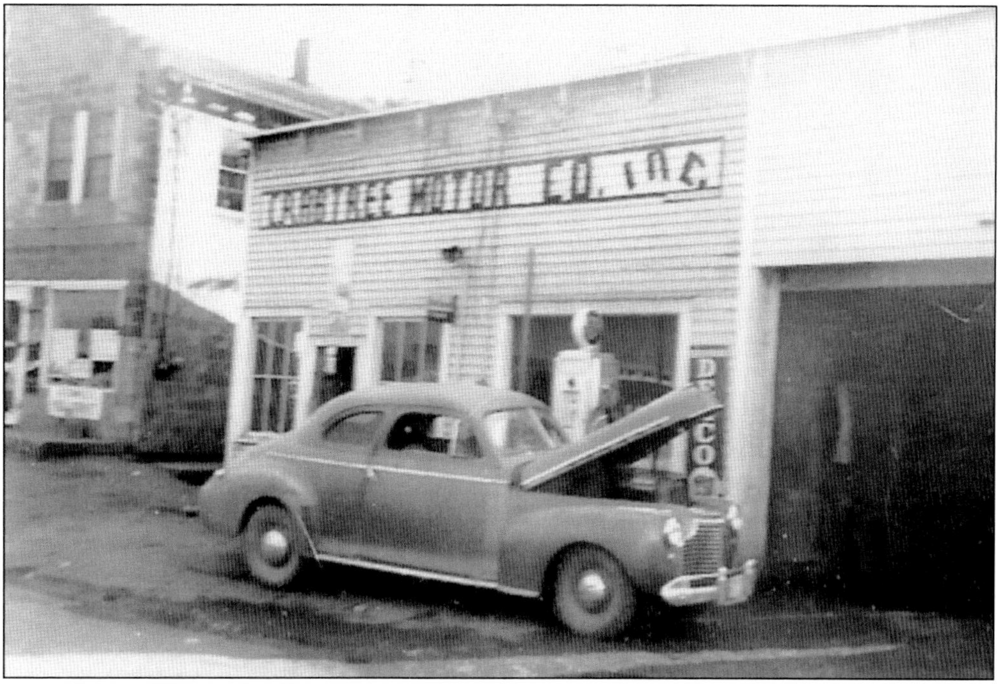

The Crabtree Motor Company, Inc., sign shown here in downtown Honaker was the first wall sign ever painted by Carl B. Jessee Sr. He painted it at the age of 15 in the year 1945. He was paid $5 for his work. This business later became Crabtree Buick in Bristol. (Courtesy of James C. and Nellie R. Jessee.)

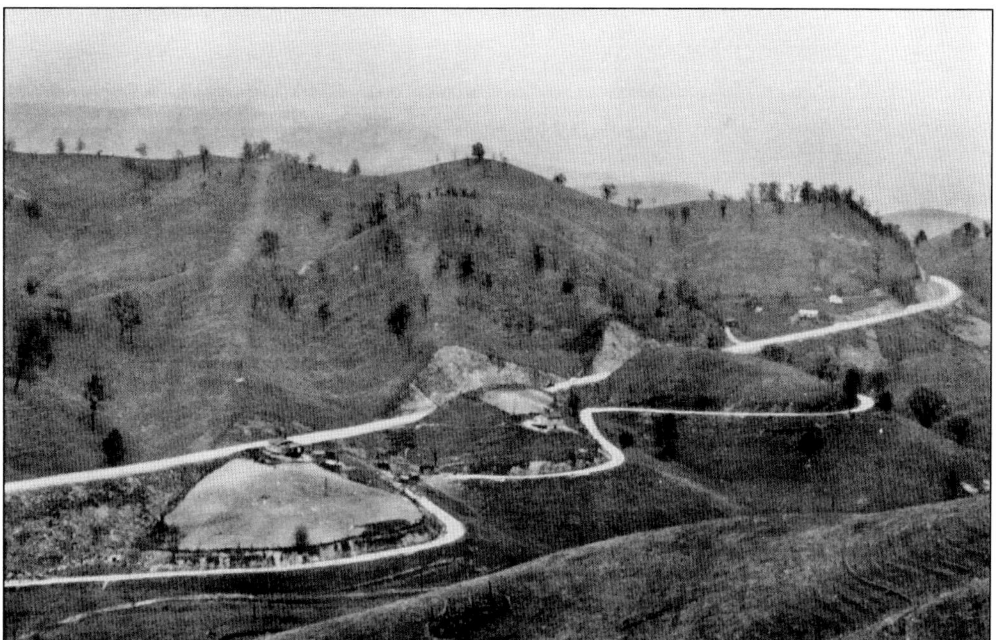

This aerial view of Honaker was taken in 1947 or 1948. It is a view of Route 80 at the Doubles. It shows the old road and the newly opened road between Rosedale and Blackford. (Courtesy of RCPL, provided by F. B. Gent II.)

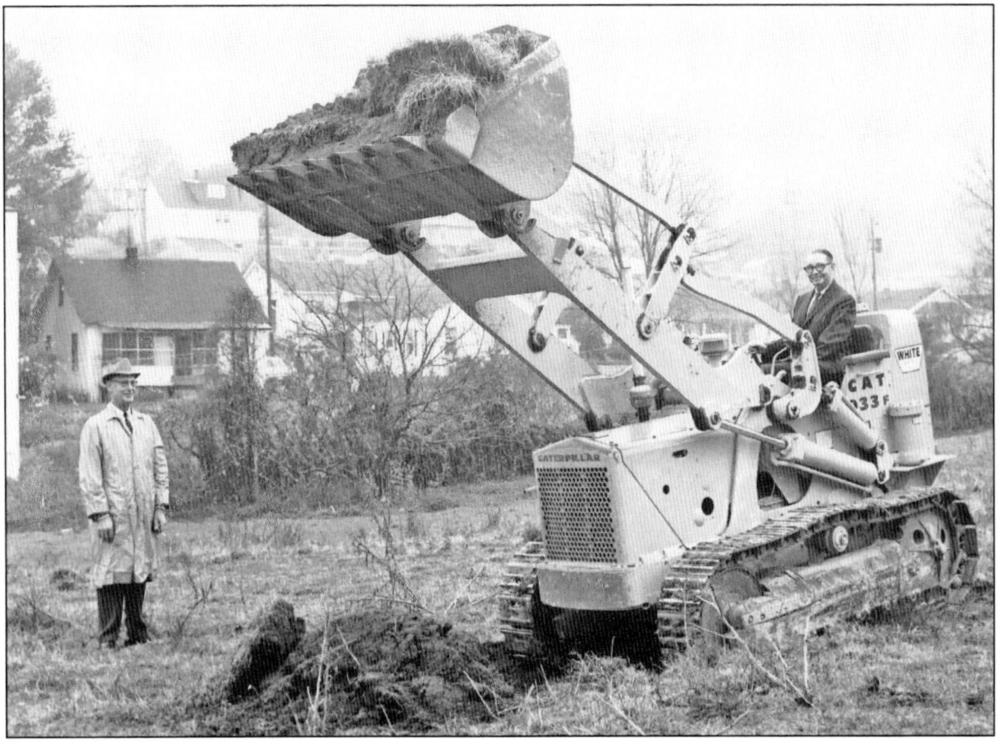

James S. Easterly shovels the first load of dirt in preparation for the new telephone company building to be constructed in the early 1940s. (Courtesy of Jim Easterly.)

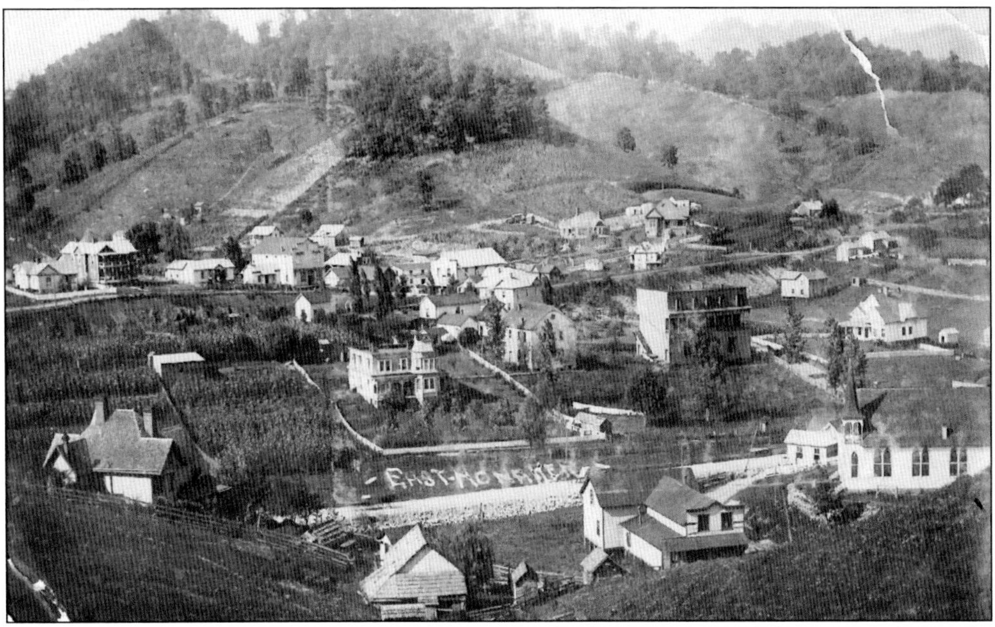

This postcard reflects East Honaker around 1900. The lower portion of the picture shows the Dr. Burke home, the livery stable, the Red Flag Store, and the First Baptist Church. Behind the words "East Honaker" are the college buildings and the Tom Davis home. The upper portion of the postcard shows homes on both sides of the railroad tracks. (Courtesy of HHM.)

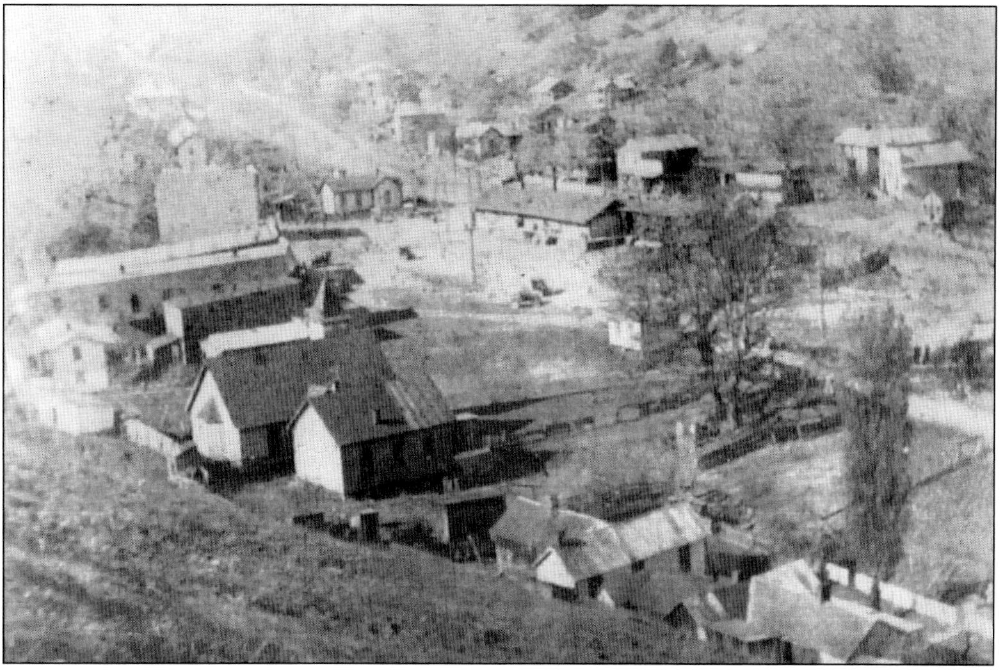

Reflected in this photograph is West Honaker in the early 1900s. The building on the left with the bell tower is the First Methodist Church. Beyond the church is the Honaker Flour and Grain Company. The first election for town offices was held there. Also in the picture are the depot, the section house, the William Lockhart home, and the general store. (Courtesy of HHM.)

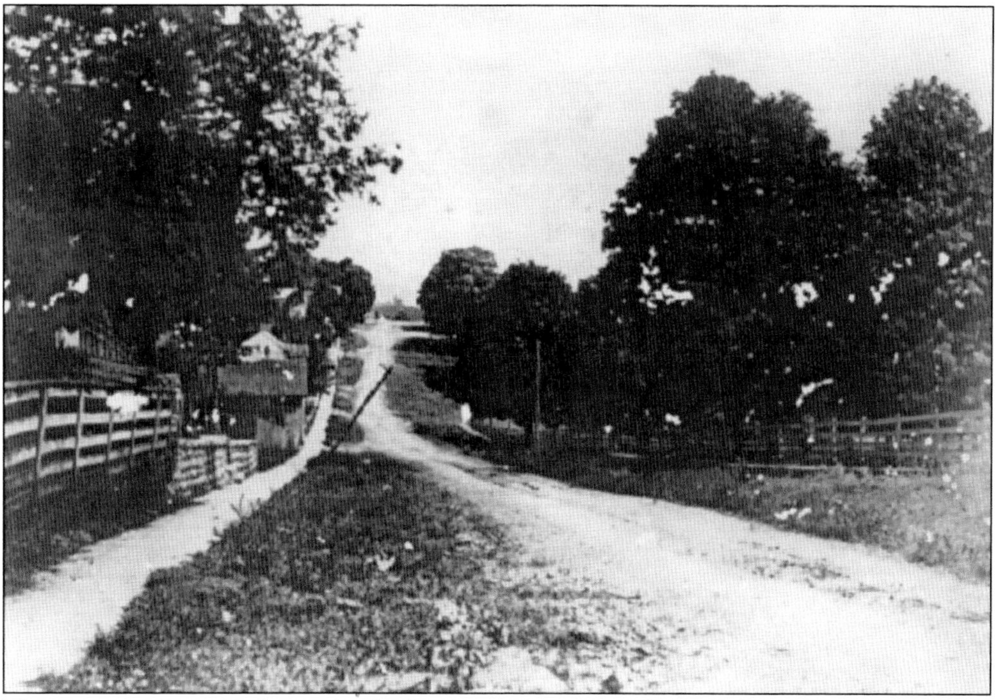

This picture reflects Highway 19, which is Main Street in Lebanon. This picture was taken in 1910, when the roads were still unpaved. (Courtesy of RCPL, provided by Barry Hess.)

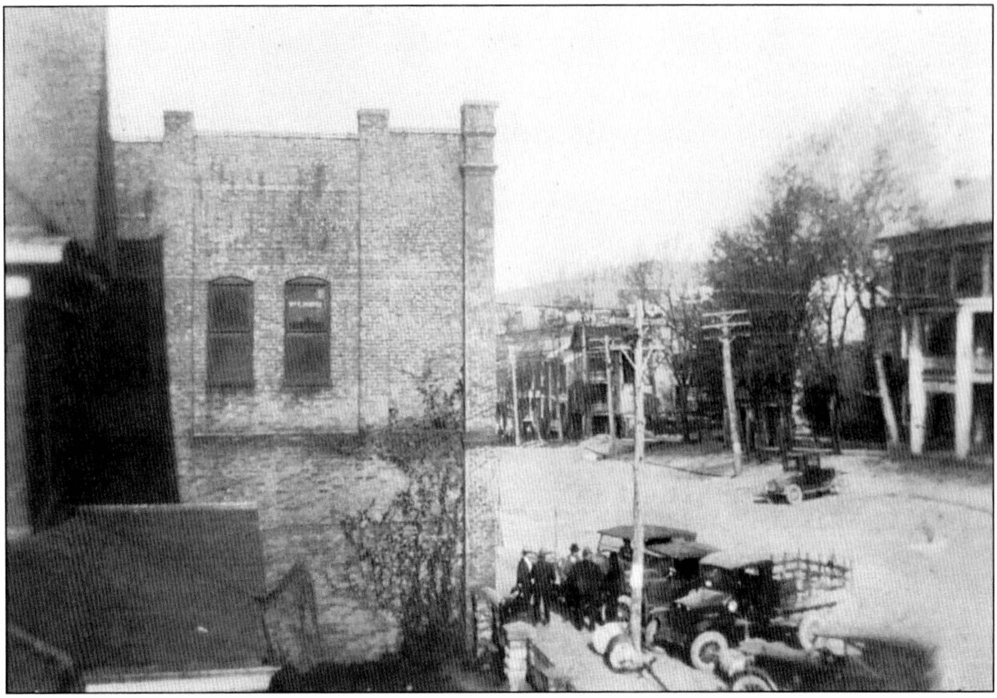

This scene is downtown Main Street, Lebanon, in the early 1900s. This location is near the Russell Theater. (Courtesy of James C. and Nellie R. Jessee.)

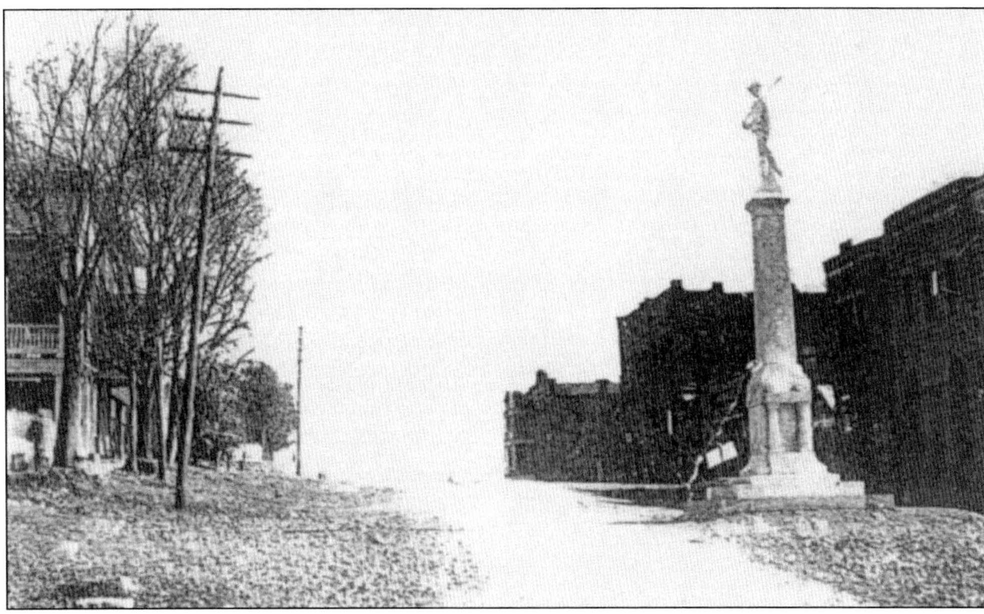

Lebanon in the 1920s reflects a postcard view of the Confederate Soldier Memorial when it was located in the middle of the street. The memorial was to honor and remember the valor of the 13 companies of men who in 1861 left Russell County. Many never returned to their families and loved ones. In 1914, the statue was placed in the middle of the intersection of Court Street and Route 19. In 1944, it was moved to the south side of the street. (Courtesy of RCPL, provided by James C. and Nellie R. Jessee.)

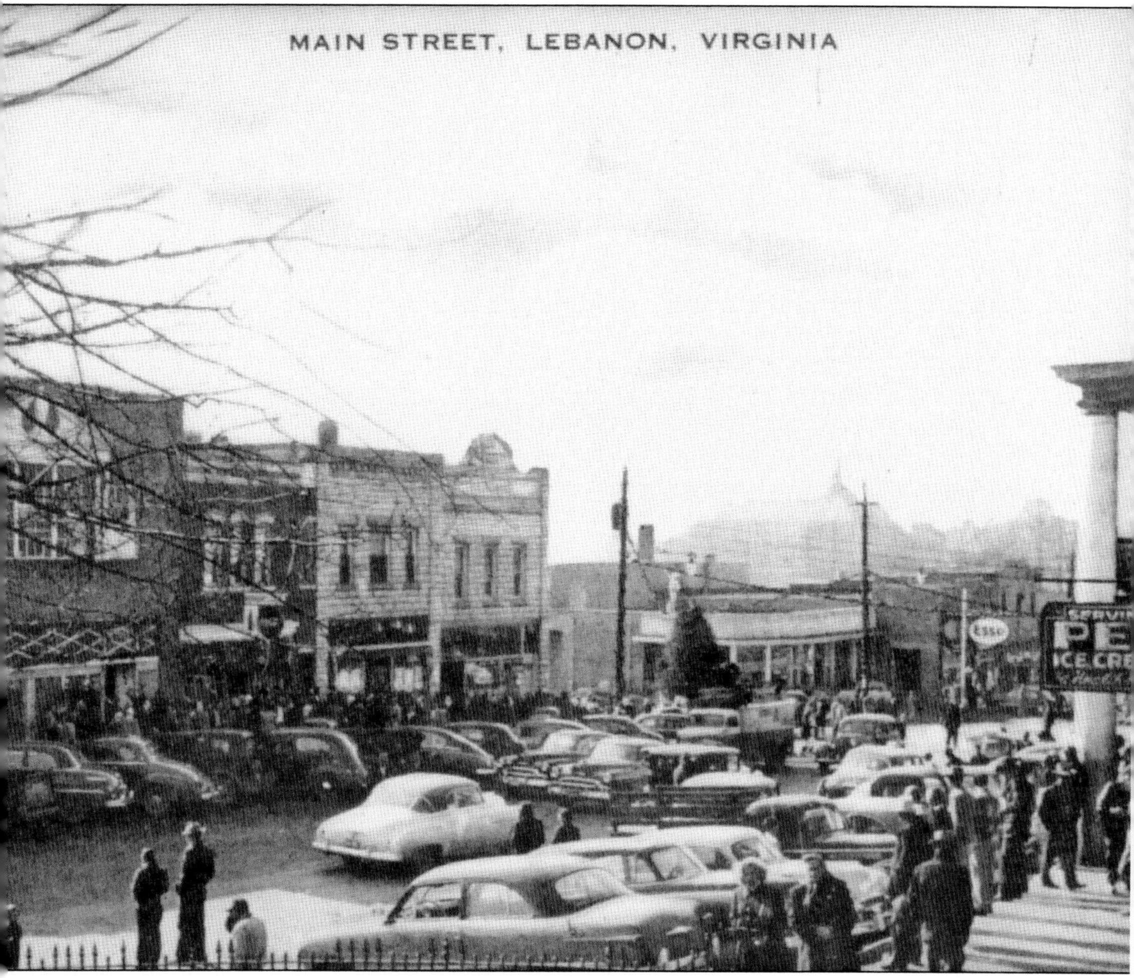

A Lebanon street scene in the 1940s is reflective of a Saturday or Sunday, when the local folks gathered in town. It was an opportunity to shop and get caught up on the local news and events. Folks would dress to see and to be seen. Socializing revolved around the church and trips to town. (Courtesy of RCPL, provided by Dave Leonard.)

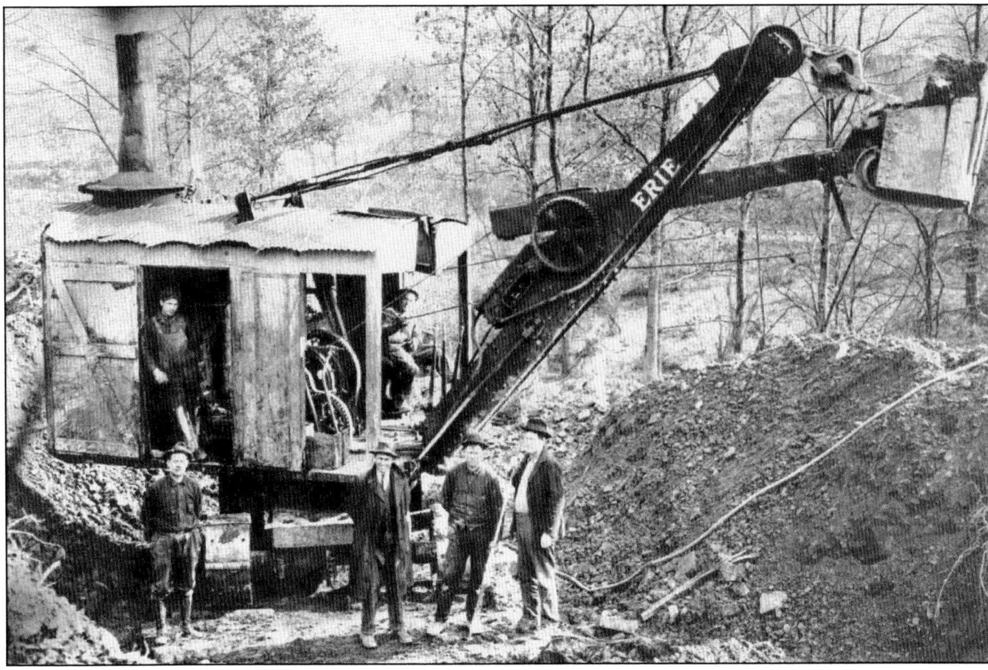

Here is a 1924 Lebanon scene of the construction of U.S. 19 between Hansonville and Lebanon. In the shovel doorway to the left is James Monroe Bolling, the equipment operator and the donor's father. On the right is Stewart Bolling, the oiler and the donor's uncle. On the ground at left is R. H. Bolling, the contractor and the donor's uncle. R. H. Bolling lived in Norton. (Courtesy of RCPL, provided by Kenneth Bolling.)

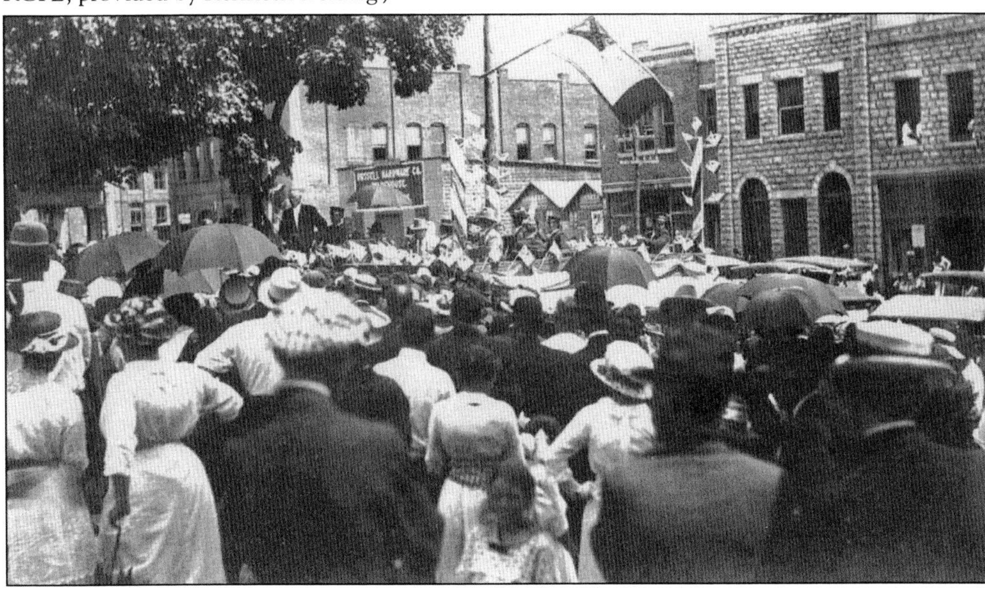

Reflected here is Lebanon in the early 1900s. This scene is looking north on Main Street at East Side Street. Prior to the beginning of the 20th century, Saturday was go to town to "trade" day. Farmers traded crops, crafts, and eggs for the clothing, fabrics, and sundry items they could not produce for themselves. It appears these folks have gathered to hear a speaker visible in the back of the picture to the left. (Courtesy of RCPL, provided by Ruth Whitt.)

Three

SCHOOLS AND CHURCHES

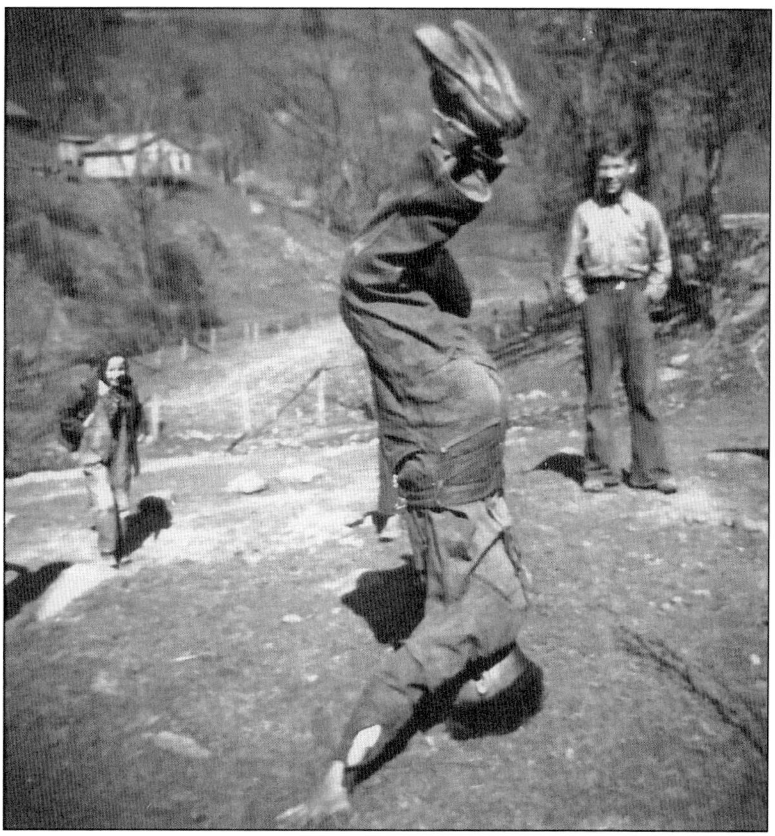

Creativity allowed the children of the day to avoid boredom. Games such as hide-and-seek, often called "Whoopy Hide," provided hours of fun at no cost. Cartwheels, standing on one's head, and arm wrestling provided fun and ways for the boys to get the girls' attention. This picture was taken in 1941. (Courtesy of HHM, provided by Kathleen R. Taylor.)

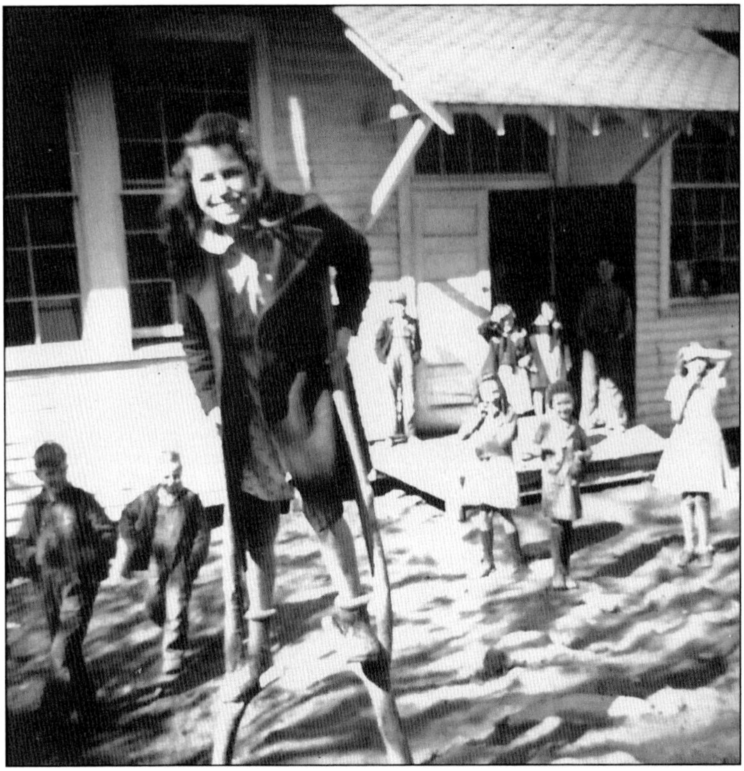

There were two breaks during the school day. One was in the morning and one in the afternoon. Lunch usually lasted 45 minutes to an hour, providing the children with time to eat as well as a recess for games and exercise. Walking on stilts was just one of the many forms of entertainment. This picture is from 1941. (Courtesy of HHM, provided by Kathleen R. Taylor.)

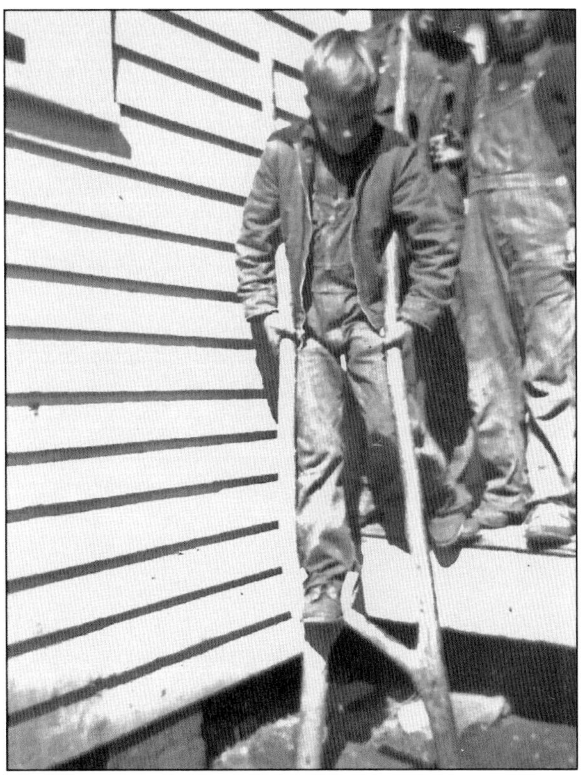

Walking on stilts demanded balance, usually acquired through lots of practice. This image is from the year 1941. (Courtesy of HHM, provided by Kathleen R. Taylor.)

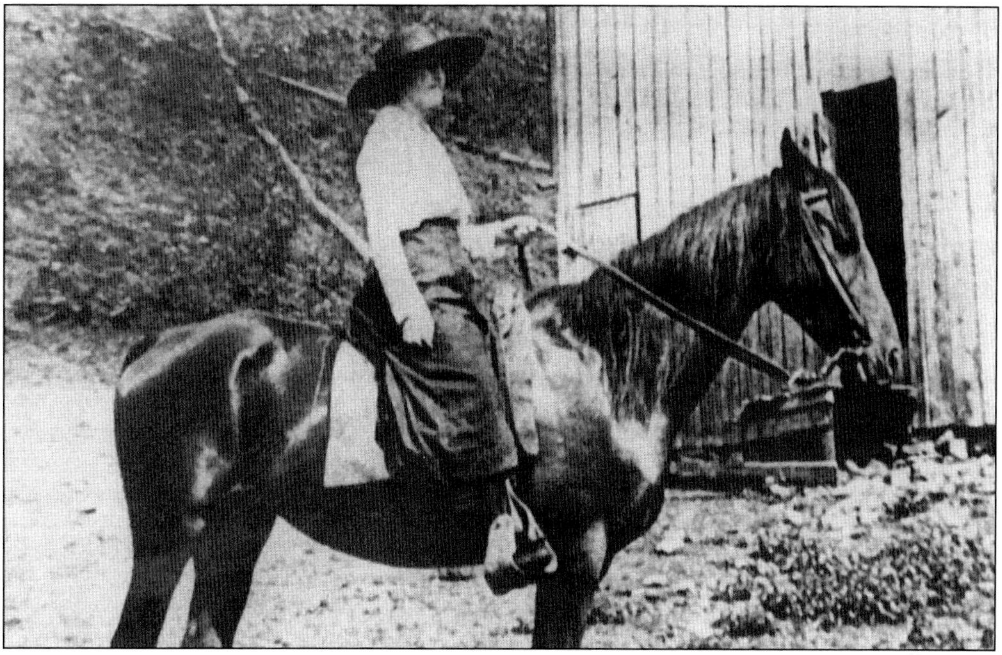

This picture shows Rebecca Ann Munsey Gibson. She was Fred Gent's great-aunt. In this 1920 photograph, she is sitting in the saddle on her horse Nancy. She was preparing to leave Dickensonville to teach school at either the Sulfur Springs School or the Stony Point School. Gibson was the mother of Dorothy Gibson. (Courtesy of RCPL, provided by Fred Gent.)

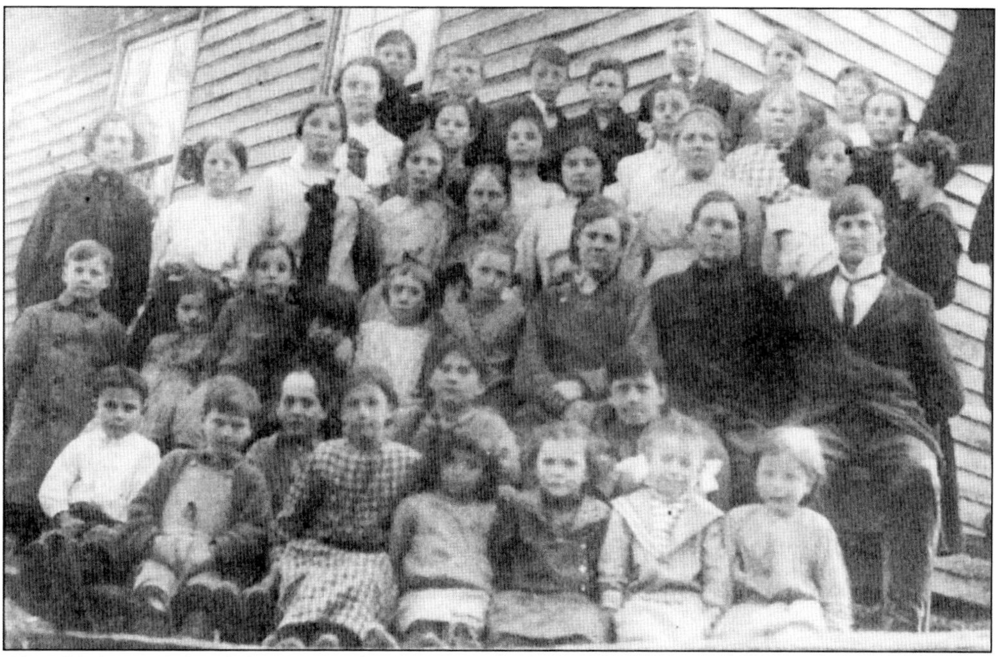

The old Artrip School about 1910 shows a variety of age groups. At the time, a number of different age groups may have been taught at the same time or divided into individual groups. The only individual able to be identified here is Glen William "Bill" Sykes. He is in the back row, the third one to the left of the corner. (Courtesy of James C. Jessee.)

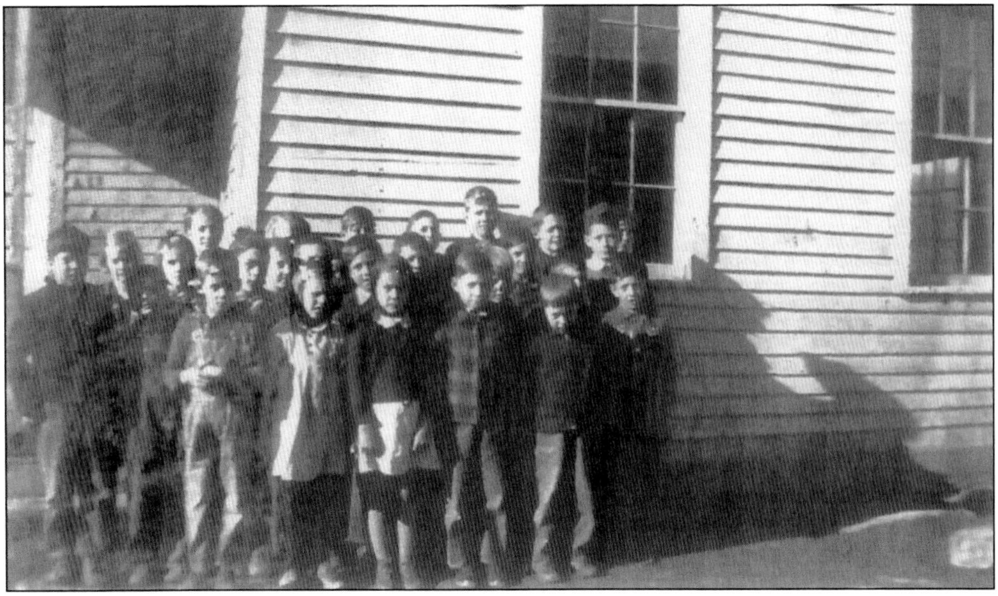

Spruce Pine School in the 1940s, located on Route 640, River Mountain Road near Blackford, strove to educate its students. Included in this photograph from left to right are Harold Hess, Bill Harris, Ruby Hess, Viola Hess, Douglas Honaker, Billy Taylor, Billy Honaker, Ruth Taylor, Ruth Hubbard, Raymond Harris, Joe White, Joe Taylor, Mary Ellen Hess, Irlon Honaker, J. B. Justice, and Clyde Taylor. (Courtesy of RCPL, provided by James C. Jessee.)

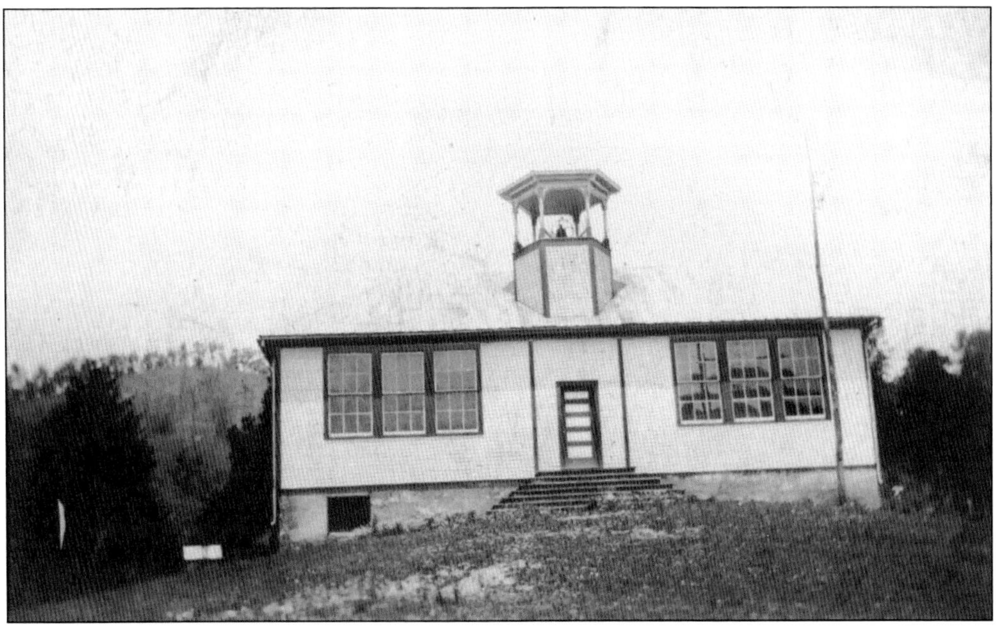

This photograph of Carbo School was taken in 1920. The school was built around 1890 to 1900 from Park Sutherland's estate. As school enrollments increased, larger schools began to emerge, bringing with them separate classes and grade levels. (Courtesy of RCPL, provided by Karen Sutherland.)

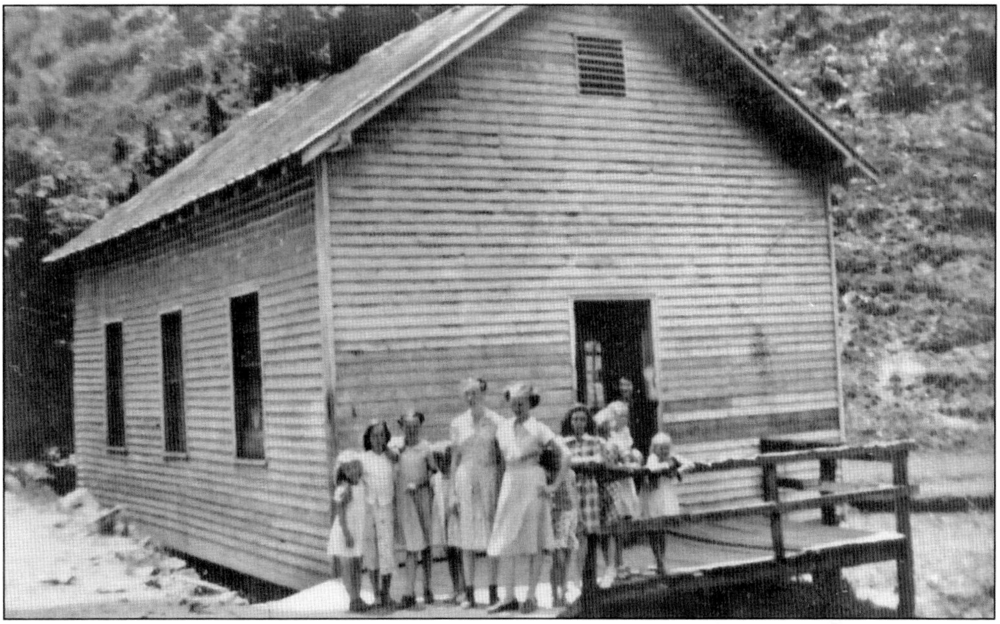

Castle Run School, pictured here in 1882, provided education for its pupils. Most children who received any schooling were taught at home by their parents prior to the existence of one-room schools. Local families began to "pool" their children to share the expense of paying a teacher. This enabled the children to receive what became known as a "schoolhouse" education. This practice resulted in the younger and older children being taught together. (Courtesy of Russell County School Board.)

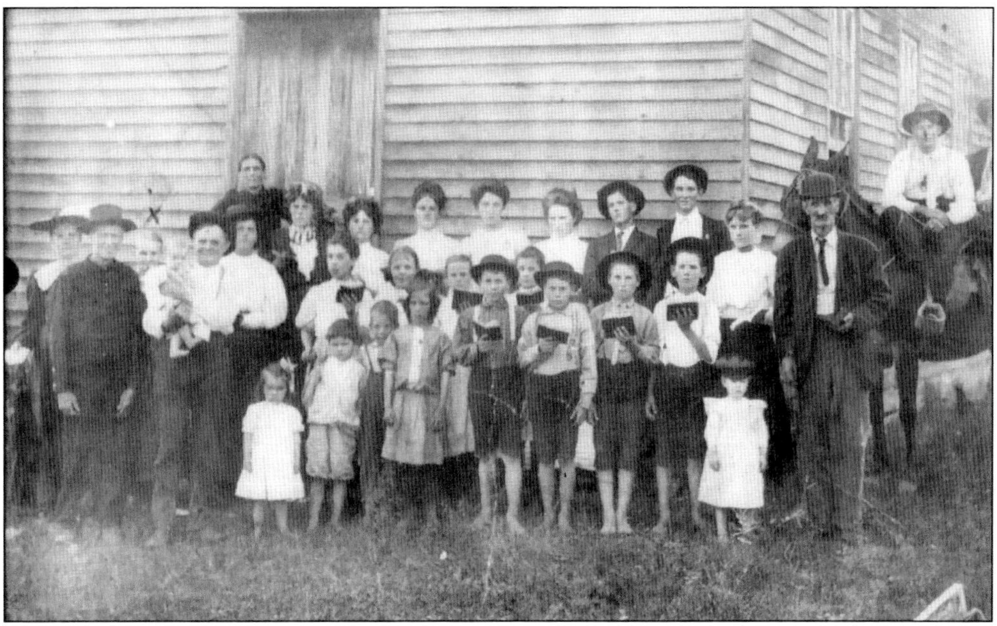

In this picture of the Cleveland School in the late 1800s are both children and adults. In the early days, a schoolhouse was used for church services on Sunday. Schools were used to host other social events as well. It is not known if this was a church service or a special school activity that brought the parents and siblings of the students to school. (Courtesy of James C. and Nellie R. Jessee.)

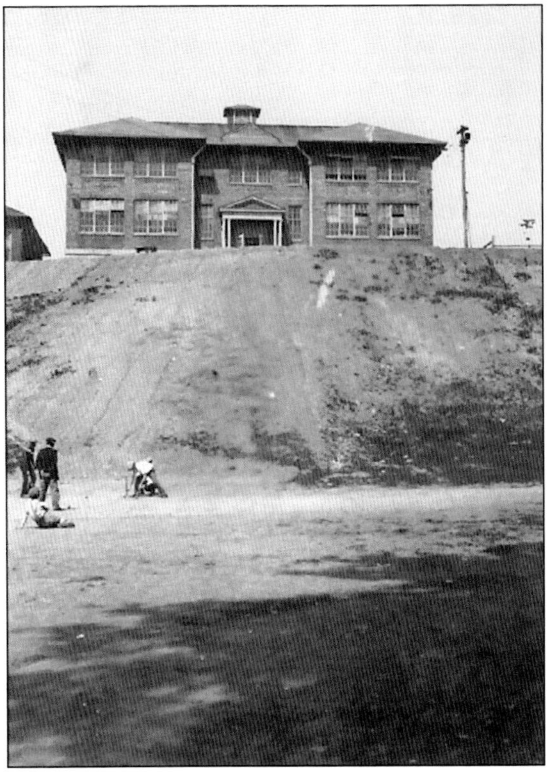

This 1925 picture of Cleveland High School reflects the extended education becoming available. There were no school attendance laws, so many children did not complete the seventh grade. Parents who wanted to ensure that their children had more schooling sent them to stay with family who lived near a high school or sent them off to a boarding school. (Courtesy of Mrs. Ralph Owen.)

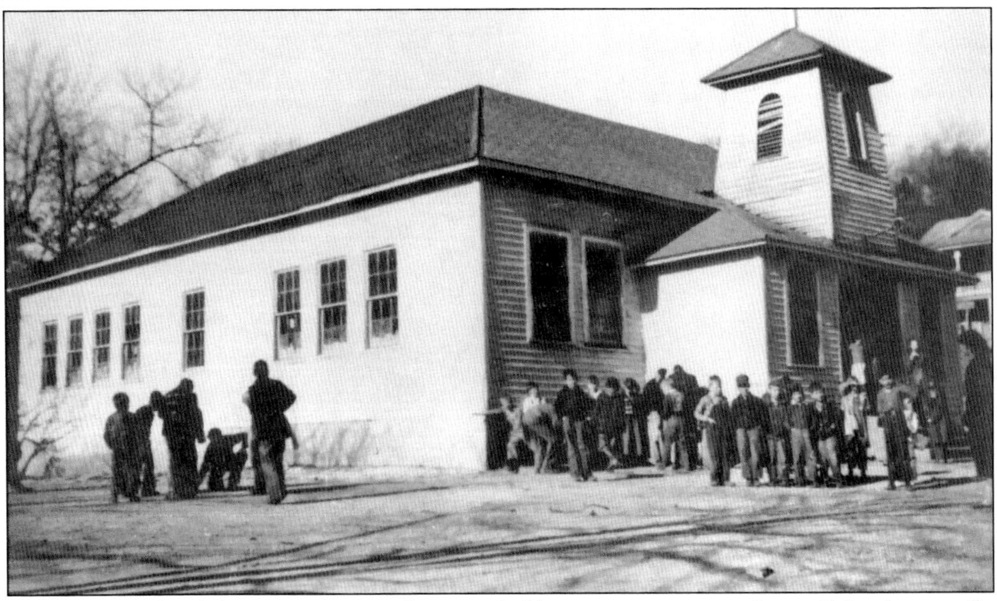

Clinchfield School, here in 1918, was large and able to serve many students. School generally began once the crops had been harvested. It then let out for the year in the spring prior to the planting of the crops. It was vital that families grow the foods and keep the livestock necessary to meet their needs. With the coming of the railroads, many times the head of the household sought work in the coal mining or lumber industry, leaving the farming for the wife and children. (Courtesy of Russell County School Board.)

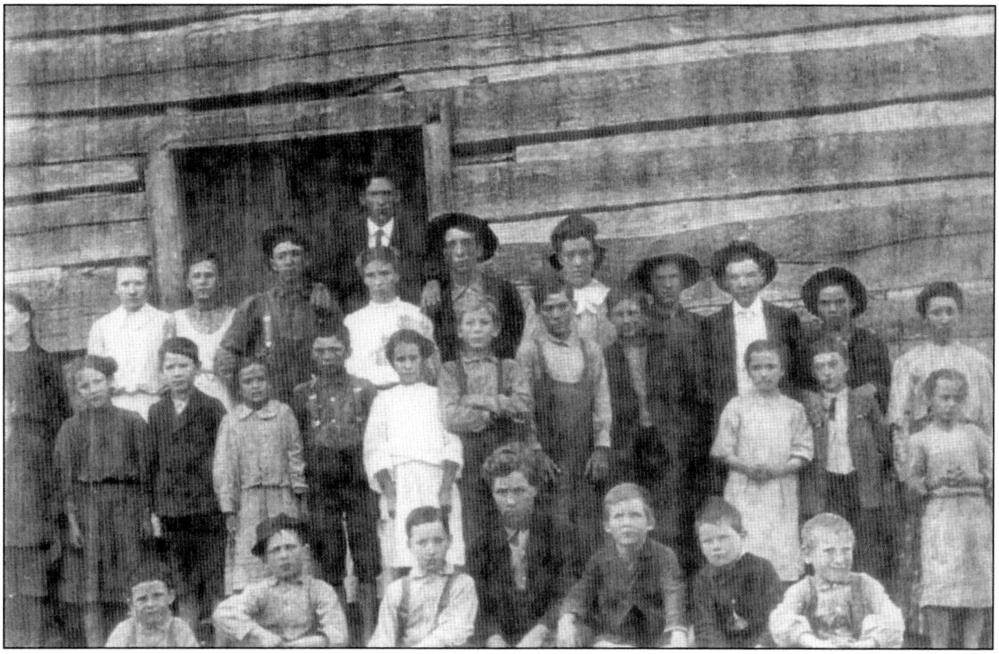

Early schools were often constructed of logs with the cracks filled in with clay mud. The floors consisted of planks, and the roof was generally made of boards. This picture of the Corners School was taken in 1900. The only student identified here is Fred Jackson. He is on the back row, third from the right in the white shirt. (Courtesy of RCPL, provided by James C. Jessee.)

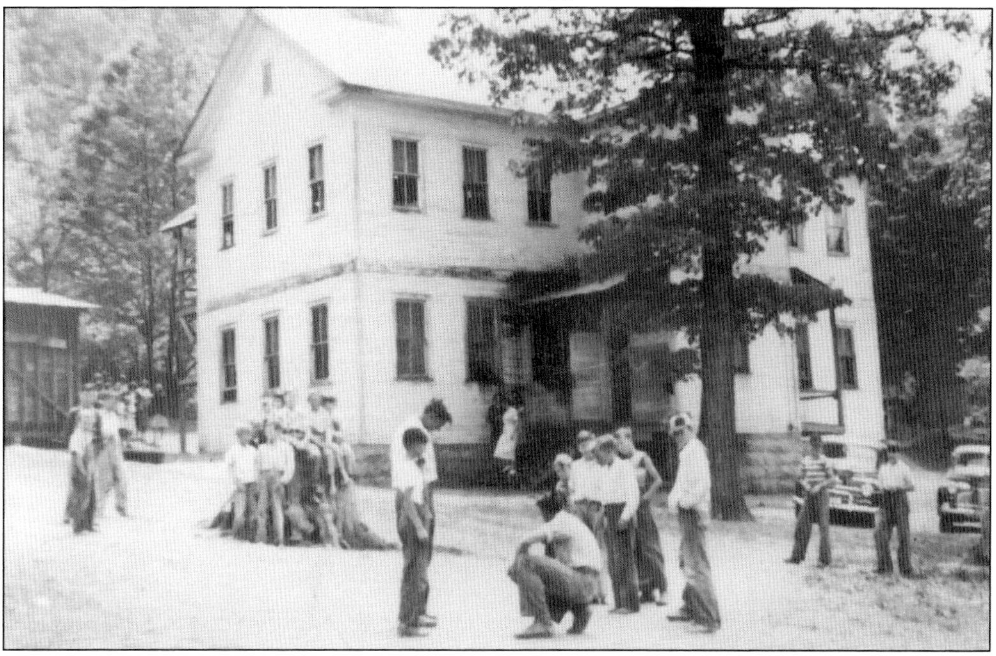

Here is the Crossroads Elementary School in Moccasin in 1915. At recess, a favorite game for many boys was playing marbles. The boys may play for fun or for "keeps." A boy might come to school with a few marbles and leave with a pocketful. This was often frowned upon by the parents, who thought it seemed a little like gambling. (Courtesy of Russell County School Board.)

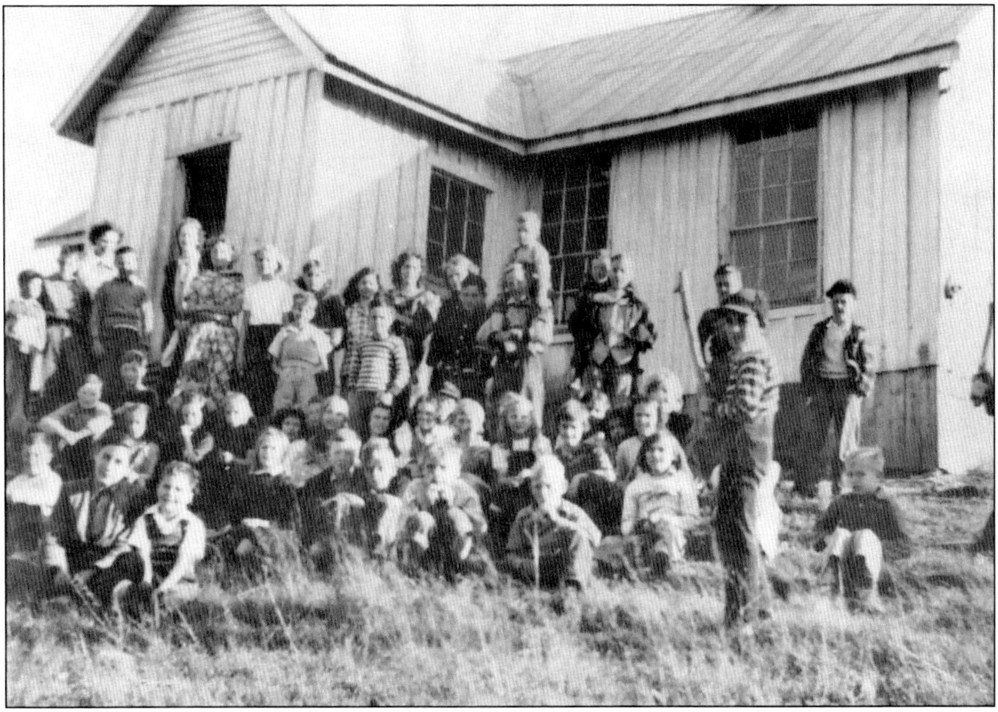

Located between Dickensonville and Hansonville was the Sulphur Springs School. This picture was taken in 1880. (Courtesy of RCPL, provided by Russell County School Board.)

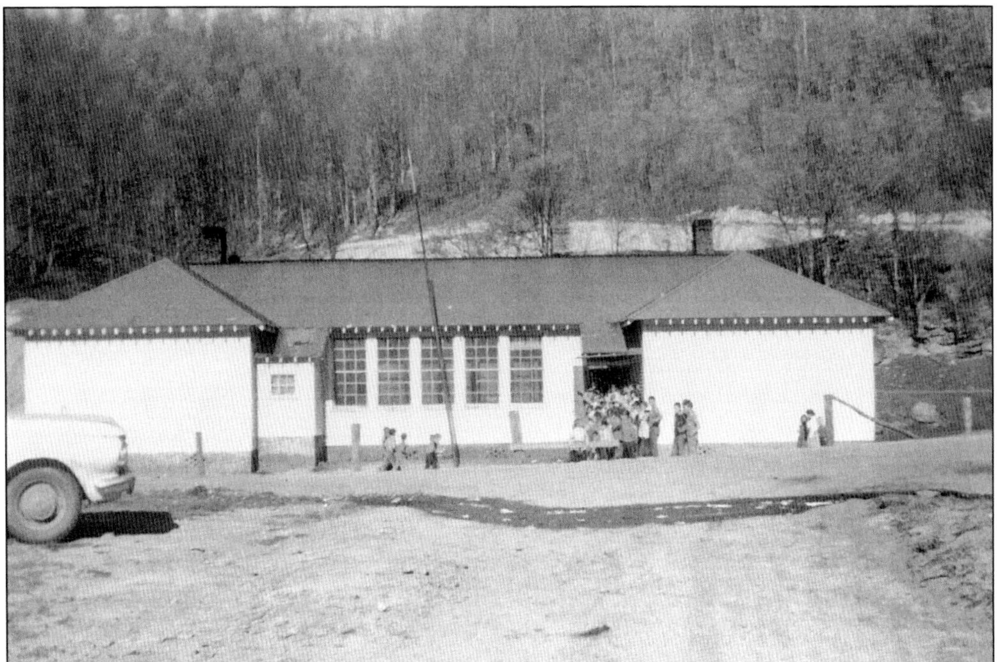

This picture taken in 1963 depicts the Drill Elementary School. The school was closed in 1964 and the students traveled by bus to attend the new Honaker Elementary School. (Courtesy of James C. and Nellie R. Jessee.)

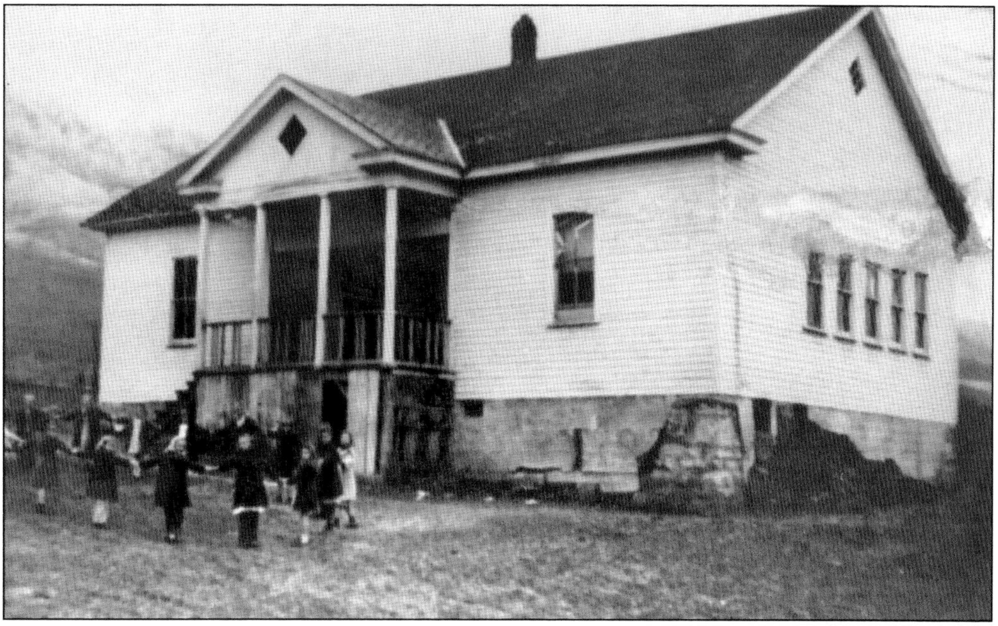

The Elk Garden school is shown in 1917 as the children enjoyed their recess. A favorite game of the children was "Farmer in the Dell." Girls and boys formed a circle as they would sing and walk about; a farmer was often selected by the teacher. The farmer would then choose a wife, the wife would then choose a child, and so on. (Courtesy of RCPL, provided by Russell County School Board.)

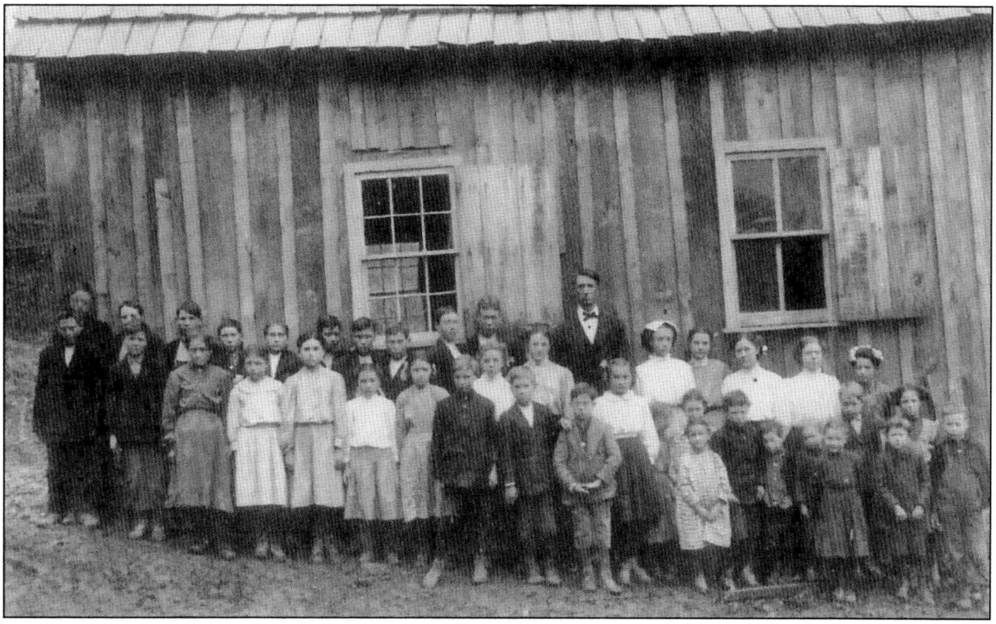

Schools were generally named for the person who donated the land or for the local community. Children often walked miles to attend school, often barefooted until cold weather. After getting shoes for cold weather, the children would sometimes take them off, weather permitting—their little toes knowing freedom for so long did not find the shoes nearly as comfortable. This is the Finney School in the late 1800s. (Courtesy of RCPL, provided by James C. Jessee.)

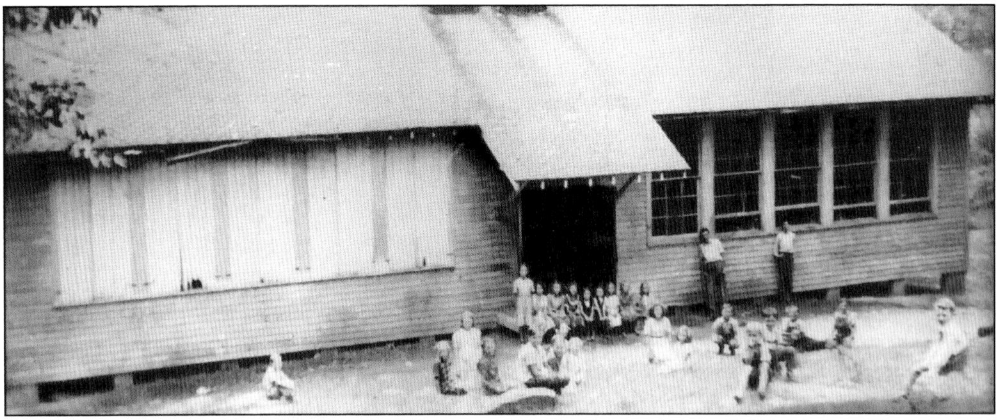

Taken in 1923, this picture is of the Hess Creek School. The students took time from their school day to pose for this picture. (Courtesy of Russell County School Board.)

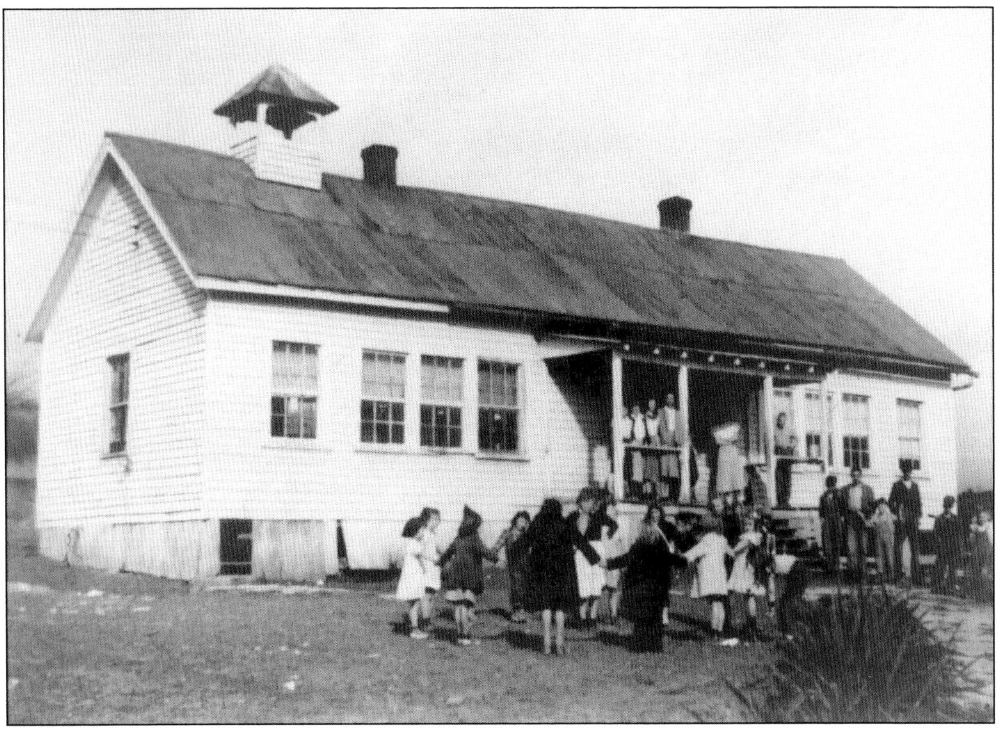

High Point School in 1905 captures its students on film as they participate in recess activities. Perhaps they were playing one of the walking and singing games such as "London Bridge" or "Farmer in the Dell." High Point School was located on Route 71. (Courtesy of RCPL, provided by Russell County School Board.)

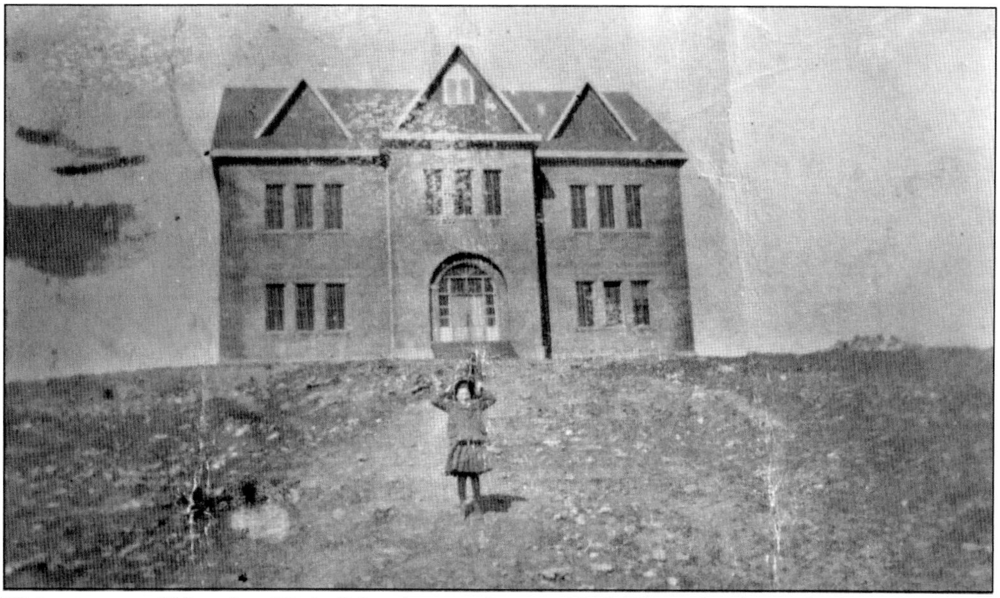

This picture of Honaker High School was taken in 1907. The school was built on Fairmont Street around 1904. The child in the picture is unidentified. (Courtesy of RCPL, provided by Kathleen R. Taylor.)

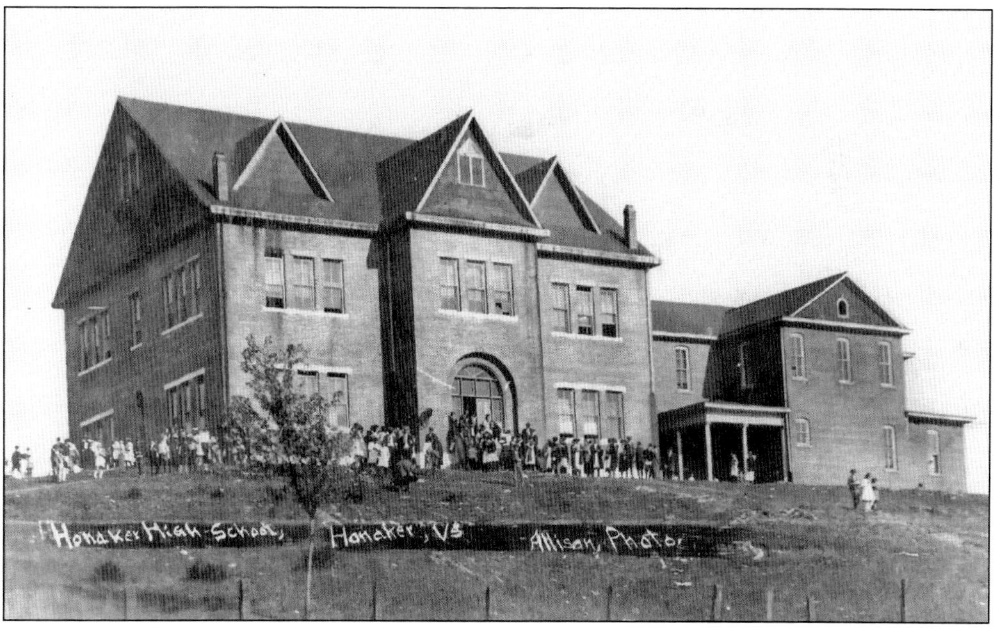

This picture of Honaker High School was taken in the 1920s. The school had four classrooms on each floor. The addition was built in order to offer a music department. In the 1918–1919 school year, it became a four-year high school. In 1927, a new school was built. (Courtesy of RCPL, provided by James C. Jessee.)

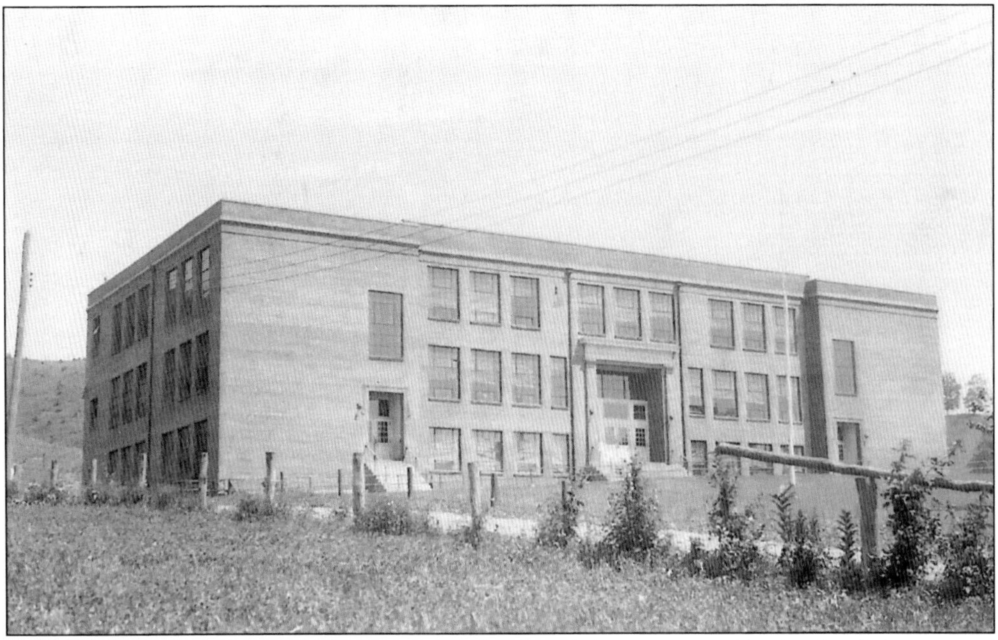

In 1927, this new school was built in Honaker. It offered elementary and high school classes until 1952, when the present-day high school was built. This photograph was taken in 1932. (Courtesy of HHM, provided by Kathleen R. Taylor.)

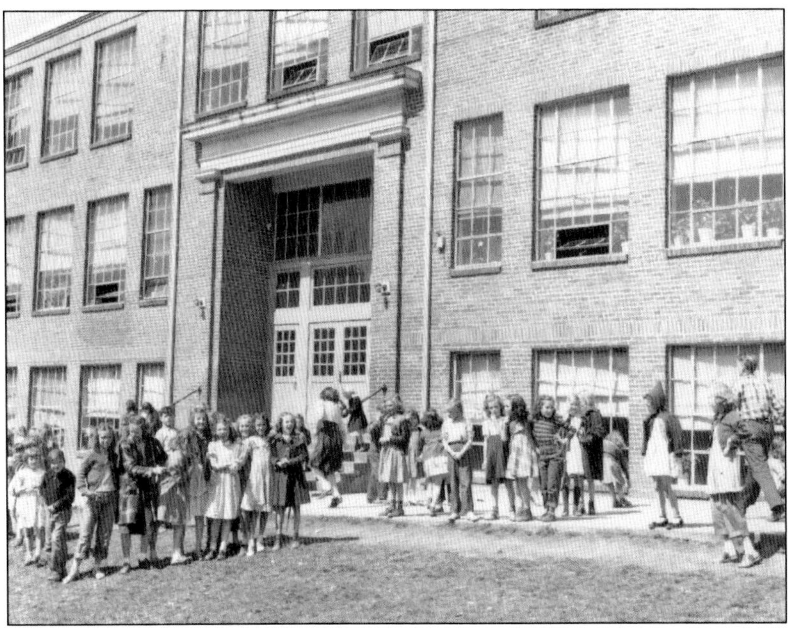

This is an image of Honaker High School in 1950, before it was replaced in 1952 by the current high school. (Courtesy of RCPL, provided by Claude E. Griffith.)

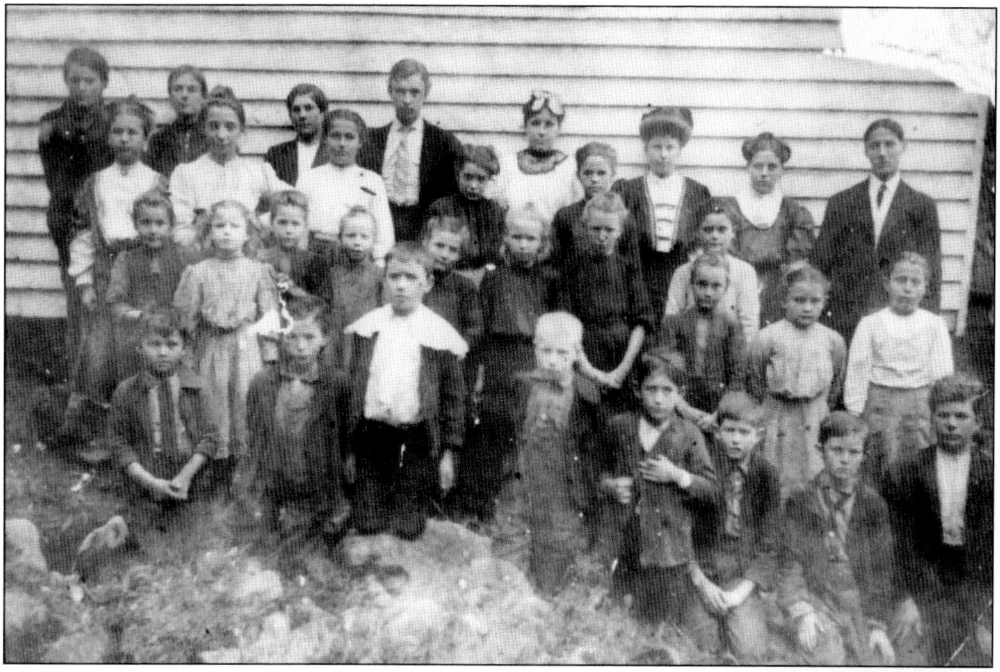

The Rasnake School in the Clinchfield area of Dumps Creek was photographed here 1900–1905. The school was located at the foot of Sourwood Mountain. From left to right are (first row) Holland Kiser, Doris Grizzle, Ray Breeding, Fred Kiser, Billy Grizzle, Walter Grizzle, Seldon Grizzle, and Garrett Breeding; (second row) Efie Taylor, C. Tempance Breeding, Doro Taylor, Lulo Kiser, Winnie Breeding, Farris Rasnake, Pinkie Rasnake, Ada Taylor, Jutish Rasnake, and Casia Rasnake; (third row) Dosha B. Breeding, Celia Taylor, Ida Rasnake, Winnie Grizzle, and Lillie Rasnake; (fourth row) Arnold Rasnake, Frank Breeding, Russell Skeen, Earl Breeding, Mary Skeen, Snoda Breeding, and Sada Rasnake. The teacher was Stafford Rasnake. (Courtesy of RCPL, provided by Lester Watson.)

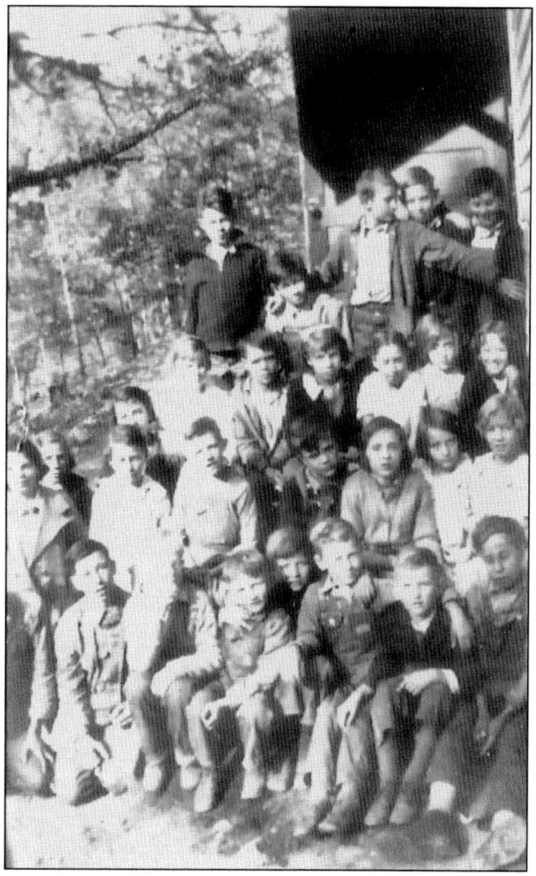

The Horton Ridge School students are pictured here about 1935. Their names are not known, but they no doubt used the early knowledge gained in this schoolhouse setting to prepare themselves to go forth into the future with a greater chance for opportunity. (Courtesy of James C. and Nellie R. Jessee.)

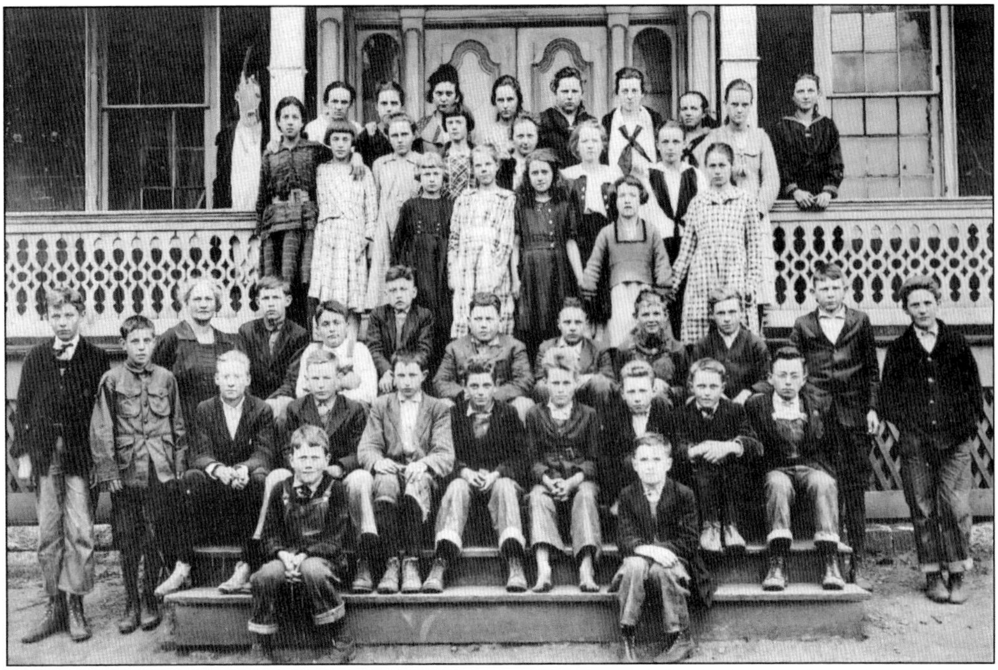

Depicted here are the students in the fifth and sixth grades of the Lebanon State School. This picture was taken in 1919 when their teacher was Julia Fugate. (Courtesy of RCPL, provided by Betty Fugate.)

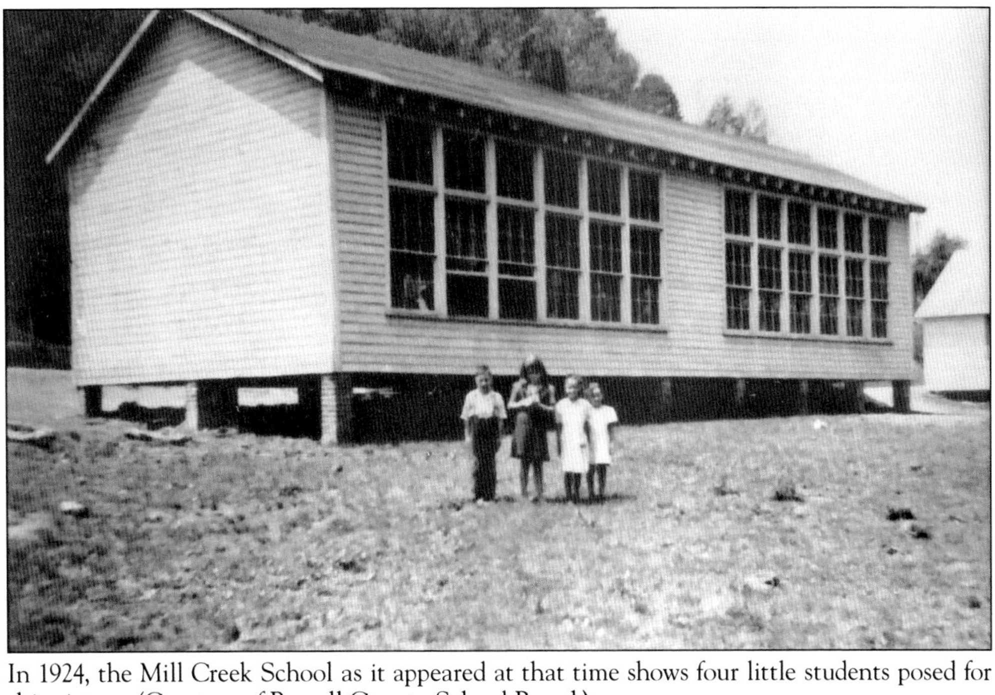

In 1924, the Mill Creek School as it appeared at that time shows four little students posed for this picture. (Courtesy of Russell County School Board.)

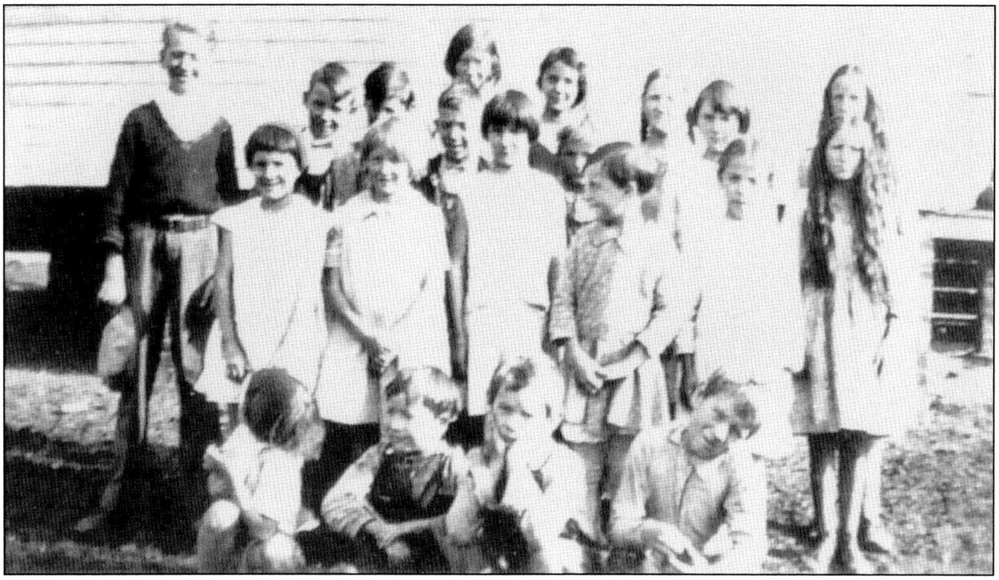

It is told that when this one-room school was built, Penn Barrett, unable to obtain a bell through the school board, had the matter solved for him by his wife. She solicited $16 from friends and neighbors in the community. She then ordered one from the Sears and Roebuck catalog. This 1930 picture of the Penn Barrett School does not show the school bell, but it surely had one. Pictured here are, from left to right, (first row) Geraldine Coleman, Claude Peck, and Carl and Gilmer Yates; (second row) Lois Barrett, Louise Coleman, Vaughn Barrett, Charlene Thompson, Gladys Griffith, and Mary Ann Peck; (third row) Paul Cox, Buford Thompson, Lloyd Coleman, Howard Griffith, Clarence Coleman, Malcolm Barrett, and Gemima Peck; (fourth row) Pauline Fife, Helen Coleman, and Nannie Griffith. (Courtesy of RCPL, provided by James C. Jessee.)

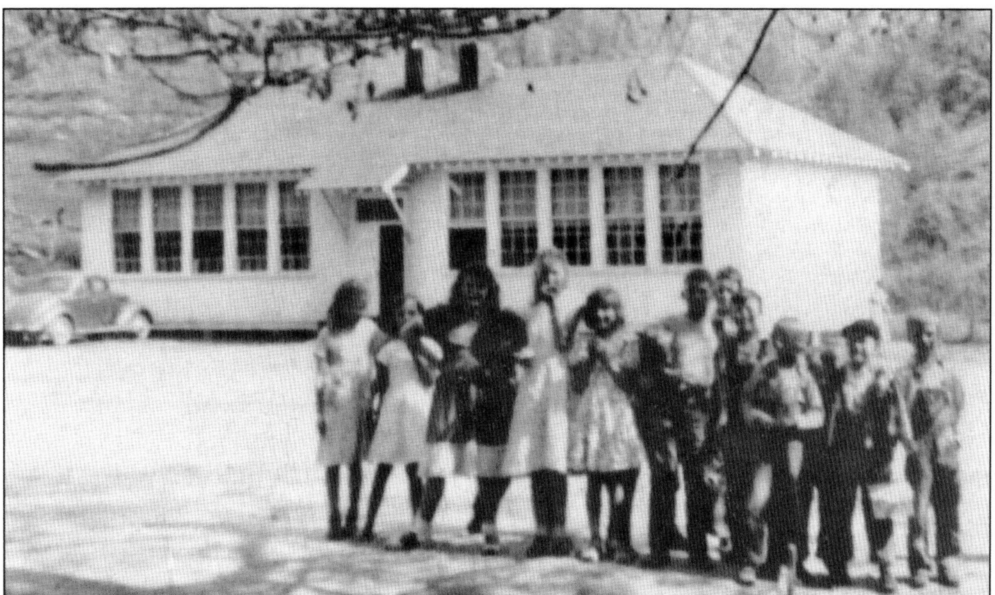

The Pine Creek School is pictured here as it appeared in 1924. As cars and buses came into greater use, many of the schoolchildren had options and were no longer required to walk to school. (Courtesy of RCPL, provided by Russell County School Board.)

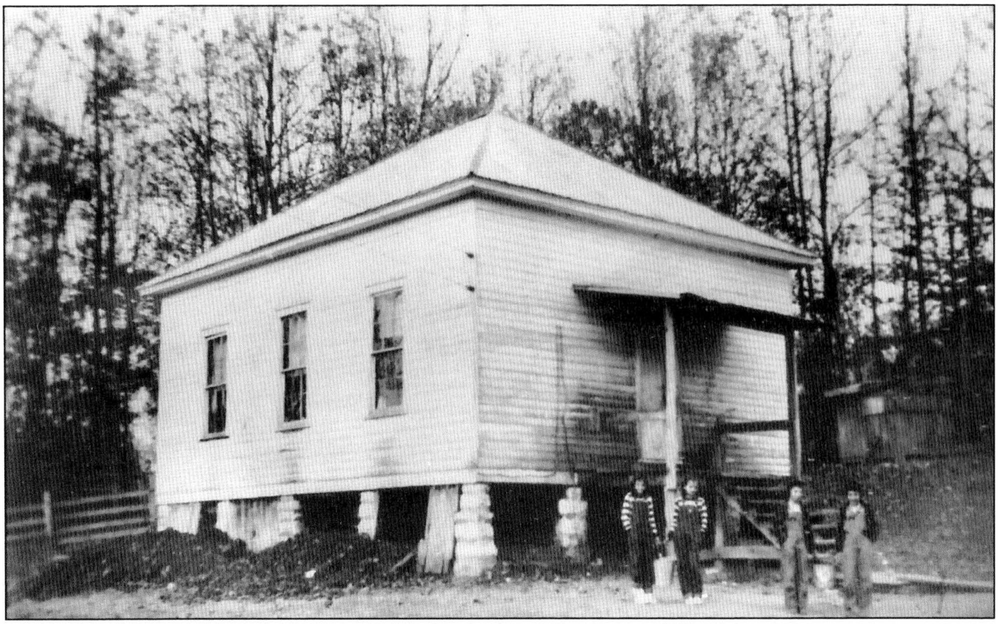

Coal was usually provided by the county, but the children, usually the boys, were responsible for gathering the wood needed to start the fires. Sometimes a child may have been paid 5¢ or 10¢ a day to come in early and start fires. Water would be brought in a large bucket with a big dipper, often with each person using the same dipper. These pupils are attending the Spring City School in 1919. (Courtesy of Russell County School Board.)

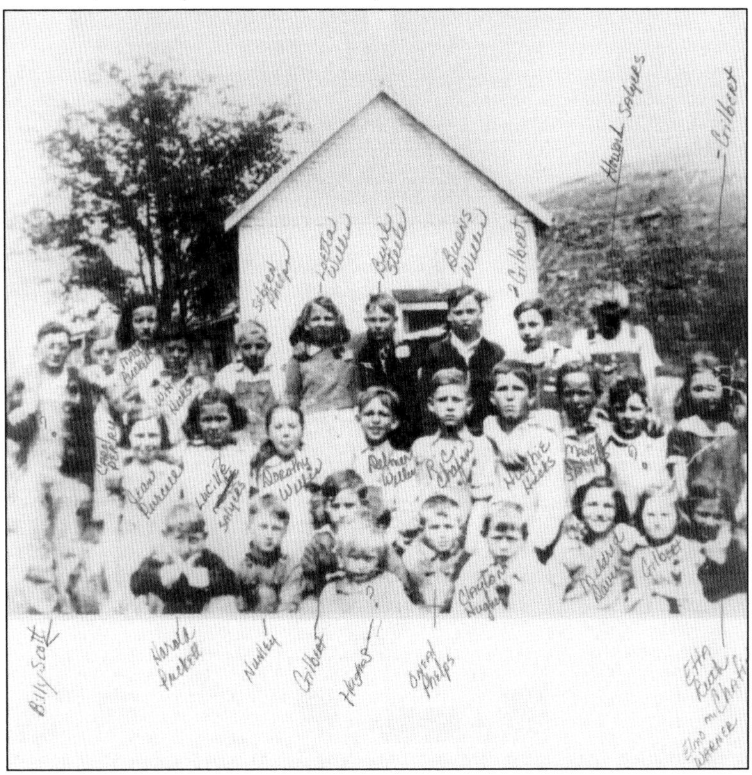

The pupils of the Stony Point School on Route 71 in the late 1930s are reflected here. The Guy B. Davis Store, next to the Stony Point School, was once owned and operated by "Cooney" Davis and his wife, Pauline. One of Pauline's chickens used to lay eggs under the schoolhouse. The school kids would find the eggs and take them to the store and trade them for candy. (Courtesy of RCPL, provided by Mildred Davis.)

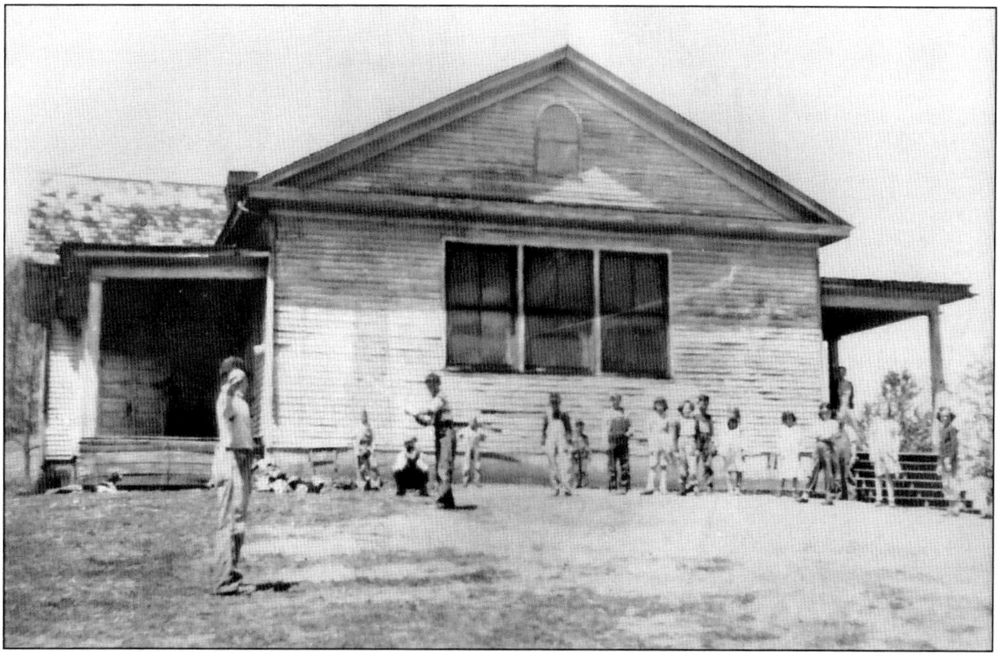

These young students take time out for recess and a friendly little game of baseball at the Sunny Point School in 1918. (Courtesy of Russell County School Board.)

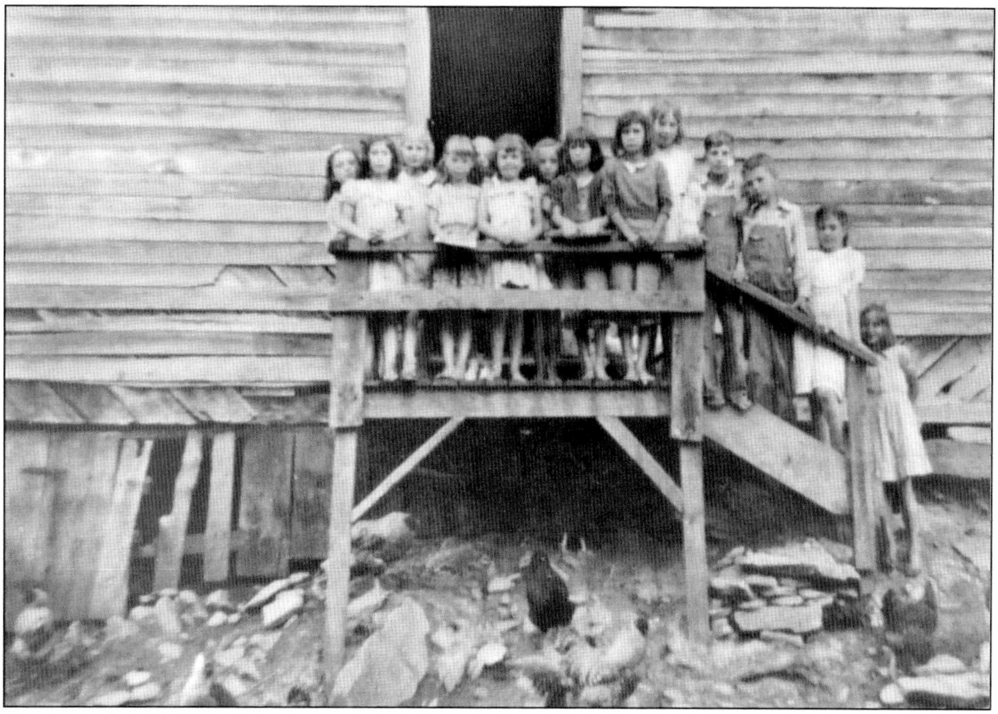

At the Whited School in 1919, these children take a break from their studies to pose for this picture. Students studied reading, writing, and arithmetic. Spelling, multiplication tables, and poems were memorized and recited before classmates. (Courtesy of RCPL, provided by Russell County School Board.)

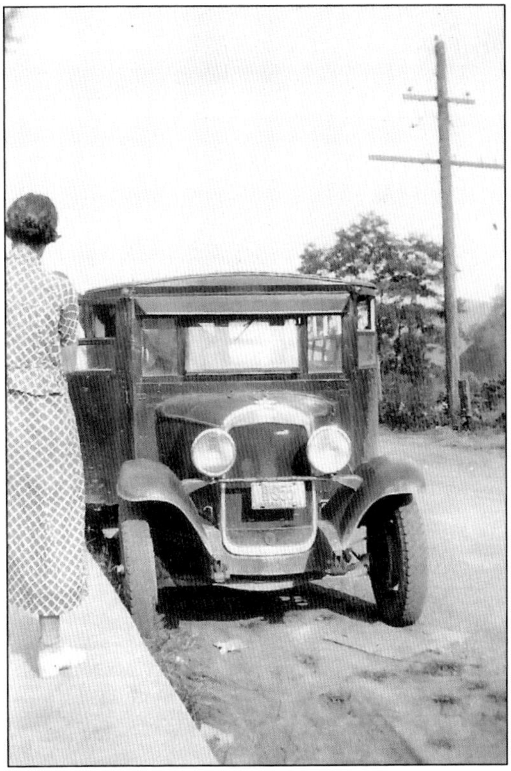

The "Old Red Goose" was the name given to the school bus that ran from Honaker to Pine Creek. The driver was Hollis Ball. This picture was taken in 1935. (Courtesy of HHM.)

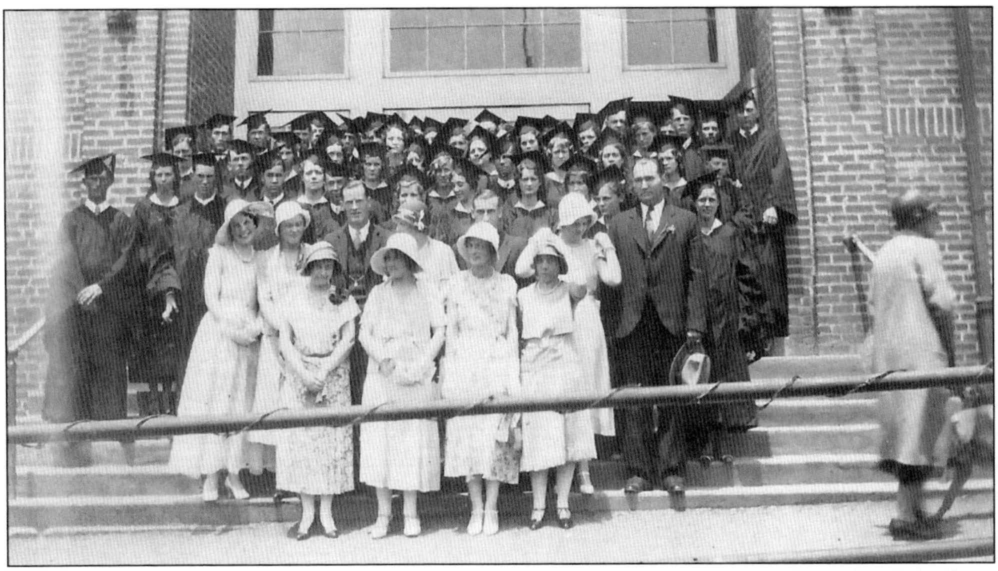

The graduating class of Honaker High School is pictured here in 1932. This school, built in 1927, was the second high school in Honaker. Hazel Beatrice Compton Fuller (eighth from left, third row) graduated in this class. She was so determined to graduate that she rode a horse from Coulwood to Finney so she could catch the train to Honaker every morning and then repeated the same process in reverse to get back home each day. At the time, it was only necessary to complete 11 grades in order to graduate. Evelyn Ball Hobbs was also a graduate of this class and later returned to the Honaker High School as a math teacher. (Courtesy of RCPL.)

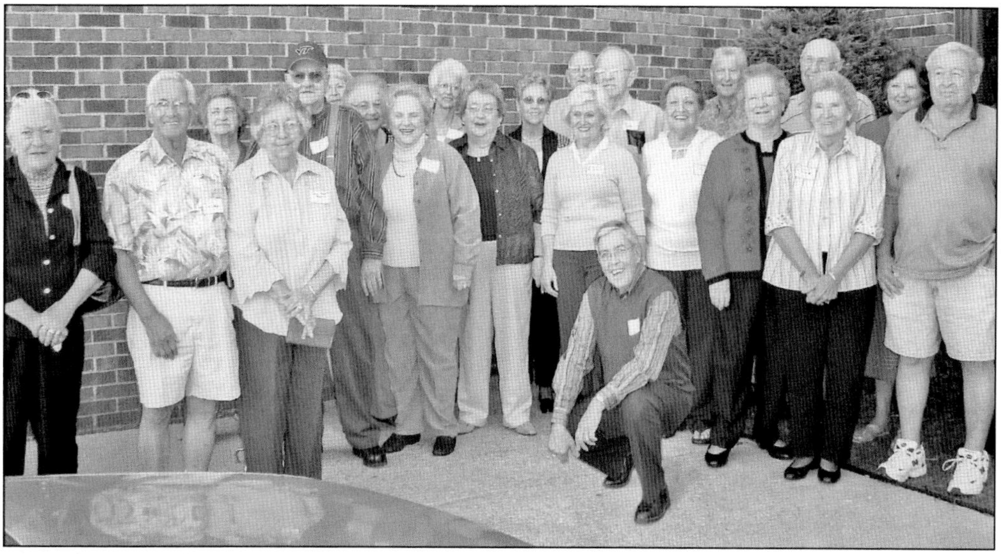

The Lebanon High School class of 1952 at their 55th reunion included, from left to right, (kneeling) class president Leon W. Castle; (first row) Shirley Harcum McDaniels, Donald Lasley, Virginia Carpenter Fogleman, Con Puckett Jr., Betty Vandyke Childers, Nancy Stinson Herndon, Ann Sykes McClanahan, Virginia B. Ferguson, Reva Litton Keith, Frances Mitchell Harlan, and Roy Davis; (second row) teacher Daisy Campbell, Nancy Aker Cross, Regina Fields Robinson, Edith Sutton Gibson, Bernice Kimberlin Keesling, Kenneth Garrett, Paul Price, Douglas Buckles, Tommy Whited, and Wyolodean Hughes Steelman. Billy Owens is not pictured. (Courtesy of Jerry Lark.)

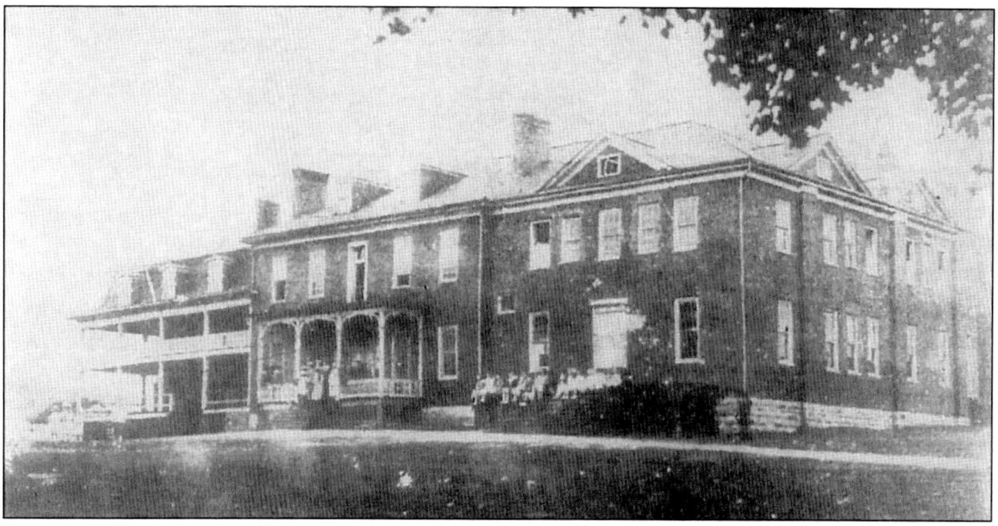

Russell College was established in Lebanon in 1892. The Russell College 14th annual catalog indicates that the school year began on September 3, 1906, and concluded with the commencement sermon on May 20, 1907. This early college catalog indicates that Lebanon in Russell County is known for the cultural refinement and morality of its citizens. The catalog further states that there are no saloons in Lebanon or in Russell County. This catalog also claims "shoddyism" is considered unacceptable and further that those best trained have the best chance in life—that life, education, and a "genuine sterling character" are all worthwhile. (Courtesy of RCPL, provided by James C. and Nellie R. Jessee.)

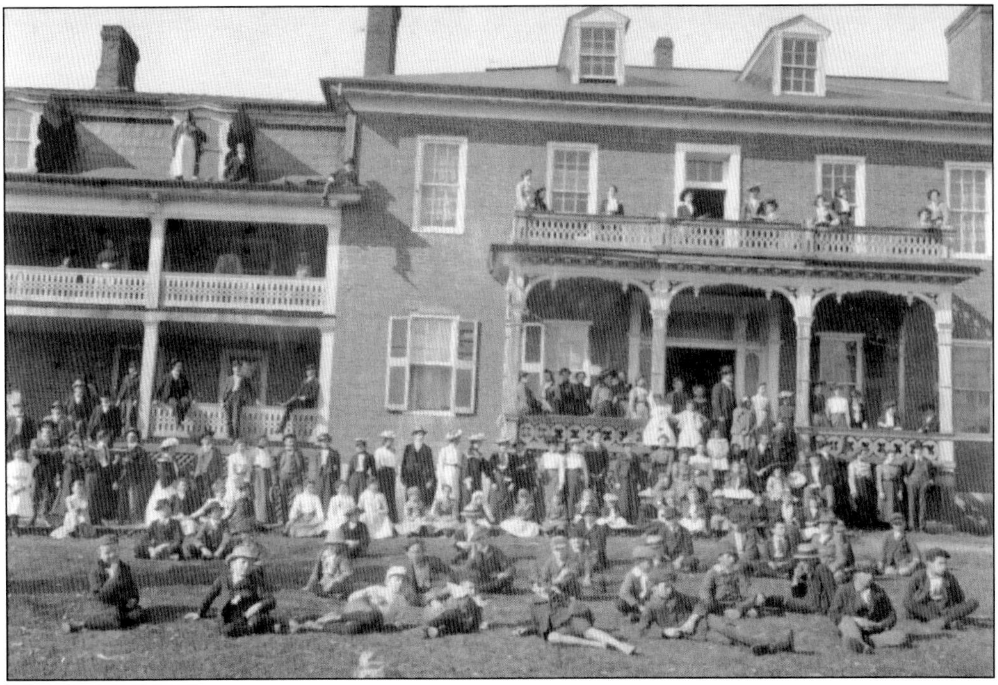

This picture of Russell College was taken in 1900. (Courtesy of RCPL, provided by Marquerik Walden.)

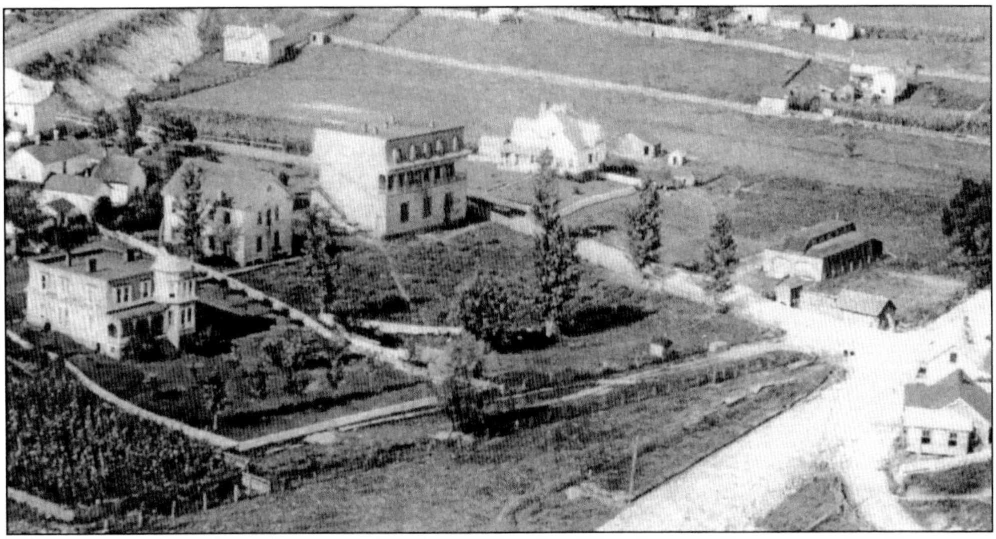

Opened in 1897, Old Dominion College was located in Honaker. In the picture, Old Dominion College is the building with the fence and also includes the two buildings to the right of it. In addition to academics, the school served the cultural needs of the students, faculty, and local people. Music, art, public speaking, plays, public recitals, and special classes were offered. Alson Hutton and his wife, Margaret "Maggie" Kendrick, founded the school, with Maggie's father, John M. Kendrick, having built the school. Prior to founding the school, Alson Hutton lived in Glade Spring and was founder and principal of Southwest Virginia Female Institute, which was moved to Bristol and in 1920 became what is now known as Virginia Intermont College. (Courtesy of HHM.)

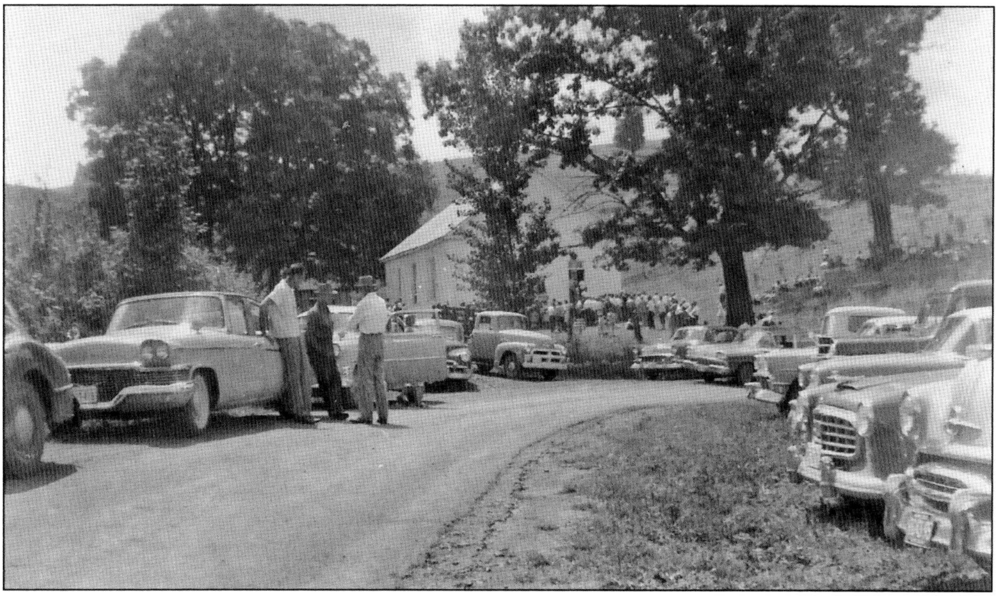

New Garden Primitive Baptist Church is the oldest church in Honaker. Pictured here is an association meeting in October 1959. In 1813, Martin Honaker and his son Nicholas donated the land for the church. It became the first church in Honaker. It served three denominations until the 1860s. The Missionary Baptists, the Primitive Baptists, and the Methodists worshipped together in the same church. The Primitive Baptists remained when the other two left. (Courtesy of Diane Fuller.)

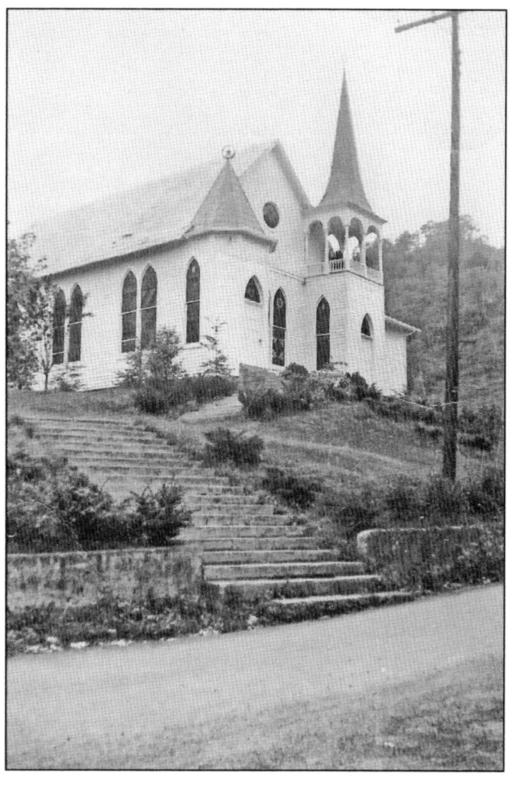

The First Baptist Church is one of the oldest buildings in Honaker. Early members recall carrying lanterns on the way to attend the night services. Dr. and Mrs. M. O. Burke supervised the planning and building of the church. Dr. John Lockhart is said to have been concerned about the construction of the steps, as he had big feet, and requested that the steps be deep enough to place his feet straight when climbing them. His daughter, Gaynelle Lockhart Albert, stated later that her father had been satisfied with the results. (Courtesy of HHM.)

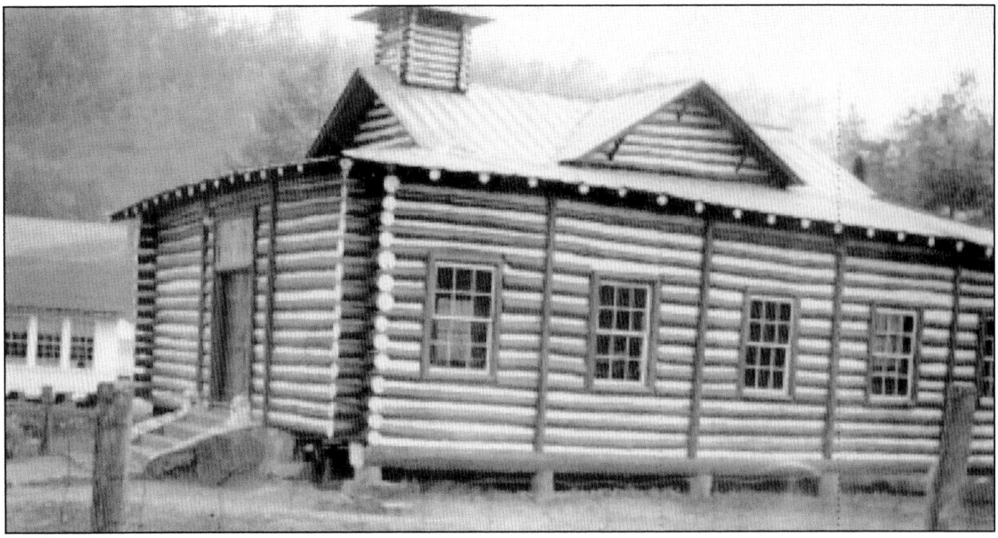

On July 29, 1934, Pine Creek Community Log Church was dedicated. This little church was built during the Great Depression, when money was scarce, for a little more than $500. With Fred Gent donating the land and Emma Martin donating the logs, it was built by hand by its membership. Since there were many denominations in the Pine Creek area, it was decided that the church would be non-denominational and would meet in the name of one Savior—Jesus Christ. This is still the practice to this day. Mae Wells Ball has been credited with accumulating and maintaining the rich history of this church, as its very existence brings hope and peace to those who worship there. (Courtesy of Judy A. Hess.)

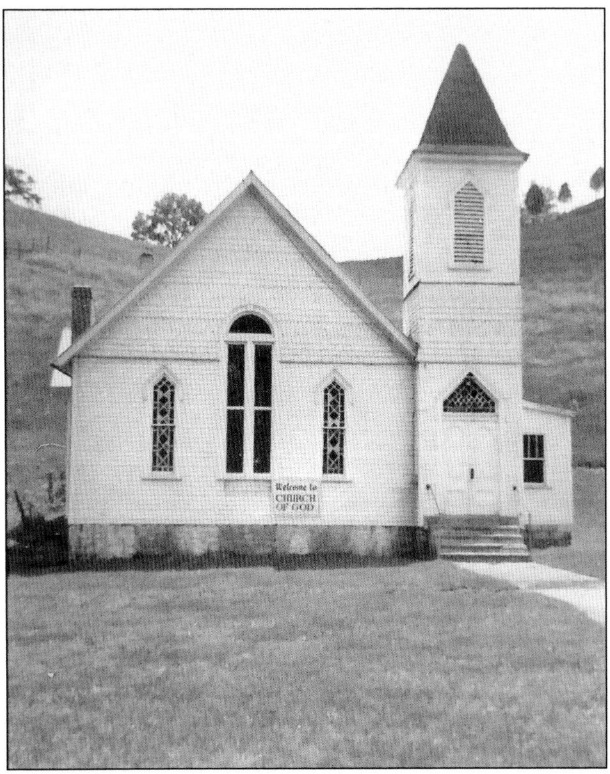

First Methodist Church in Honaker was built in 1901 near the train depot. Notice the bell tower. Bells were an important form of communication. The ringing of bells might announce a marriage, the birth of a child, an emergency, the passing of a neighbor, or the very obvious—a call to worship service. (Courtesy of HHM, provided by Kathleen R. Taylor.)

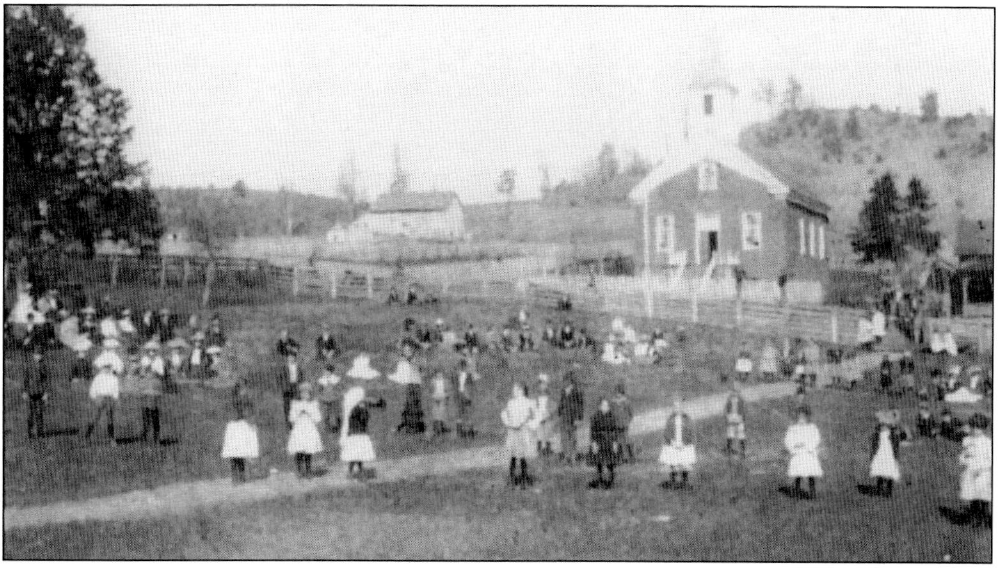

Following issues surrounding the subject of missions among the members of the Glade Baptist Church, located two miles west of Lebanon, it was decided the mission group would build a new Baptist meeting house in the town of Lebanon. This church was built in 1854 and became known as the Missionary Baptist Church. The Glade Hollow Church began meeting at the new church. It was later agreed that the Glade Hollow Church would then become the Lebanon Baptist Church of Christ, organized on April 27, 1856. William N. Huff became the first pastor. (Courtesy of RCPL.)

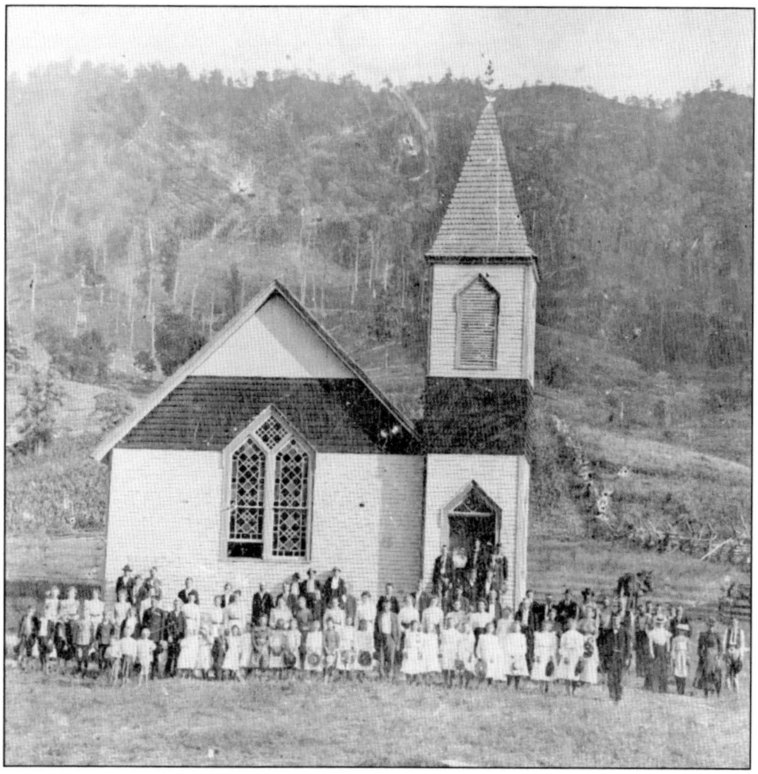

This picture is of the Bascom Methodist Church when it was built on Route 657 "up" Big Cedar Creek. Notice the large congregation dressed in their "Sunday go to meeting" best. Attendance and dressing for church were important to folks of the day. The church was the center of the community's life and was a source of pride for its community and congregation. Most attended. (Courtesy of RCPL, provided by Alma Lester.)

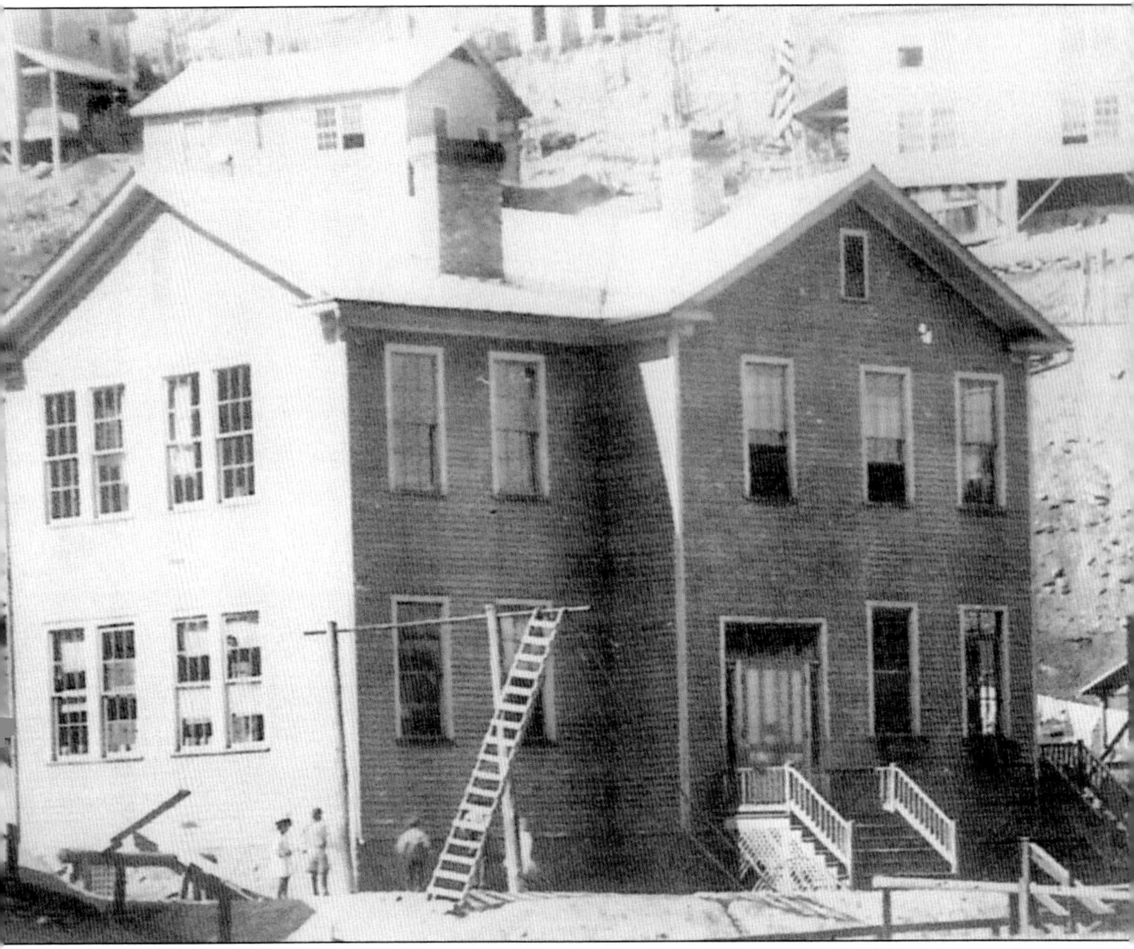

The Wilder School building served the needs of the Wilder community. Wilder was a coal-mining town. The Clinchfield Coal Corporation was active there from 1910 until 1930. After the coal operations closed down, many families moved to Dante and Clinchco to continue working for the Clinchfield Coal Corporation. During the most active operations of Clinchfield, Hungarians, Italians, Greeks, and Polish would regularly arrive on the trains from New York to work in the mines. Many stayed and made this their home. The individual families and ethnic groups brought with them their recipes and culture. These all meshed together to create a rich cultural blend. Often in the school, the teachers found themselves teaching students who struggled with the English language. (Courtesy of RCPL.)

Four

AGRICULTURE AND INDUSTRY

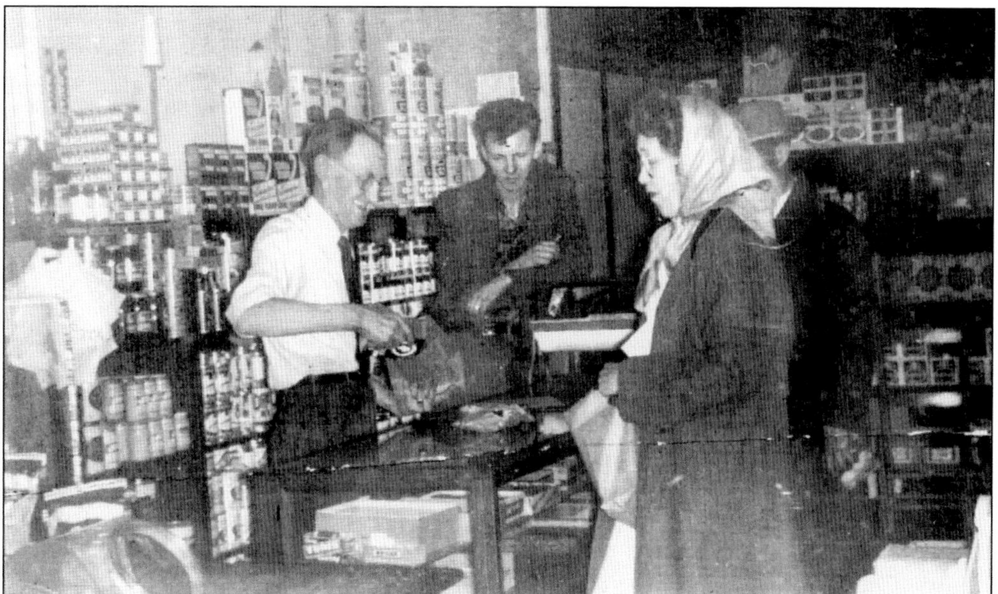

This picture of Fuller's Cash Store in Honaker was taken in 1946 after Clarence and Bea Fuller purchased the building from First National Bank. The groceries, store shelves, and display cases were purchased from Clarence Turner. Dell Fuller, Clarence's great-uncle, worked as a salesman for over 25 years. Dell and his wife, Sally Fuller, owned the Honaker Hotel. Nora Shelton is the lady in the picture. She taught third grade and lived upstairs over the store until she moved to Kingsport to live with her daughter. Anna Jackson worked in the store also. A year later, in 1947, it became a dry goods store. It remained open until 1978. (Courtesy of HHM, provided by Diane Fuller.)

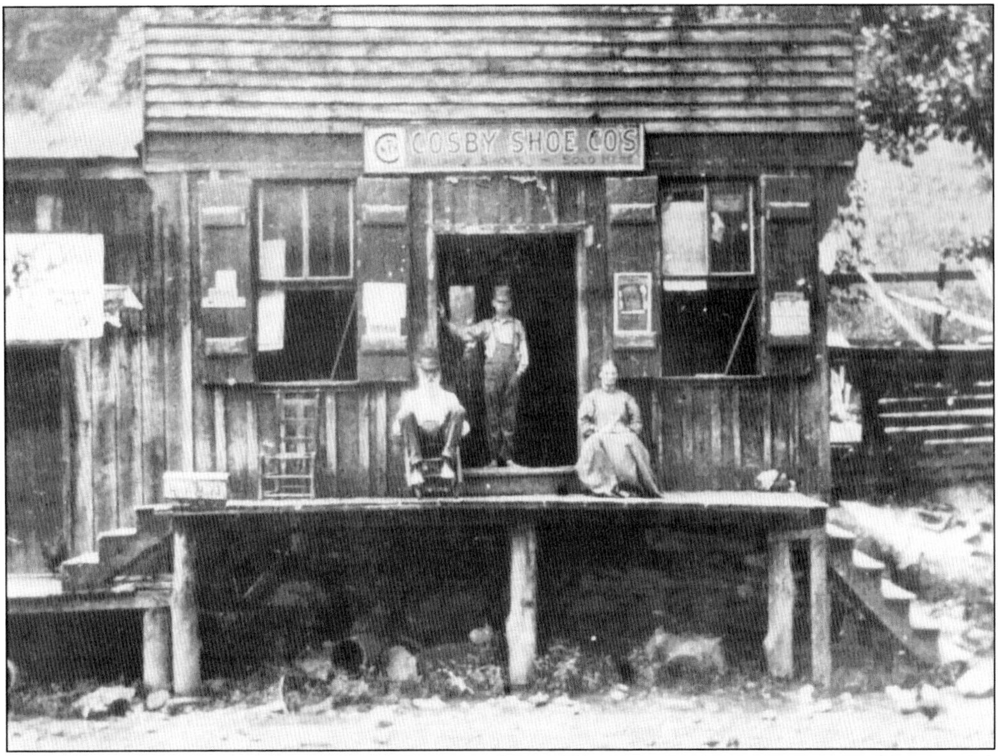

This store was located in the Moccasin section of Russell County at the intersection of Routes 613 and 676. This store was owned by Rev. Robert Cross and Katherine Statzer Cross. Their grandson Oscar is standing in the doorway. The donor of this picture is the great-grandson of Rev. Robert Cross. The chicken coop on the right was destroyed the first time Route 613 was widened. This picture was taken pre-1910. (Courtesy of RCPL, provided by Donald G. Cross Sr.)

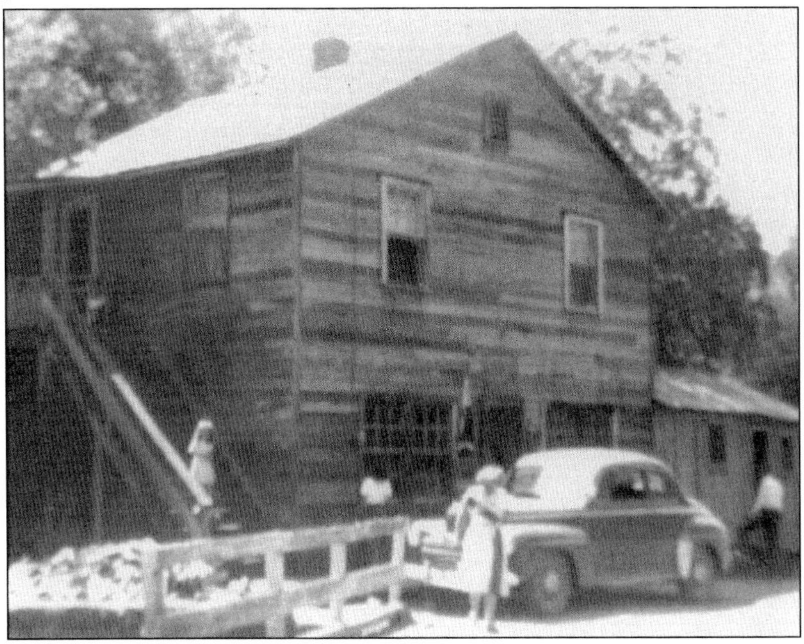

Located near Jessee's Mill, the Mill Creek Store was located at Route 645 and Route 640. Photographed here in the late 1940s, the Mill Creek Store carried most items local residents required for their daily lives. (Courtesy of RCPL, provided by Donald G. Cross Sr.)

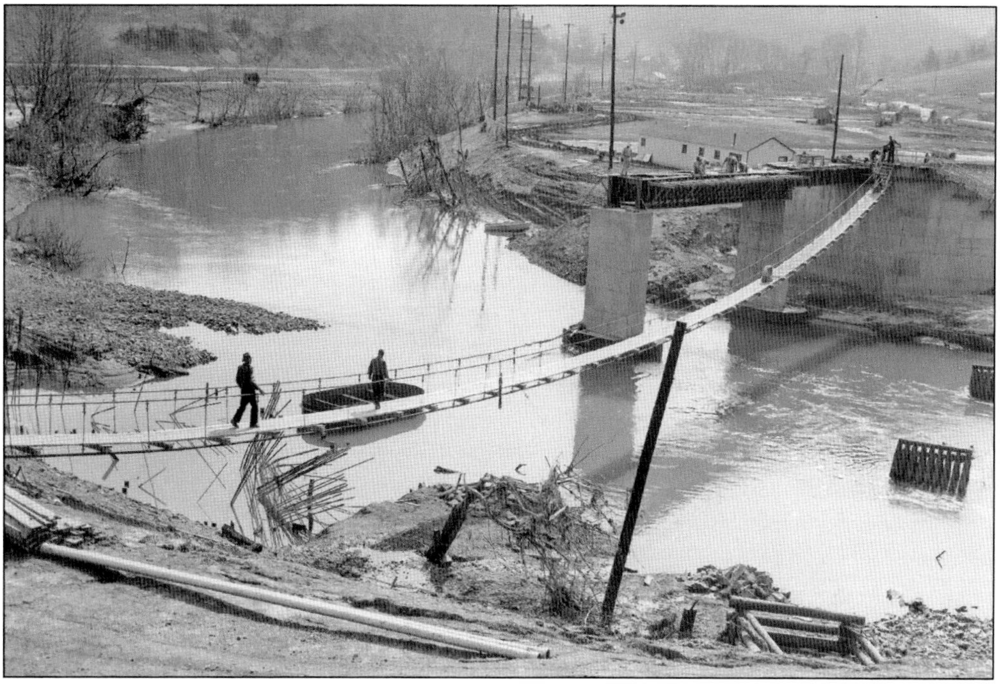

This picture taken on February 18, 1957, shows the Clinch River Plant in Carbo. The view is looking southeast showing the new suspension bridge. This plant would take coal and convert it to electricity. (Courtesy of RCPL, provided by Appalachian Electric Power.)

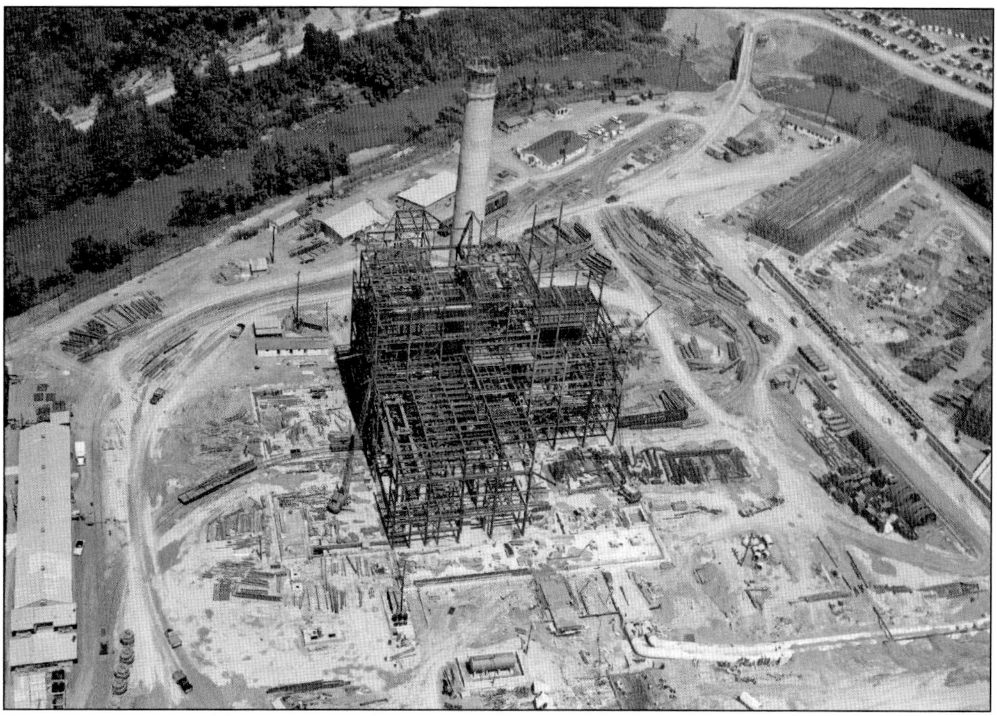

On August 27, 1957, this picture was taken of the Clinch River Plant in Carbo. This is an aerial shot looking north. (Courtesy of RCPL, provided by Appalachian Electric Power.)

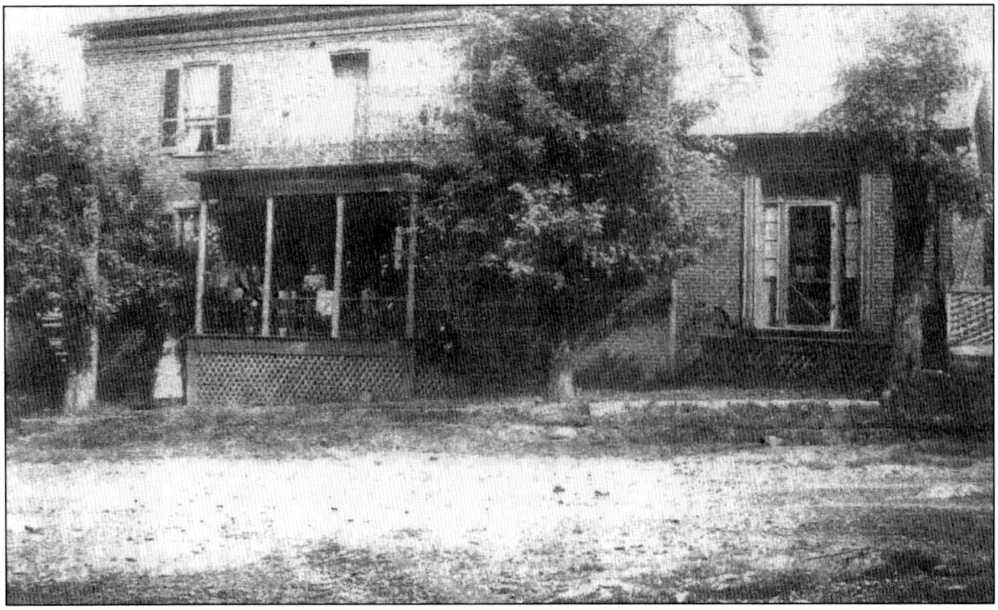

Pictured here is the Alderson Building on the north side of Lebanon. This picture was taken just after 1900. Years later, Alfred and Tom Alderson opened a store here. This store was called Alfred's and was in the section fronted with the small porch. (Courtesy of RCPL, provided by Barry Hess.)

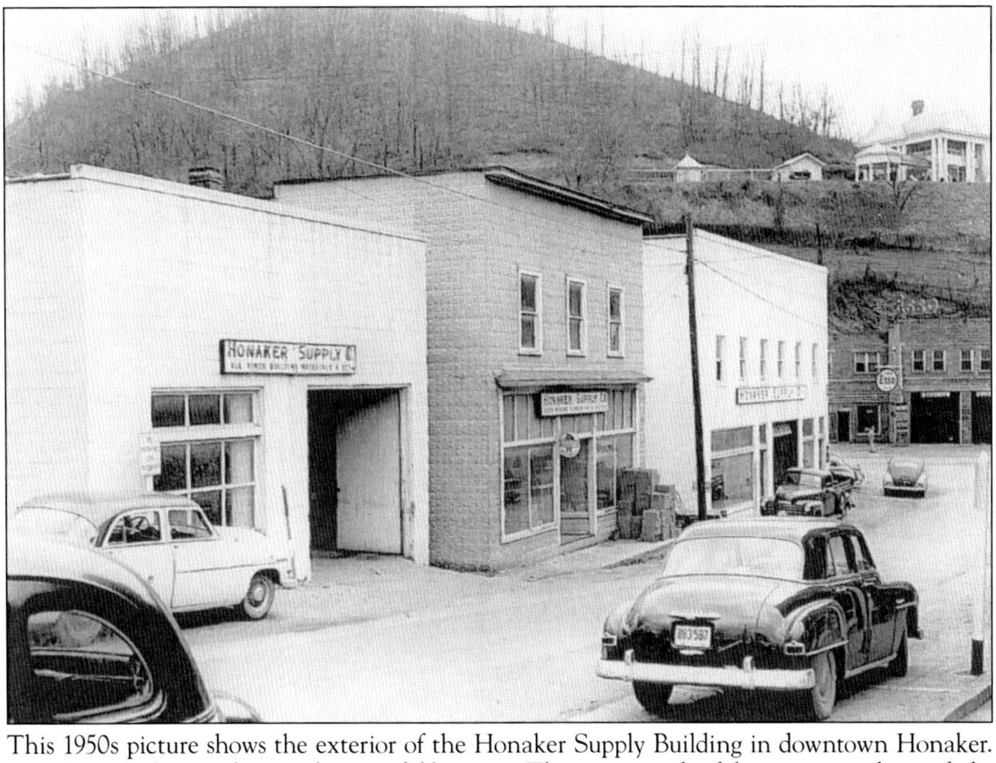

This 1950s picture shows the exterior of the Honaker Supply Building in downtown Honaker. Honaker Supply was a busy and successful business. The many needs of the customers demanded a lot of inventory and space to store and display it. (Courtesy of RCPL, provided by Barry Hess.)

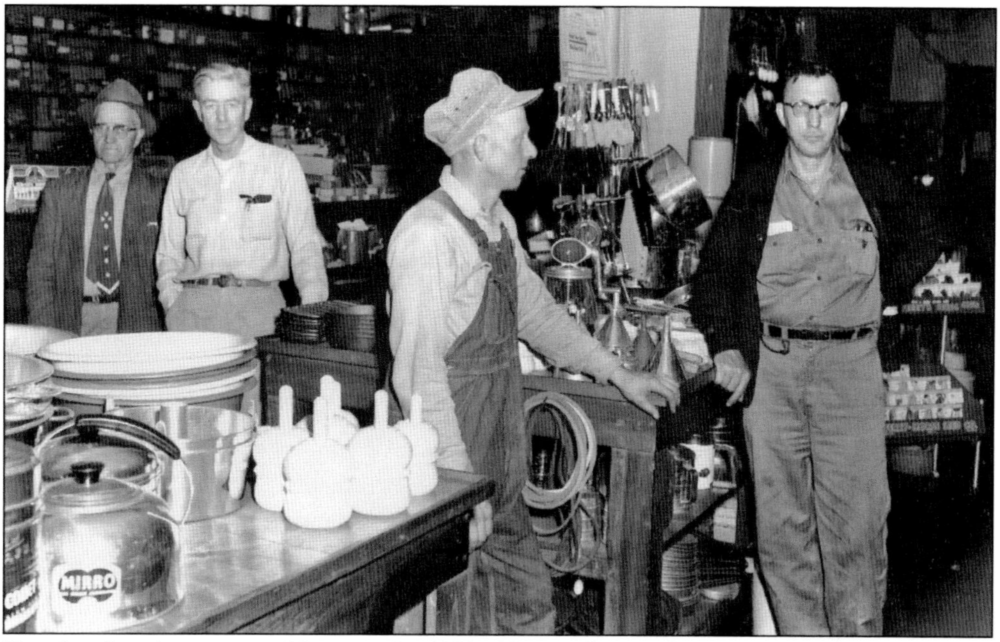

Honaker Supply is pictured here in the 1950s. Notice the ample inventory and the variety of items, including cooking and eating utensils, flour sifters, glass churns, seeds, and thermoses to mention only a few. Carefully stored on the top shelves to the left are the children's red flyer wagons, providing a great viewing advantage for little eyes. Pictured here are, from left to right, Henry Honaker, Arch Barrett (who worked here), Stanley Boyd, and Robby Smith. (Courtesy of HHM.)

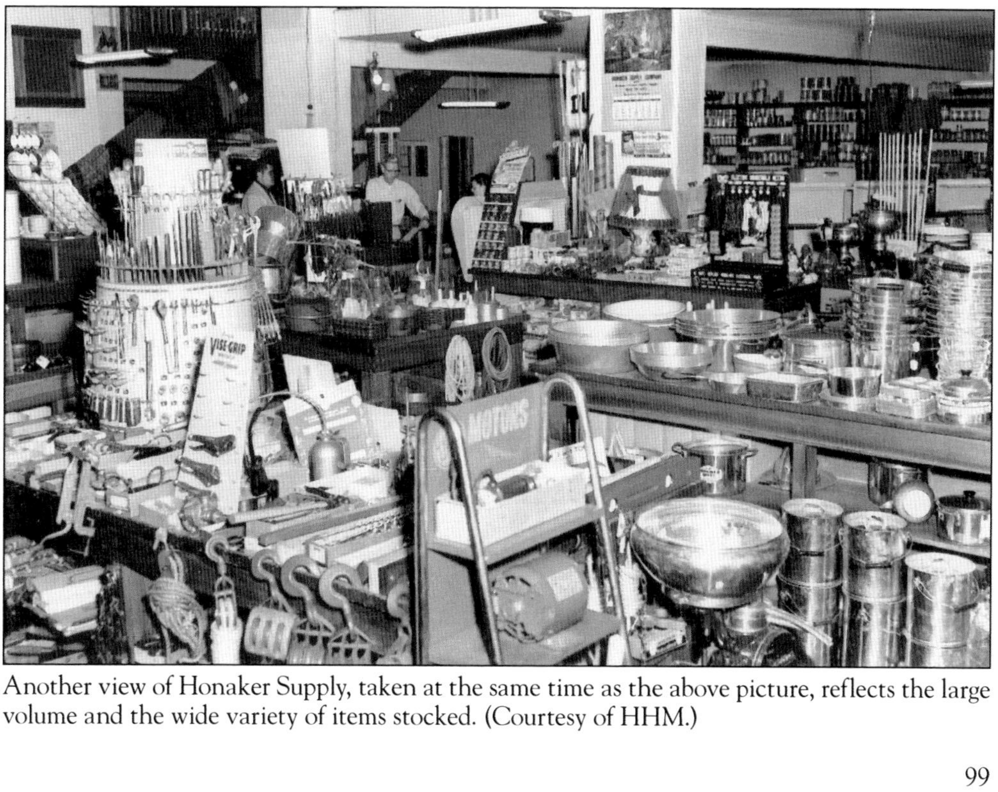

Another view of Honaker Supply, taken at the same time as the above picture, reflects the large volume and the wide variety of items stocked. (Courtesy of HHM.)

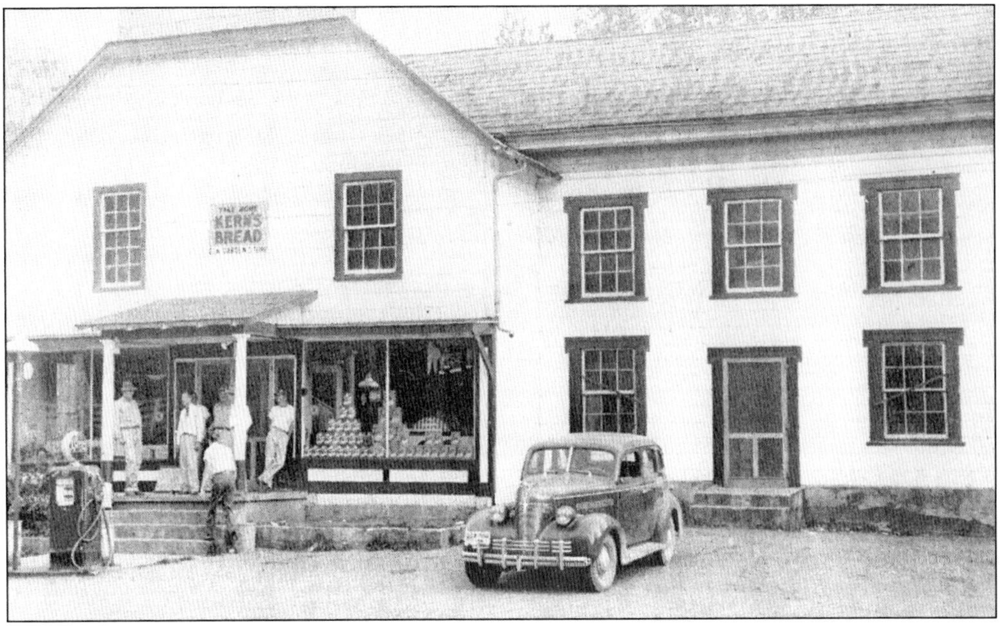

Located across the street from the Stuart Mansion, the Elk Garden Store was a part of the complex that included the post office, the mill, and the store. Despite the older vehicle parked in front of the store, it is believed that this picture was probably taken in 1960. Pictured from left to right are Richard Garrett, Jack Bondurant (former judge), Roscoe McCracken (with tie), and the postmaster. (Courtesy of RCPL, provided by J. C. Jessee.)

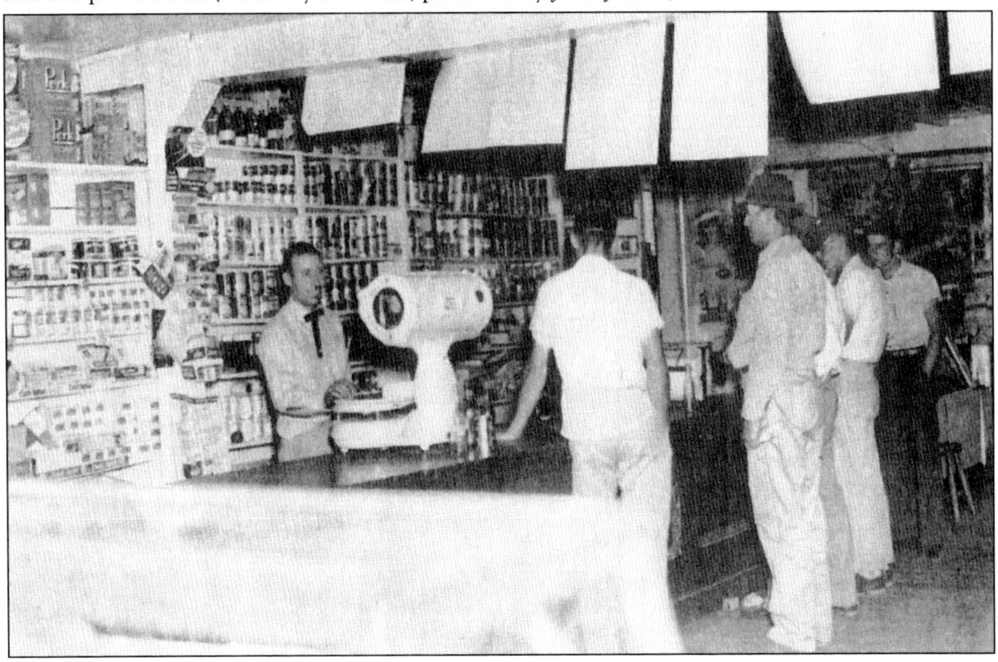

Inside the Elk Garden Store, this picture provides a glimpse of the many grocery items available. Roscoe McCracken, the man behind the counter, is the manager. The customers are, from left to right, unidentified, Jay Garrett, unidentified, Richard Garrett, and Robert Mutter. (Courtesy of James C. and Nellie R. Jessee.)

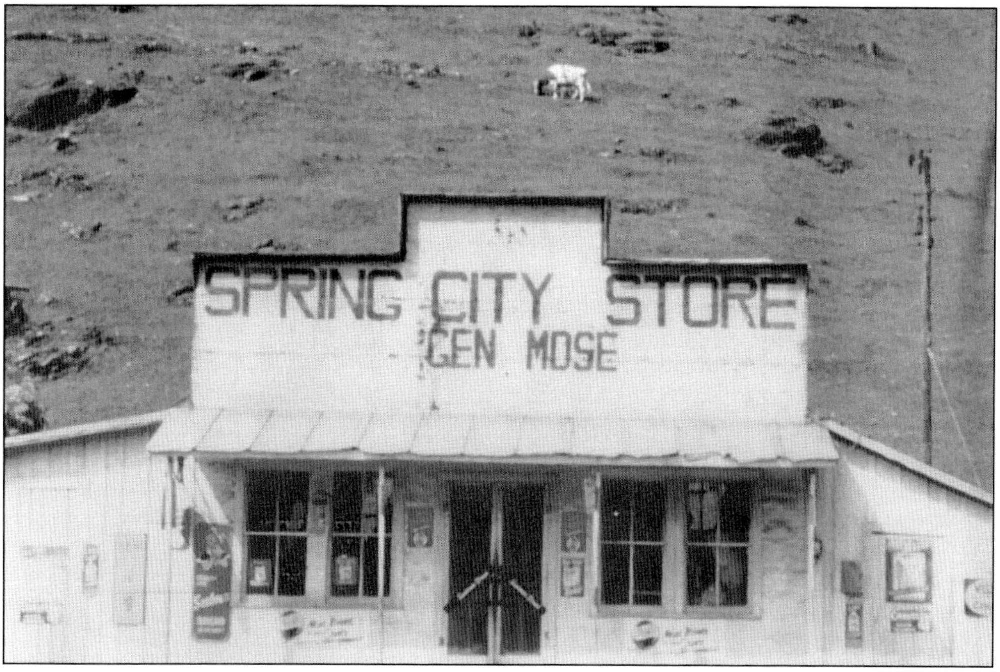

The Spring City Store, with its classic general store charm, was owned by C. W. Puckett, the grandfather of Ginny Fuller, Sen. Phillip Puckett, Mike Puckett, William Fuller, Rebecca Smith, Dr. Daniel Gilbert, Linda Bedwell, and others. The store was run by Callie Puckett, wife of C. W. Puckett, and Grace Fuller, wife of William Fuller. The store closed around 1950. (Courtesy of Sen. Phillip Puckett and Ginny Fuller.)

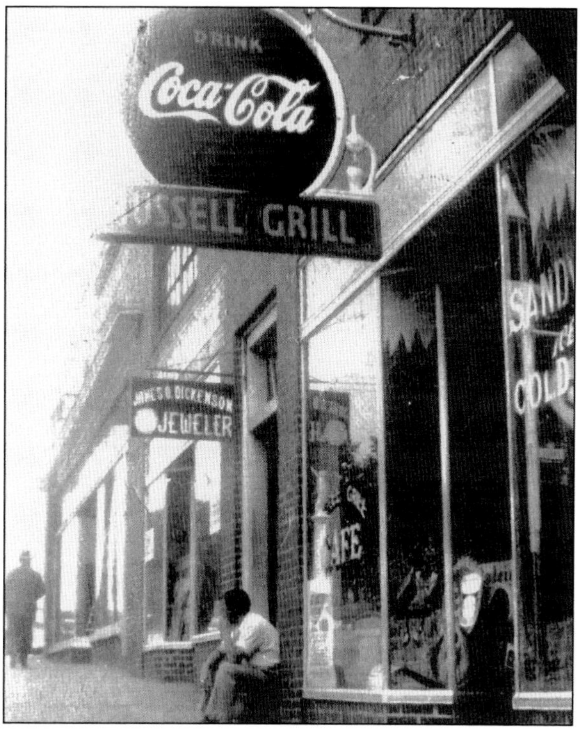

Russell Grill was located in downtown Lebanon on Main Street near the theater. This 1954 picture captures it as it looked at that time. The Russell Grill was lovingly known also by the name "the Greasy Spoon." Its great hotdogs and the signature homemade chili that topped them made it a popular eatery. (Courtesy of James C. and Nellie R. Jessee.)

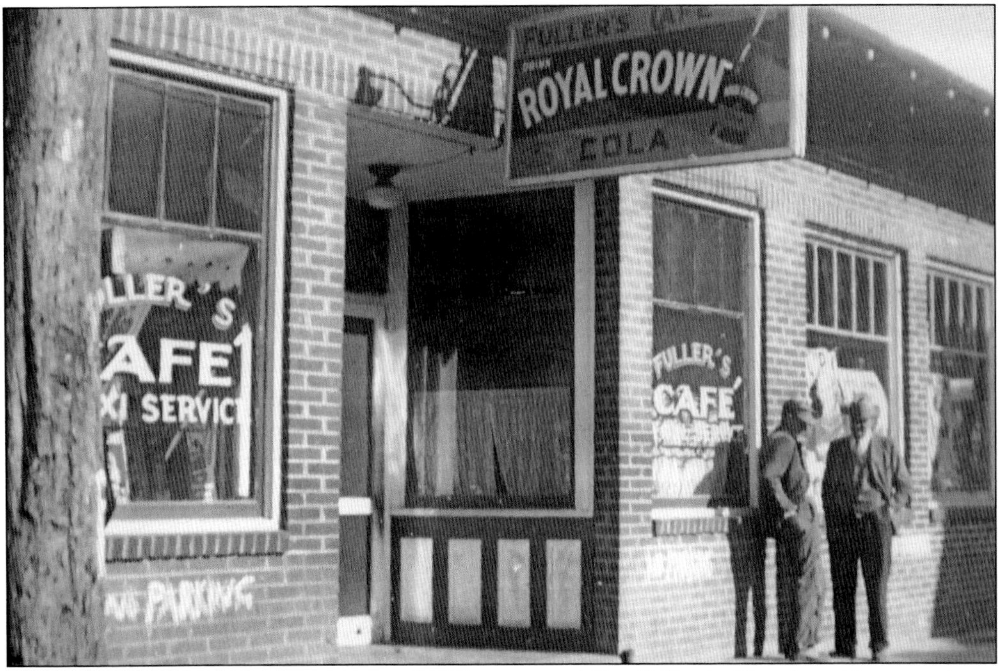

Fuller's Café and Taxi Service was run by Clarence and Bea Fuller in Honaker. Clarence drove the taxi. He always wore a tailored suit. He did a lot of what was known at the time as "hauling" his passengers to their destinations. He did local "hauling" but also traveled to Abingdon, Bristol, Kingsport, Tri-City Airport, up "hollers," or wherever his passengers needed to go. The café was a busy place. Young World War II soldiers especially enjoyed the food and the local family atmosphere there. This picture depicts it as it was around 1940. (Courtesy of HHM, provided by Diane Fuller.)

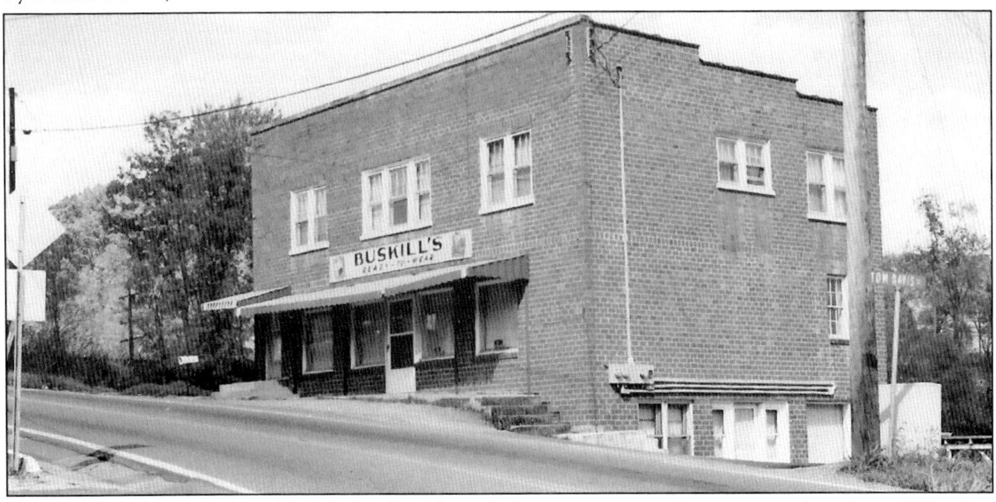

George Buskill built this three-story building in his spare time. It was completed in 1951 after four years of work. The bricks are larger than normal and were specially made at the brickyard in Richlands, Virginia. Buskill also made by hand all of thc tables, counters, and shelves used in the store. He and his wife, Lucy, operated Buskill's Ready to Wear from this location. They sold primarily shoes and children's Buster Brown clothing. This building is currently the home of HHM. (Courtesy of HHM, provided by Diane Fuller.)

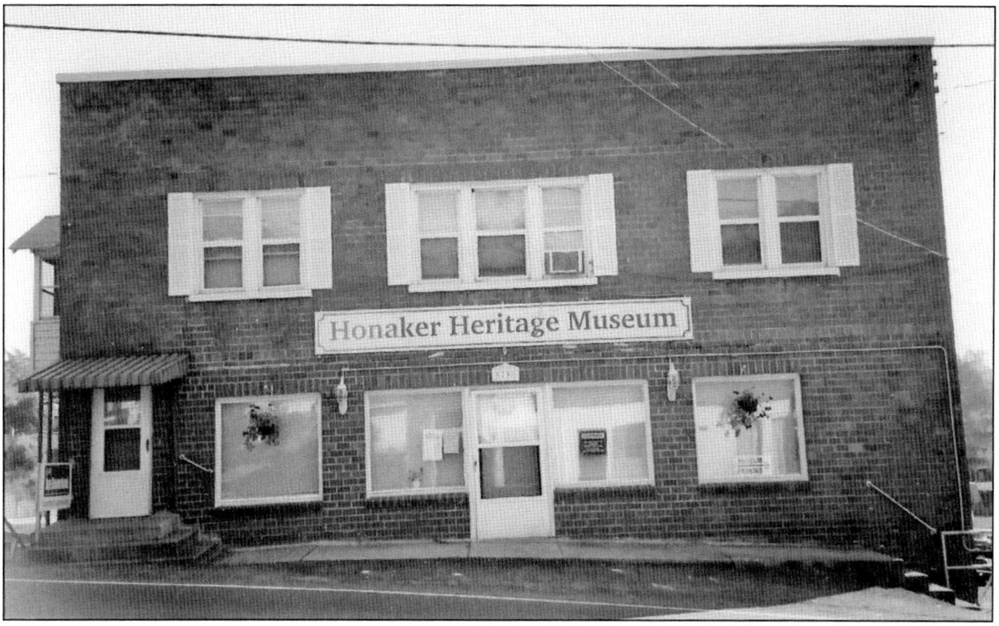

The old Buskill's Ready to Wear building exists today as home to the HHM. Inside this well-preserved landmark are all types of memorabilia from the earlier days of Russell County, carefully documented and displayed for all to enjoy. (Courtesy of Andrew Chafin.)

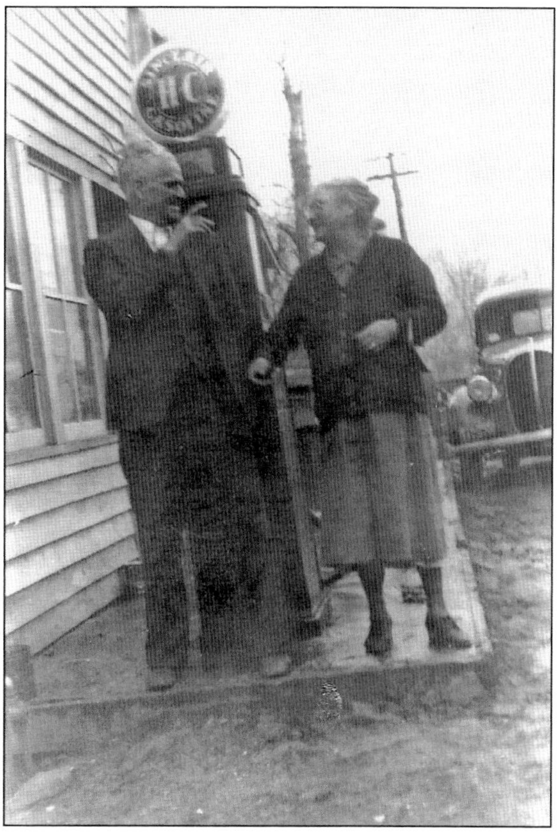

Pictured here are Frank and Belle Hale. They are standing in front of their store in Swords Creek in 1941. The demand for automobiles brought with it a need for gasoline for local folks as well as those traveling through the area. Notice the old Sinclair Gasoline sign beckoning all those passersby in need of gasoline and other travel items. (Courtesy of HHM.)

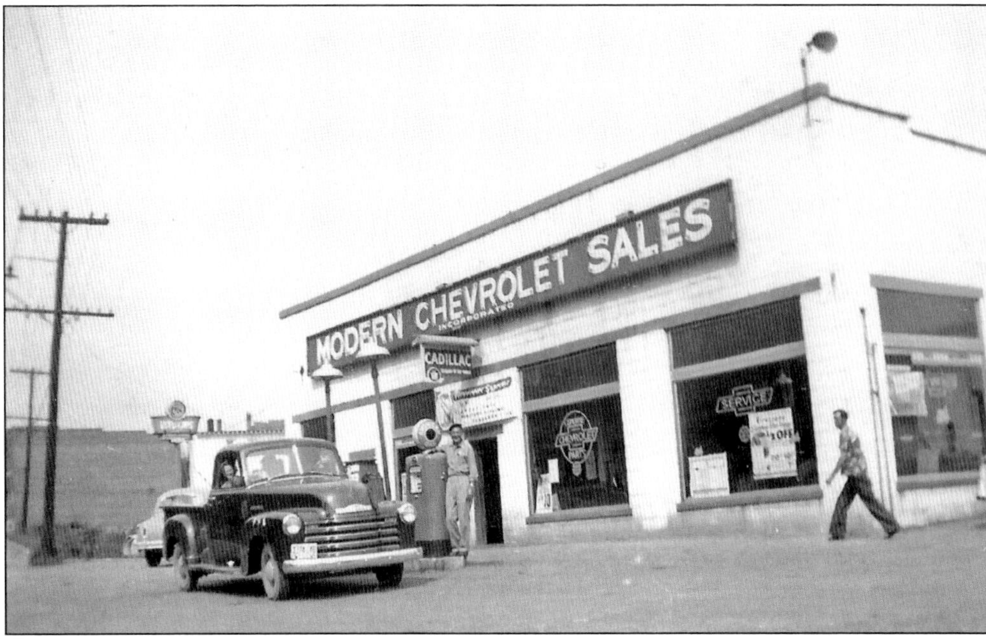

Modern Chevrolet Sales is the oldest business in Honaker. The business was started in 1934. New cars were delivered to the dealership by the Norfolk and Western Railway. This picture was taken about 1950. (Courtesy of HHM, provided by Kathleen R. Taylor.)

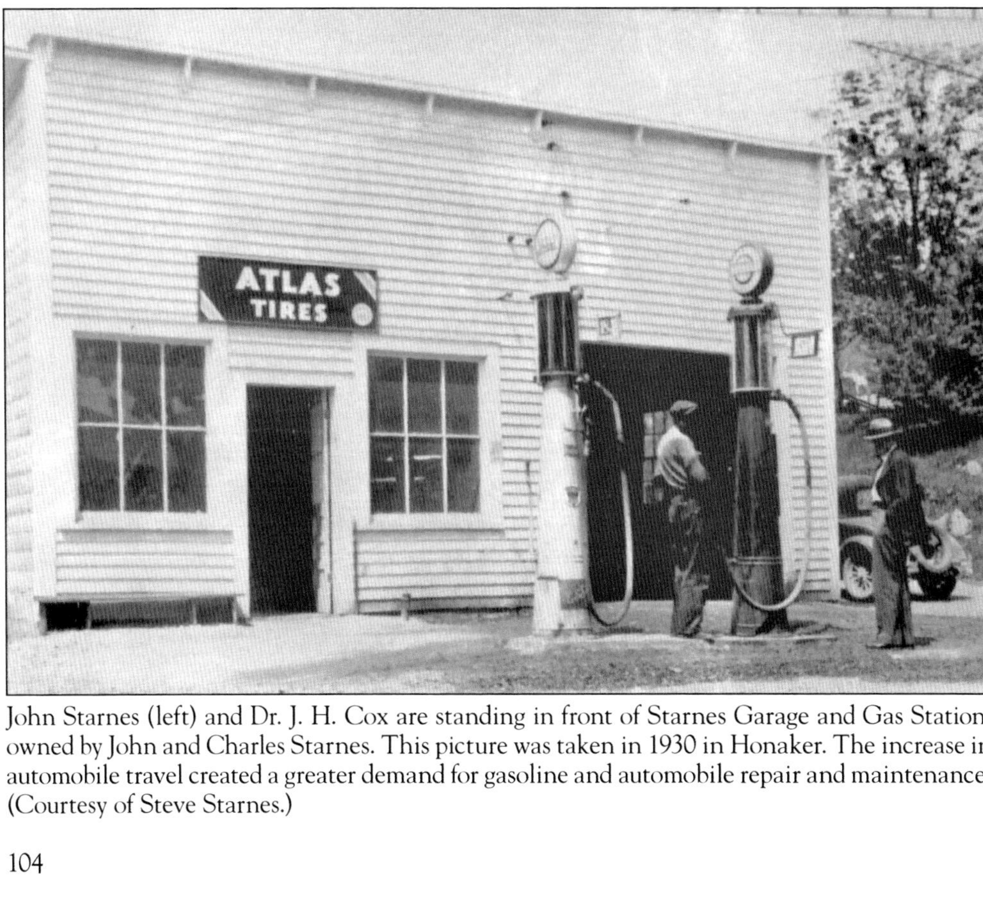

John Starnes (left) and Dr. J. H. Cox are standing in front of Starnes Garage and Gas Station, owned by John and Charles Starnes. This picture was taken in 1930 in Honaker. The increase in automobile travel created a greater demand for gasoline and automobile repair and maintenance. (Courtesy of Steve Starnes.)

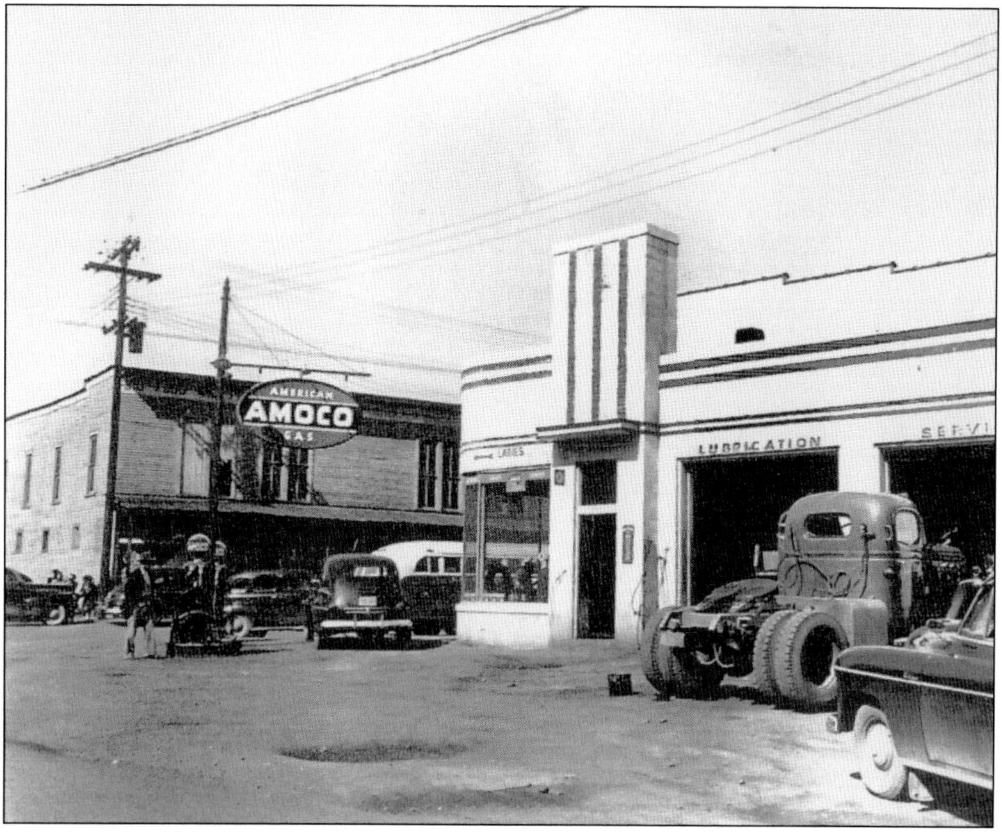

In downtown Honaker where State Route 80 turns right, this scene was photographed in the early 1950s. Notice the bus to the side of the service station. It is not known if the bus stopped for gas or if someone flagged it down for a ride. The bus route ran through Honaker on its way from Haysi to Richlands. This was not the regular bus stop, which was around the corner at the drugstore. Bus stop or not, all one had to do was flag down the bus to catch a ride. (Courtesy of RCPL, provided by Claude E. Griffith.)

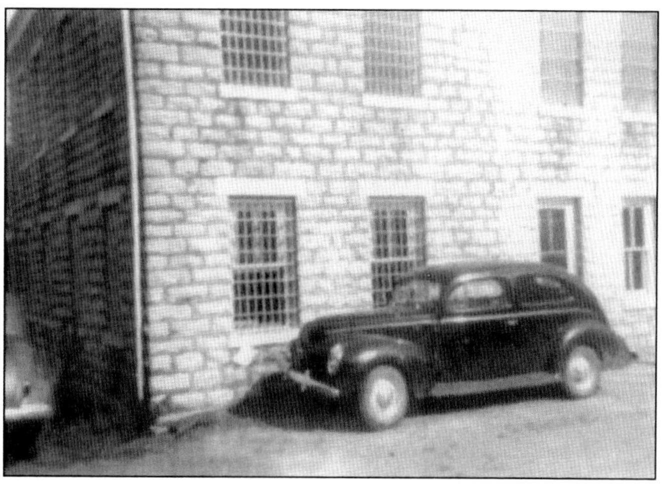

The Russell County jail, located in Lebanon, is depicted here in the early 1950s. It is still located in the same place and is a part of the courthouse complex in downtown Lebanon. (Courtesy of RCPL, provided by Donald G. Cross Sr.)

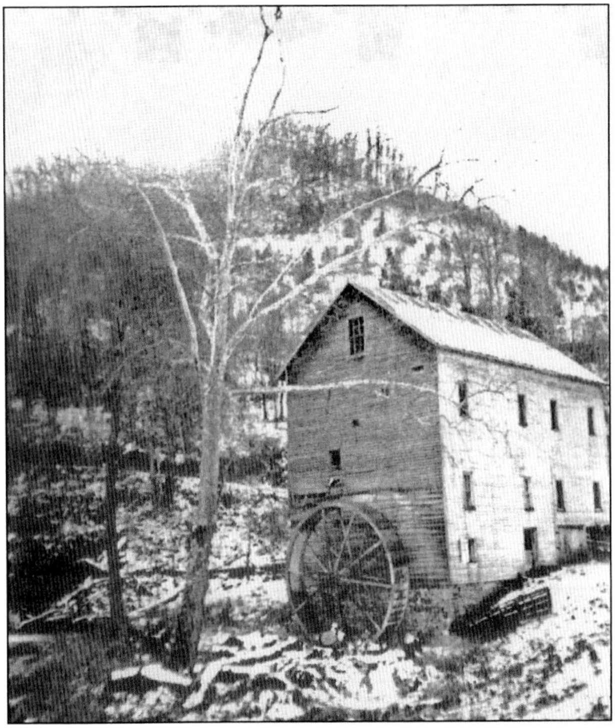

Jessee's Mill was owned by Jack Jessee, then Wiley E. Jessee. This picture was taken in the 1900s. At the end of the second century BC, the first recorded mention is made of gristmills in Europe. By 1000 AD in Europe, mills were so numerous as to seldom be more than a few miles apart. As the settlers came to the New World, they brought this knowledge with them. Jessee's Mill, located on the pristine waters of Mill Creek, closed in 1932. (Courtesy of RCPL, provided by Mildred Davis.)

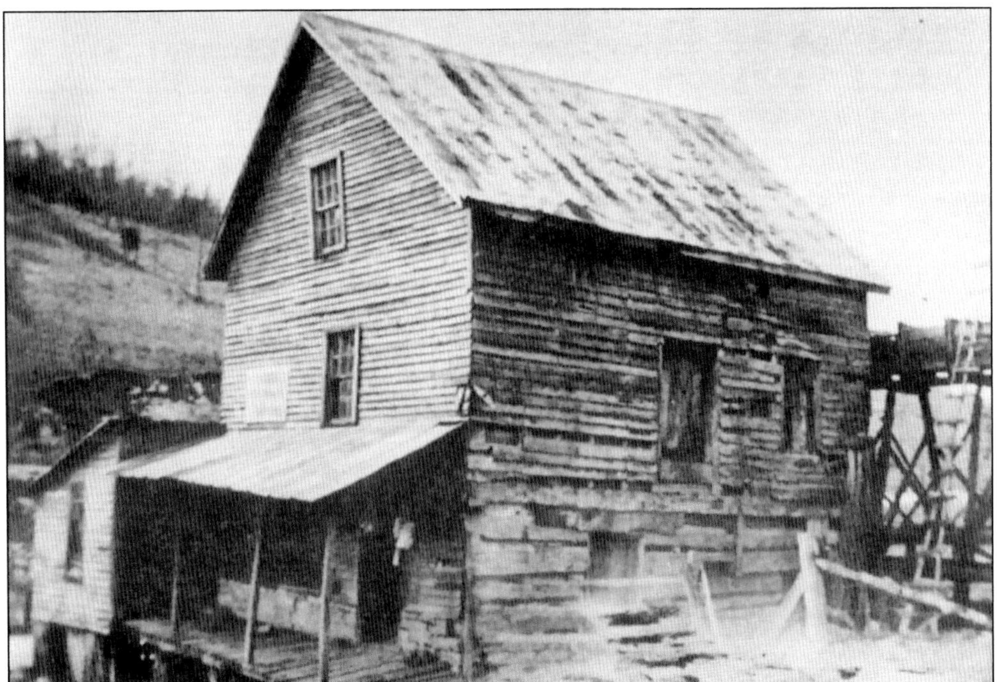

The Caleb Hawkins Mill was between Dickensonville and Hansonville. It was both a roller mill and a tanning mill. The earliest settlers of Russell County and especially the mills they built were quite a sight to the Native Americans who still occupied parts of the vast lands known as Russell County at the time. (Courtesy of RCPL.)

Located across from the Stuart Mansion in Elk Garden, the Elk Garden Mill is pictured here in the 1840s. This mill would grind corn, wheat, and feed. Mills were an important part of the community, not only providing a means in Castlewood to grind the corn, wheat, and feed grown in the area, but also serving as a gathering place. It was not unusual for the post office, voting poll, and other community services to be made available on the same site. (Courtesy of RCPL.)

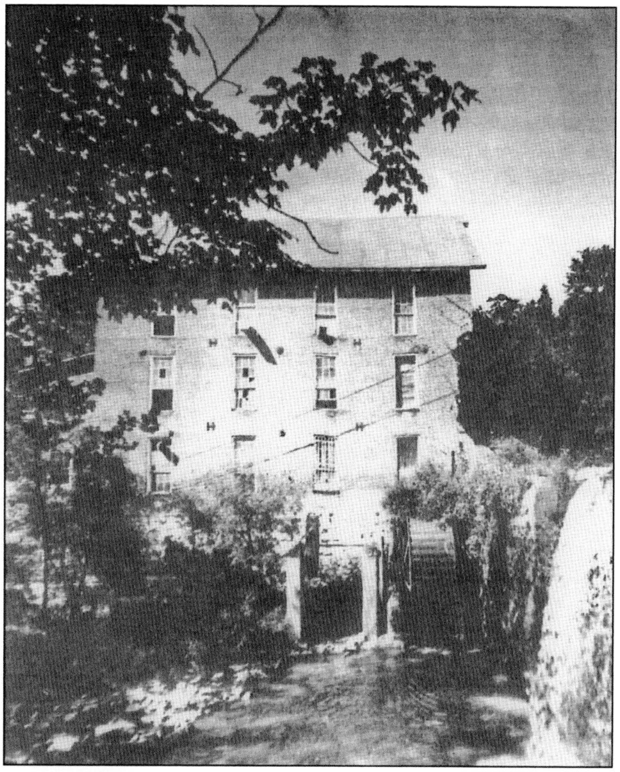

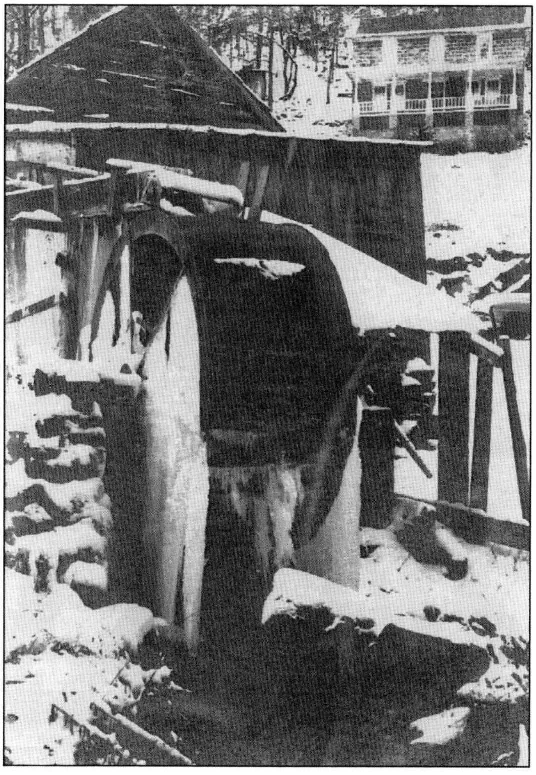

This picture was taken of the Gibson Mill prior to 1937. The Gibson Mill was located on old Route 19 at the intersection of Route 817 in an area known as Mactown. The Gibson cemetery is on the hill above, and the Johnson house is pictured in the upper right. The Johnson house was moved in 1937 or 1938. Sometimes a mill would be built with more than one foundation. This was done in order to prevent the vibrating of the wheel from damaging the main structure. (Courtesy of RCPL.)

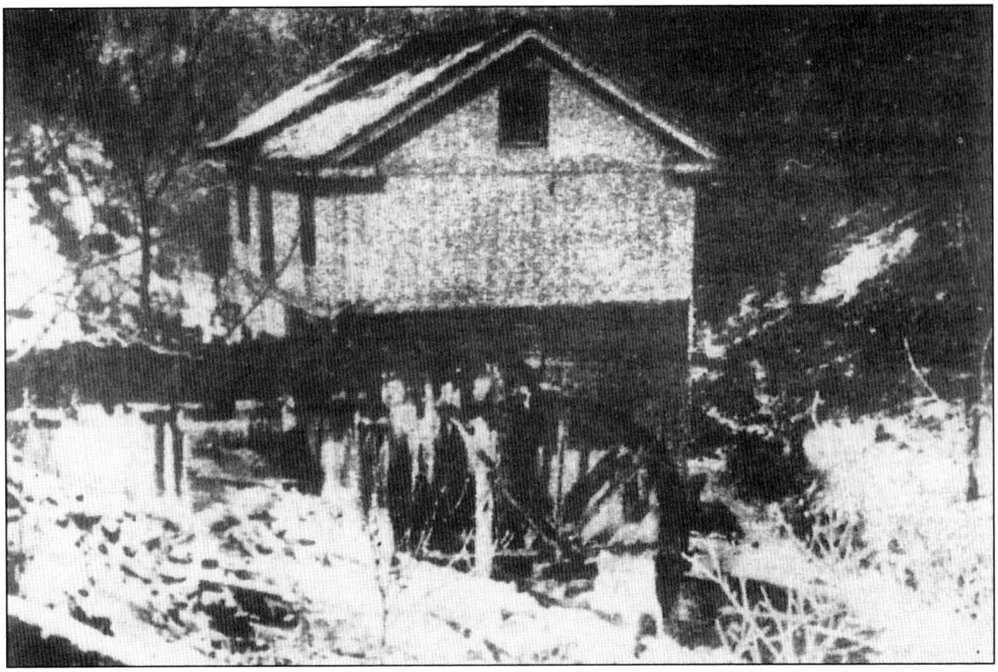

Bickley Mill, at the lower section of Mill Creek in Castlewood, is captured in this photograph. On February 3, 1832, a post office was established at the Bickley Mill. John Bickley, son of Charles Bickley, was the postmaster. This post office served the Castlewood area until February 1, 1907. A newspaper, the *Bickley Mill Post*, was published on this site for a number of years. (Courtesy of RCPL.)

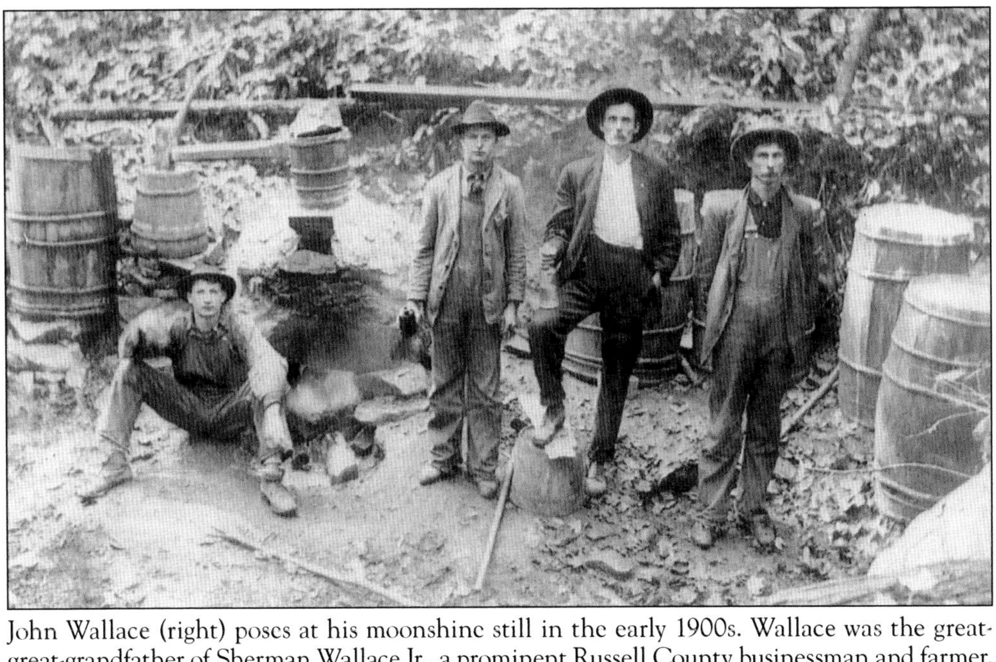

John Wallace (right) poses at his moonshine still in the early 1900s. Wallace was the great-great-grandfather of Sherman Wallace Jr., a prominent Russell County businessman and farmer. According to local historians, moonshine was available at 50¢ per gallon. The other "shiners" are unidentified. (Courtesy of Sherman Wallace Jr.)

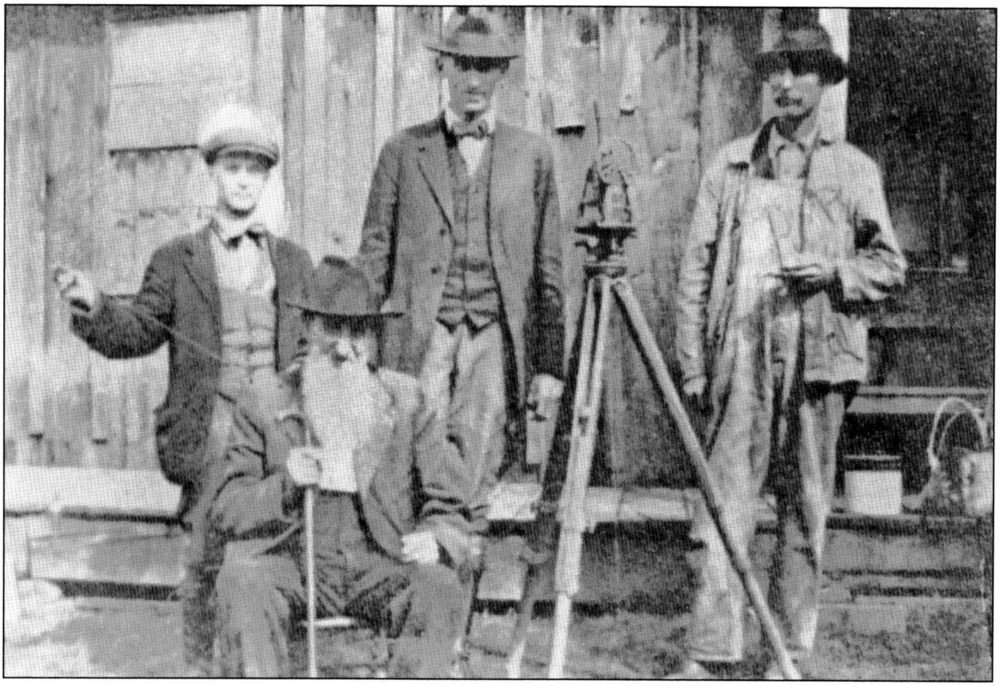

Pictured here in 1910 is a railroad surveying crew. Second from left is Paul Brown, the grandfather of Kelly Gilmer of Lebanon. On the right is Lilburn Starnes, a Russell County builder. Starnes was the great-grandfather of Steve Starnes, a Lebanon businessman who owns Gentech, a mechanical and construction company. (Courtesy of Steve Starnes.)

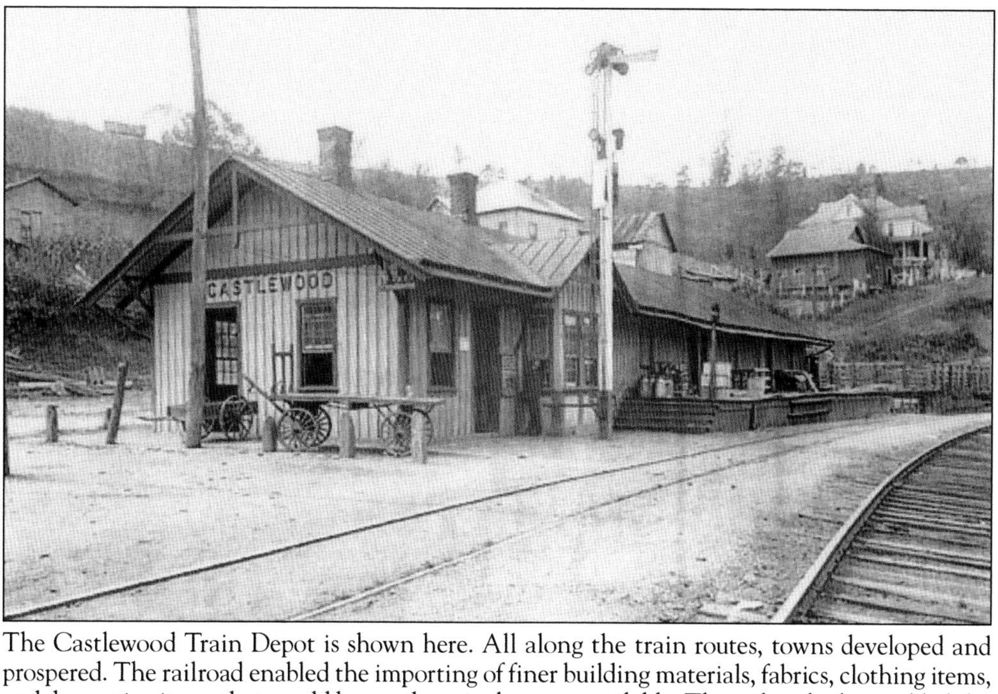

The Castlewood Train Depot is shown here. All along the train routes, towns developed and prospered. The railroad enabled the importing of finer building materials, fabrics, clothing items, and decorative items that would have otherwise been unavailable. The railroads also enabled the exporting of corn, timber, tobacco, wheat, cattle, and other livestock. (Courtesy of RCPL.)

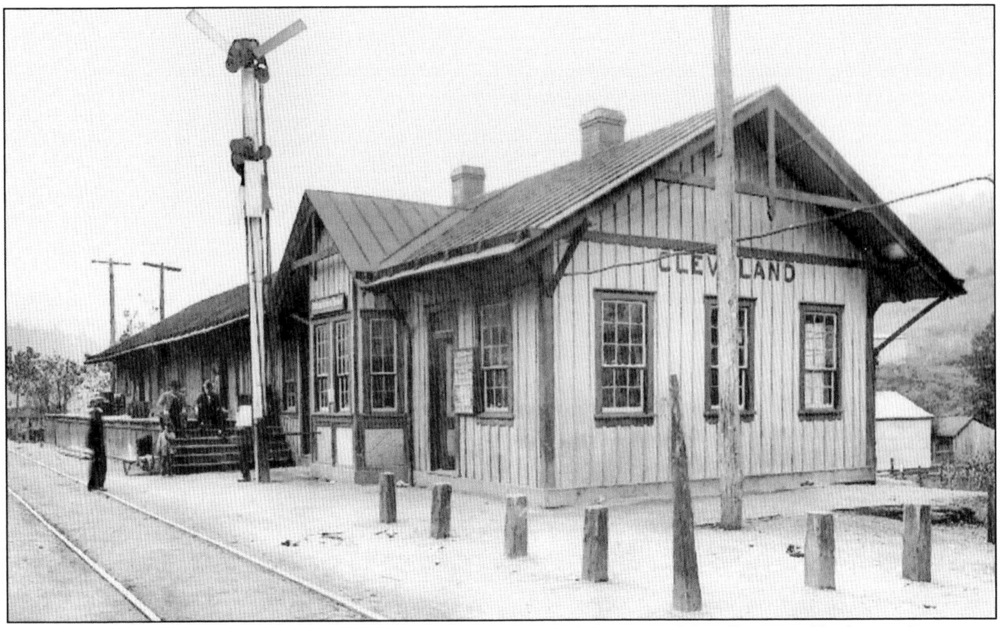

The Cleveland Train Depot, as it appeared in the early 1900s, like depots all along the route of the Norfolk and Western Railway, was equipped with all the amenities available at the time. These stations soon became meeting places. In addition to transporting freight, passenger cars opened up an entirely new method of travel. Traveling in fashion was customary. The latest fashions were displayed. Folks often came to town on Saturdays and Sundays just to watch people coming and going from the train station and to visit with friends and neighbors. (Courtesy of the Town of Cleveland.)

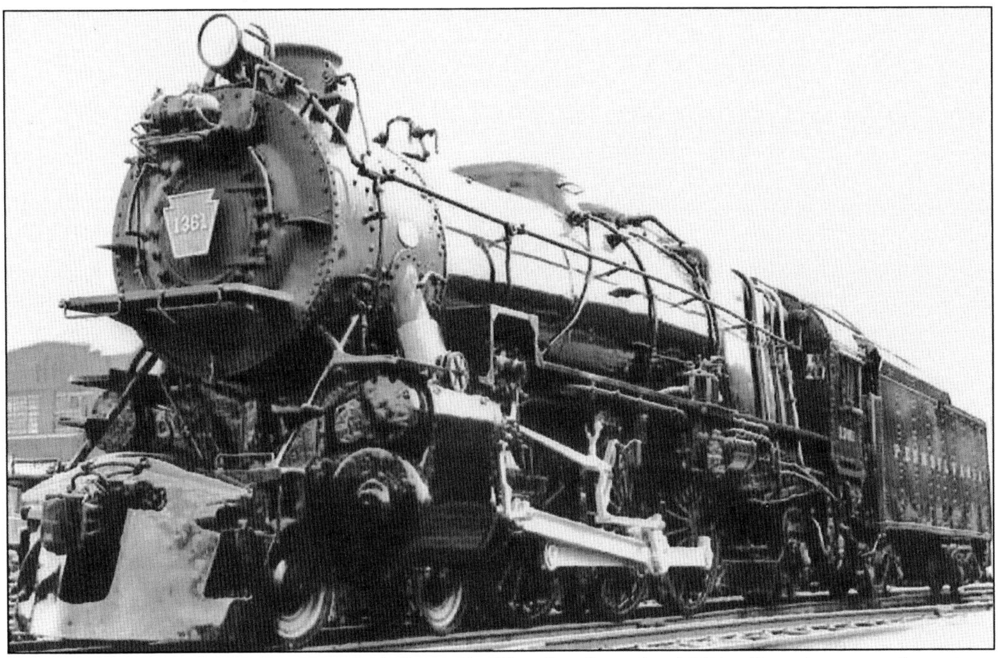

Old steam engine No. 1361 traveled through Cleveland in the 1800s. Diesel-powered engines entered the picture in the mid-1920s. (Courtesy of the Town of Cleveland.)

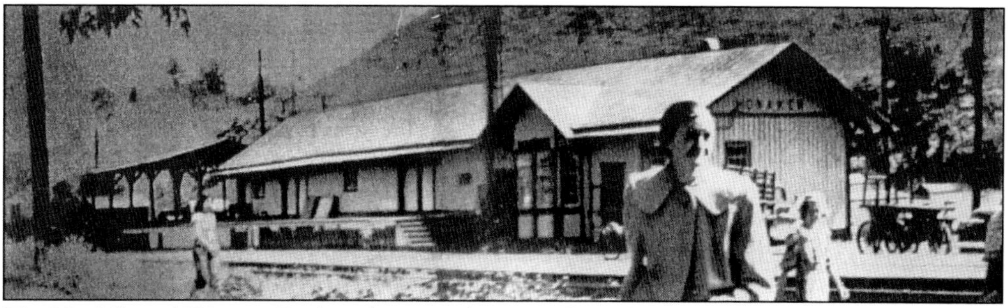

The Norfolk and Western Railway began rail service through Clinch Valley to provide access to the area in an effort to reach the great coal reserves and the vast timber resources of the area. The rail service reached Honaker in 1889. The Honaker Train Deport is pictured here. Following this, the area began to grow and prosper. The first station was an old boxcar. The first station agent was Harvey Honaker, for whom the town was named. The lady in this picture is Mrs. Dave Hess (Minnie). The girl in the background is unidentified. (Courtesy of RCPL.)

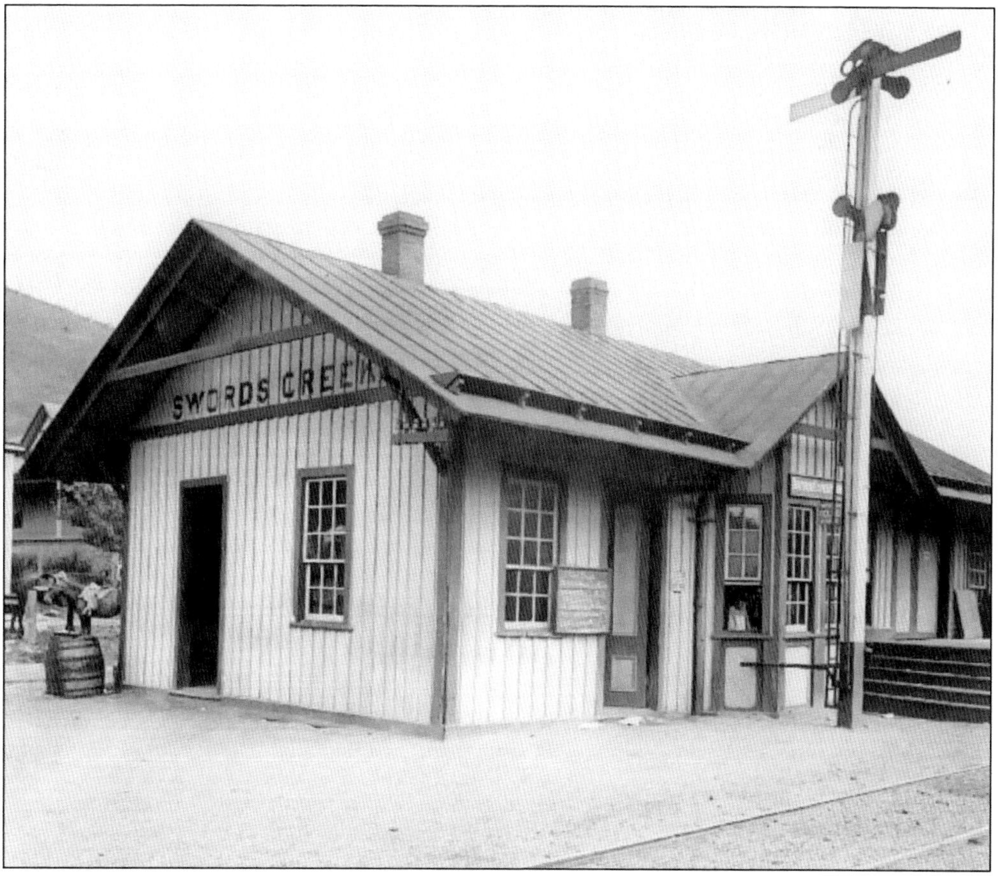

Located at Swords Creek, this railroad depot appears quiet at the moment. Many of the activities revolved around the arrival and departure of the trains. Notice the horse to the left rear of the picture. Often that was the transportation used to arrive at the station. In some towns, the timber to ship out was brought to the station by horses and placed on railroad cars for shipment. (Courtesy of RCPL, provided by Ruth Whitt.)

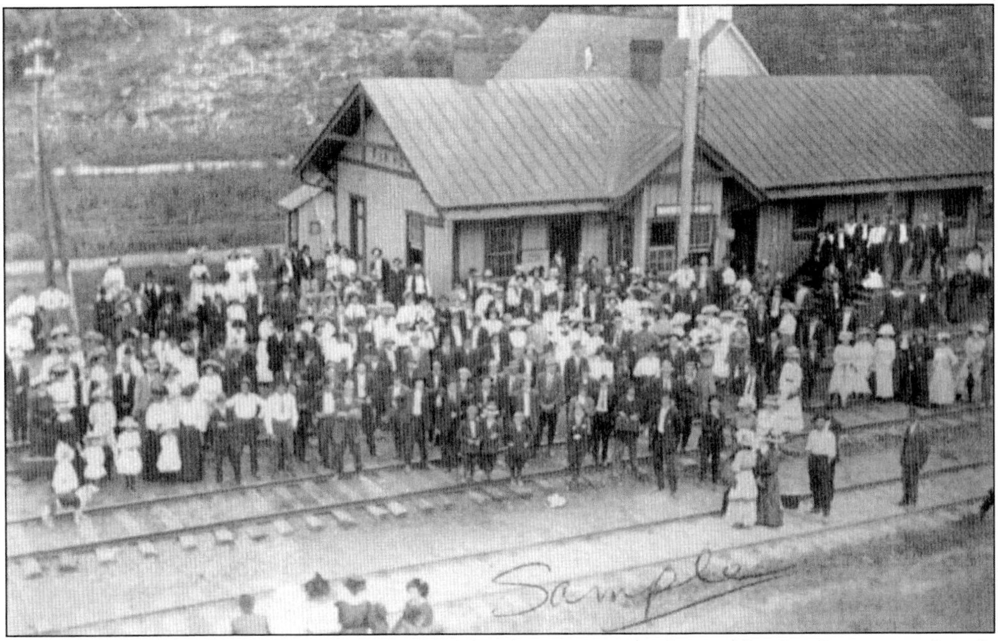

In June 1910, at Finney Depot, folks waited for the No. 5, which would take them to a church meeting in Artrip. This meeting included folks from all church groups. Judging by the number of people there, it is believed by locals that it would probably have taken three trips to get everyone there. Artrip was only three miles away, but there was not a completed road between the locations at the time. The building directly behind the train depot is the Missionary Baptist Church. (Courtesy of RCPL, provided by R. C. Sykes.)

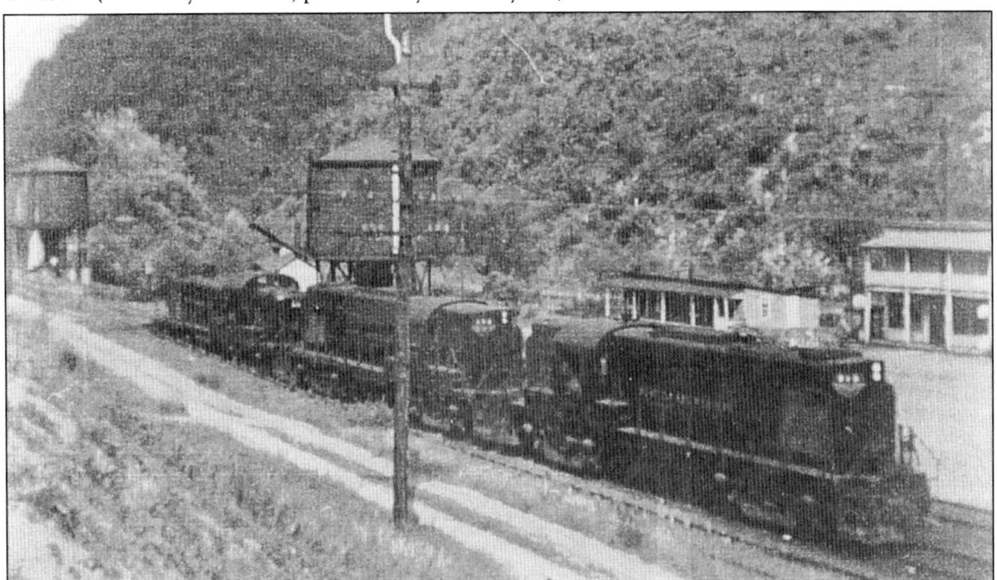

This picture memorializes the first diesel engine to pass through Finney. This occurred about 1959. The two water tanks located in Finney allowed trains to stop and fill their water tanks. This did not occur at all depots and added even more excitement to the arrival of a train. (Courtesy of HHM, provided by Kathleen R. Taylor.)

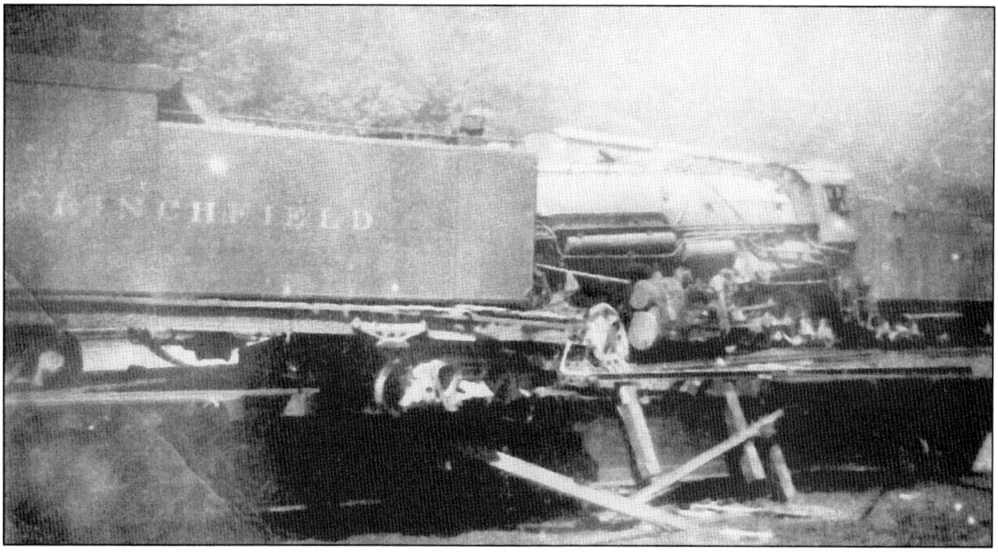

The occasional train wreck was inevitable. The railroad car is marked as Clinchfield. The date of this is unknown. Local historians indicate it is a typical view of such an event. (Courtesy of HHM.)

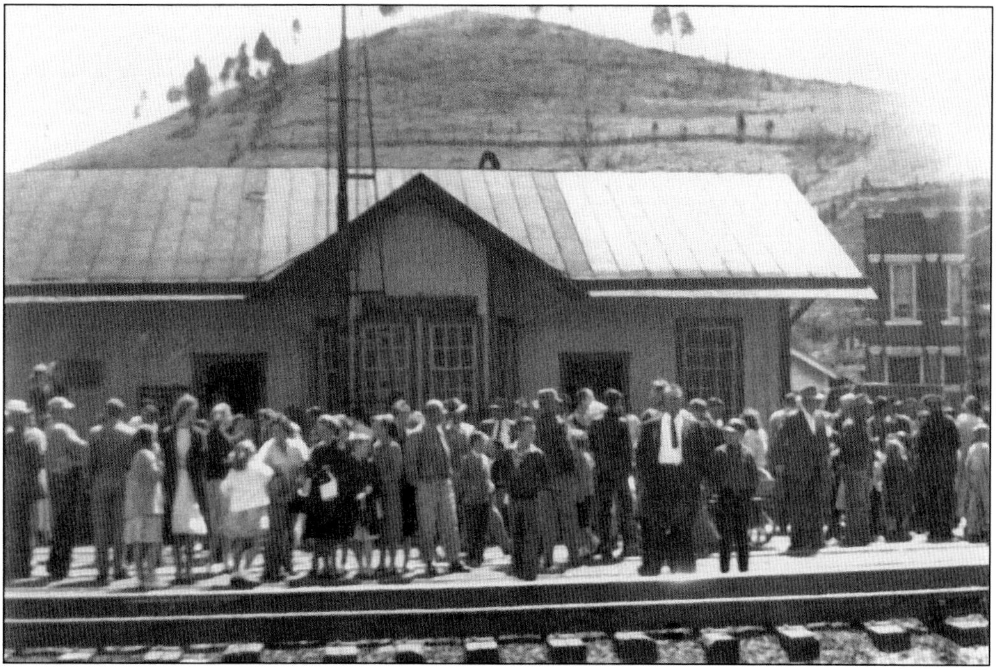

Honaker Railroad Depot is seen as it appeared on the last day of the passenger train service of the Clinch Valley Railroad from Bluefield to Norton. The time was April 1959. After World War II, there were not enough passengers to keep the passenger train running. Many now had automobiles and preferred this more flexible mode of transportation. The mail started being delivered by trucks and buses. One of Honaker's rural mail carriers, Paris Taylor, said he had to bid for the job. The Cub Scouts, leaders, parents, and other townspeople were given the opportunity to ride to Norton and back on that final trip on a Sunday afternoon. The station remained in use for freight loading and unloading. This picture was taken by Bea Fuller. (Courtesy of Diane Fuller.)

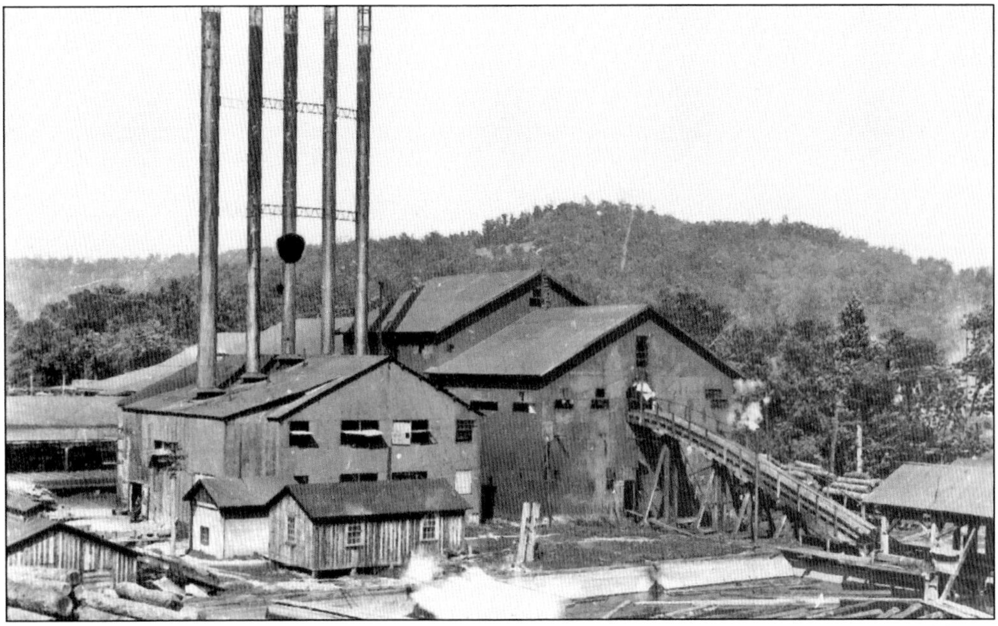

The Honaker Lumber Plant was later renamed the Putnam Lumber Company, pictured here. The Putnam Lumber Company opened on April 26, 1910. It was owned by a large corporation from Williamsport, Pennsylvania. The company moved officials in from the north. They brought with them social practices and cultural changes that impacted the lives of the locals. Many jobs were made available. The Putnam Lumber Company became the second largest lumber mill in the United States. This prosperity helped to turn Honaker into a town booming with people and business. (Courtesy of HHM.)

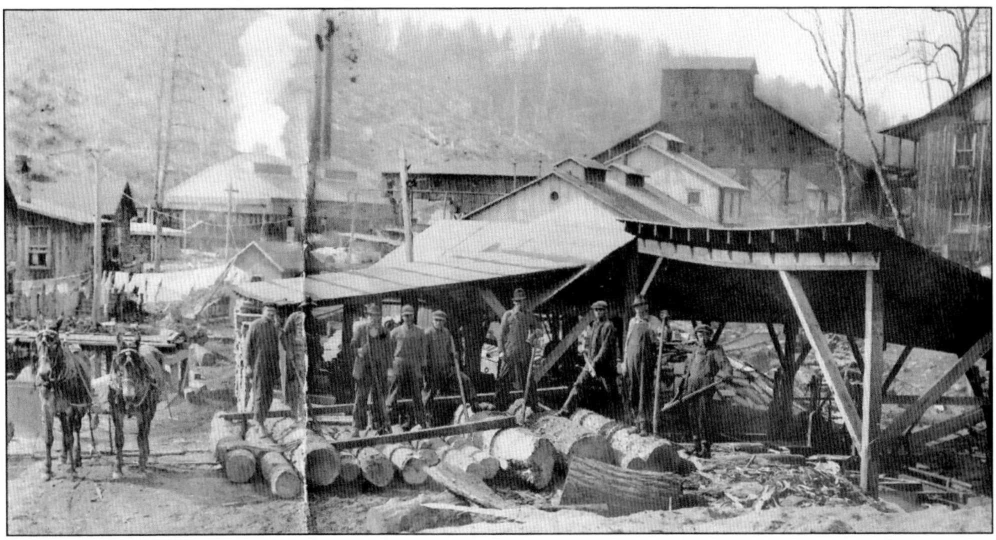

This picture postcard of a sawmill depicts the community that would develop around the work. Notice the clothes hanging on the line. Homes were often built for the families of the company officers. Many local folks were hired to work at the mills after leaving the farm for the first time to obtain outside work. Oftentimes a general store, doctor, barbershop, and post office were established at the site to serve the needs of the lumber community. (Courtesy of HHM, provided by Kathleen R. Taylor.)

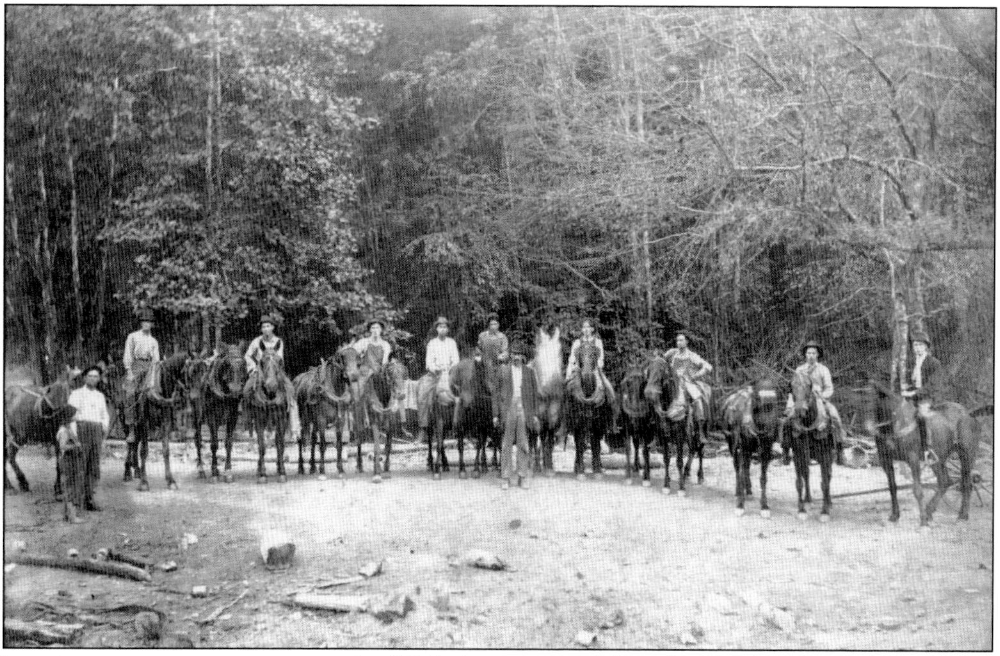

Logging camps were a common sight. With the coming of the railroads, the territory was opened up, enabling the harvesting of the rich, abundant virgin timber. Lumber crews were many. The timbering then allowed for the clearing of land to raise crops and livestock on lands previously inaccessible. (Courtesy of RCPL, provided by Claude E. Griffith.)

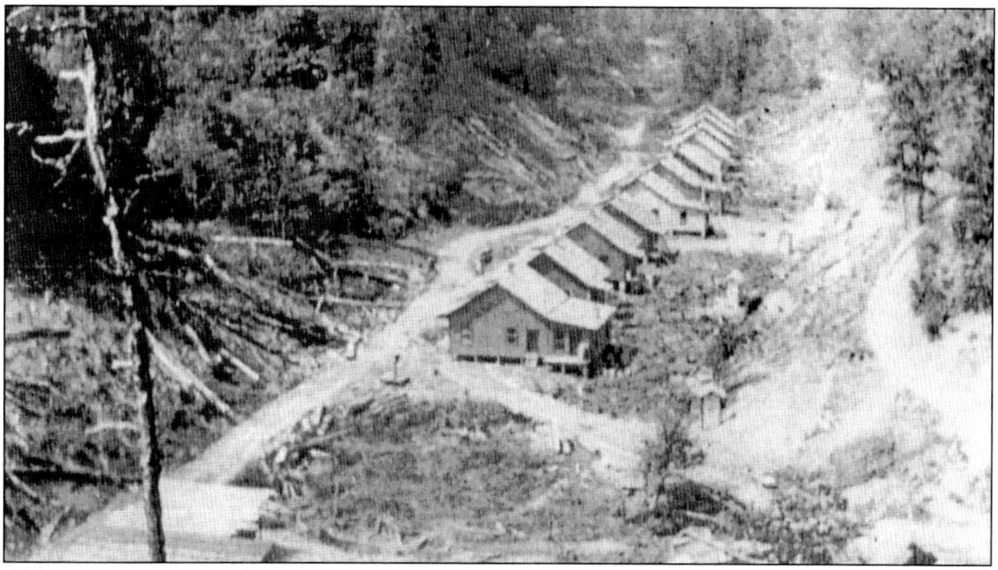

Old Banner Raven Coal Camp is seen as it appeared in 1910. Before the coal and timber industries developed, the area around Drill was thinly populated with farming families who lived off the land. The little town of Drill grew quickly as houses for miners and families were built. There were 200–300 built. Each house had a front and back porch, four rooms, and no indoor plumbing. Drill is said to have been given its name at the suggestion of Scott Israel. The men drilling through layers of rock looking for coal were rewarded when they struck what appeared to be a never-ending stream of water. (Courtesy of HHM.)

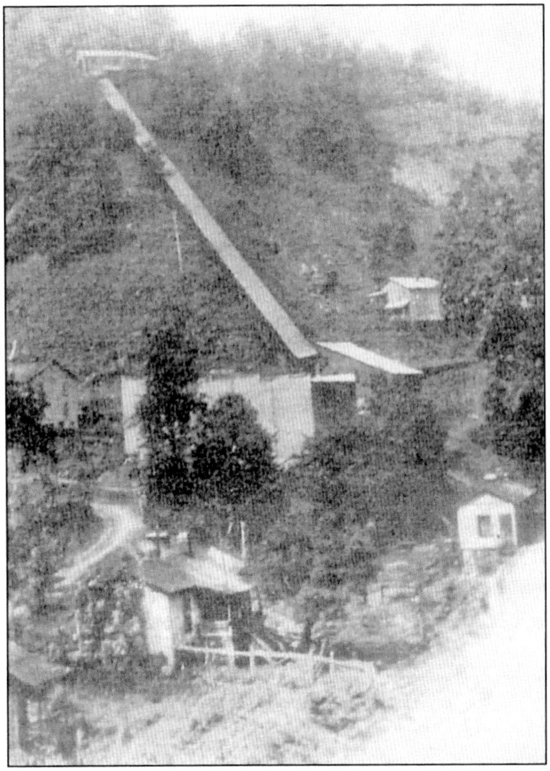

As the railroads came to the area, the rich coalfields of Russell County offered up a high-quality coal with easier accessibility than in some other parts of the country. Northern industrialists invested in removing these resources, and coal-mining towns and camps grew up along the coal-mining sites. This photograph is from Wilder. (Courtesy of RCPL, provided by Barry Hess.)

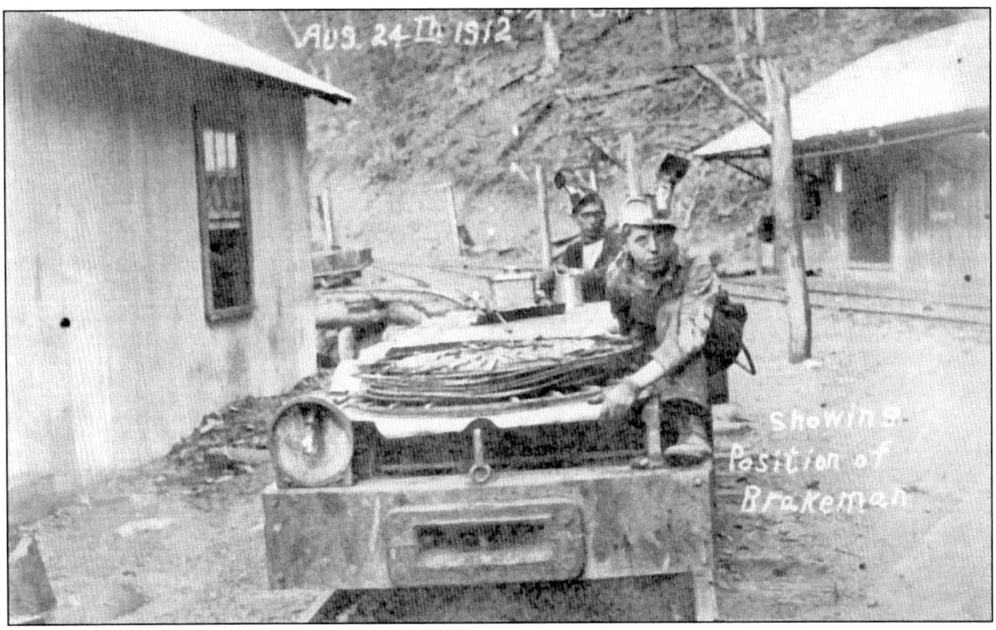

Pictured here around 1912 is a miner on a car showing the position of the brakeman. Mining provided income and a living for many who left their farms for outside work for the first time. Often the wives and children worked to keep up the chores on the farm. Others brought their families and resided in the coal camps built up around the mines. (Courtesy of RCPL, provided by Barry Hess.)

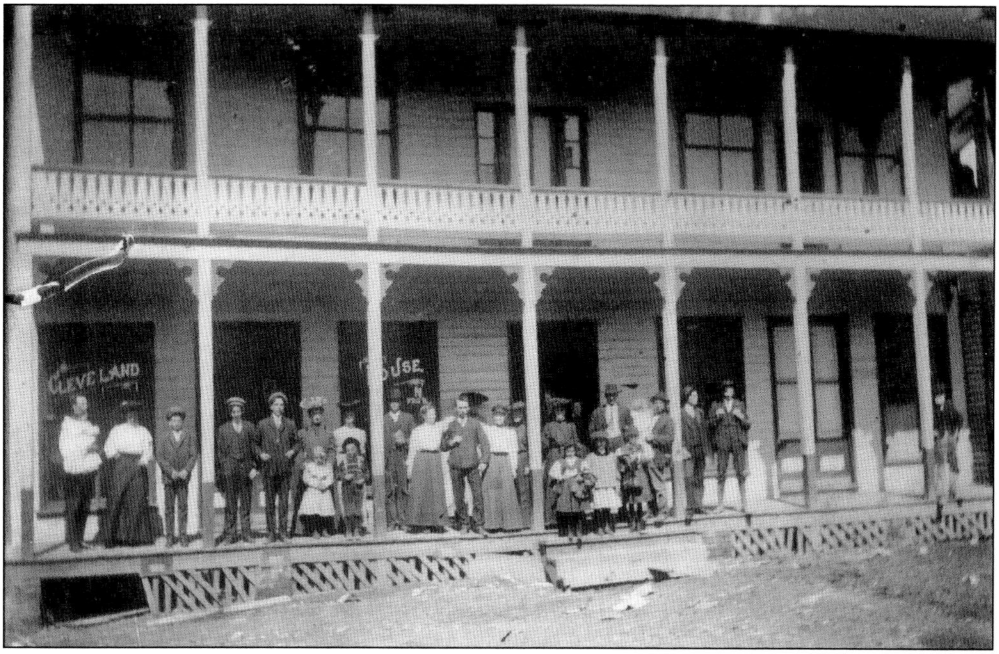

Pictured here is the Cleveland Hotel. With the business of the railroads, coal mining, and timber, the towns built up quickly. Hotels sprang up to meet the ever-increasing number of folks traveling for business or pleasure. Most hotels had a restaurant, and locals enjoyed meals there as well. (Courtesy of James C. and Nellie R. Jessee.)

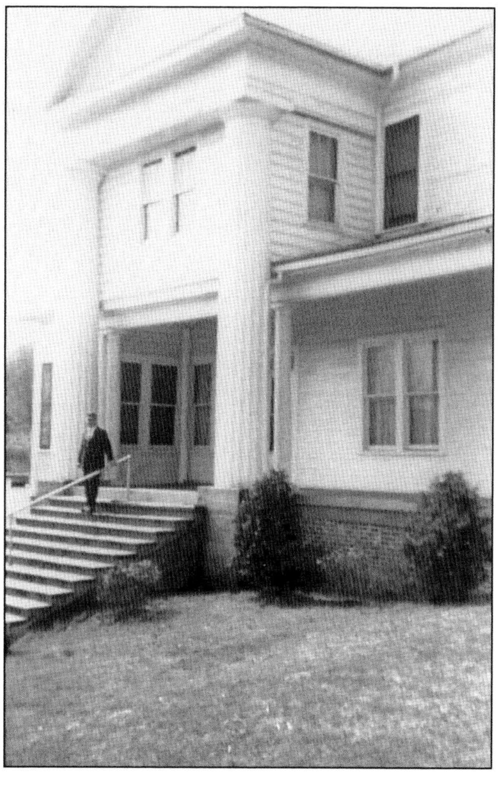

Around 1910, Napoleon Bonaparte "Bone" Honaker, son of Harvey Honaker (for whom the town was named), contracted with W. A. Strouth to build the Hotel Honaker. The man standing on the steps is Glen Owens. "Drummers" (salesman who traveled to town to sell their items), lumber and railroad officials, and later teachers often stayed here. Sally Fuller, the owner, hired pretty girls to work at the hotel. Girls from nearby Dickenson County also came to work. The girls captured the attention of local young men, and a number of marriages resulted. Real china was used in the dining room and placed properly on the table. The hotel had ice, quite a luxury at the time. One of the first public telephones, a radio, and a Victrola were some of the luxuries enjoyed by its guests. On the weekends, the townsfolk would often come to dine. The food was good, and proper behavior was always observed. The columns on the front of the hotel were removed from the Honaker National Bank building in Honaker and placed on the hotel during construction. (Courtesy of RCPL, provided by Barry Hess.)

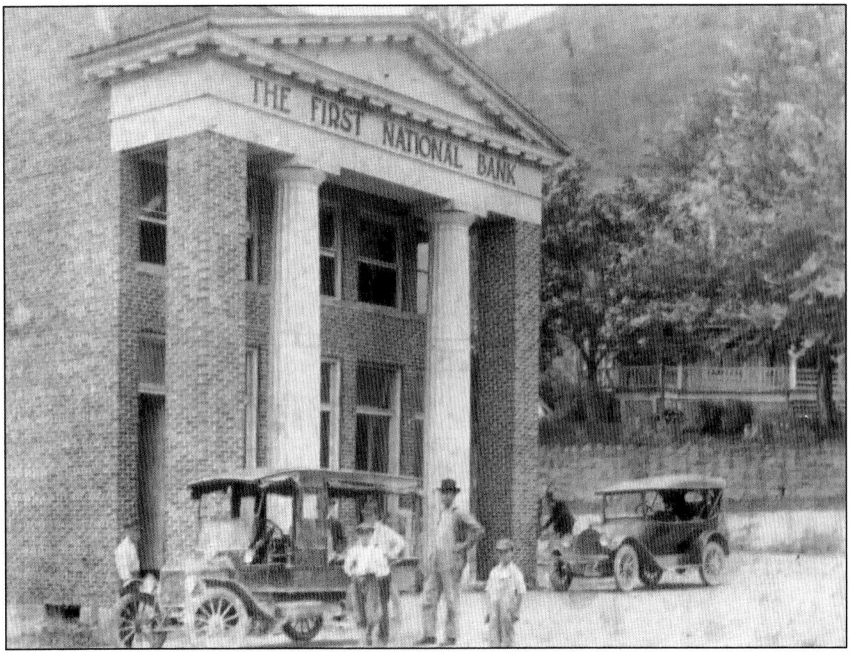

This photograph of the Honaker National Bank was taken between 1910 and 1920. It has been said that the Italians who moved to the area with the railroad construction crews helped lay the brick and stones used to build the bank. Later the bank decided to remove the columns. At the time, the Hotel Honaker was being built and its owner thought the columns would add interest to the building. Many thought it was not possible to move and install the large columns. Horsepower, manpower, and brilliant planning enabled this to occur without incident. (Courtesy of RCPL, provided by Jim Fuller.)

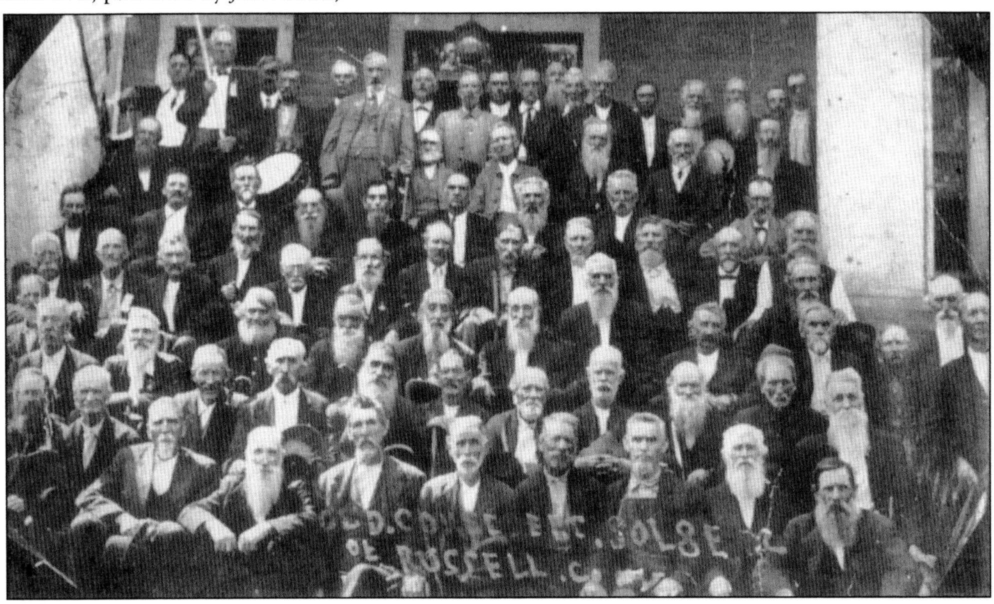

At the Hotel Honaker in 1912, these Civil War veterans of Russell County get together for a reunion. The Civil War was hurtful to the residents of Russell County, as hearts and minds were divided among friends, neighbors, and families. (Courtesy of RCPL, provided by J. C. Jessee.)

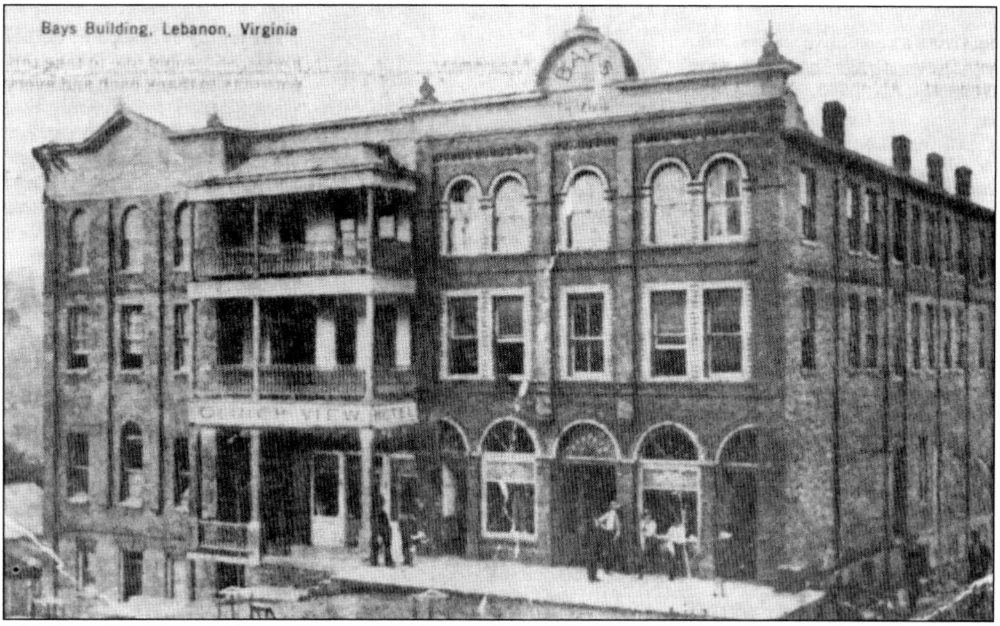

The Bays Building on Main Street in Lebanon has served many purposes over the years. At one time, it was the Clinch View Hotel. It has also served as a dental office for Dr. Davis; Dr. Daniel Trigg had his hospital there as well. It was here that Dr. W. C. Elliott began his practice with Dr. Trigg. (Courtesy of RCPL.)

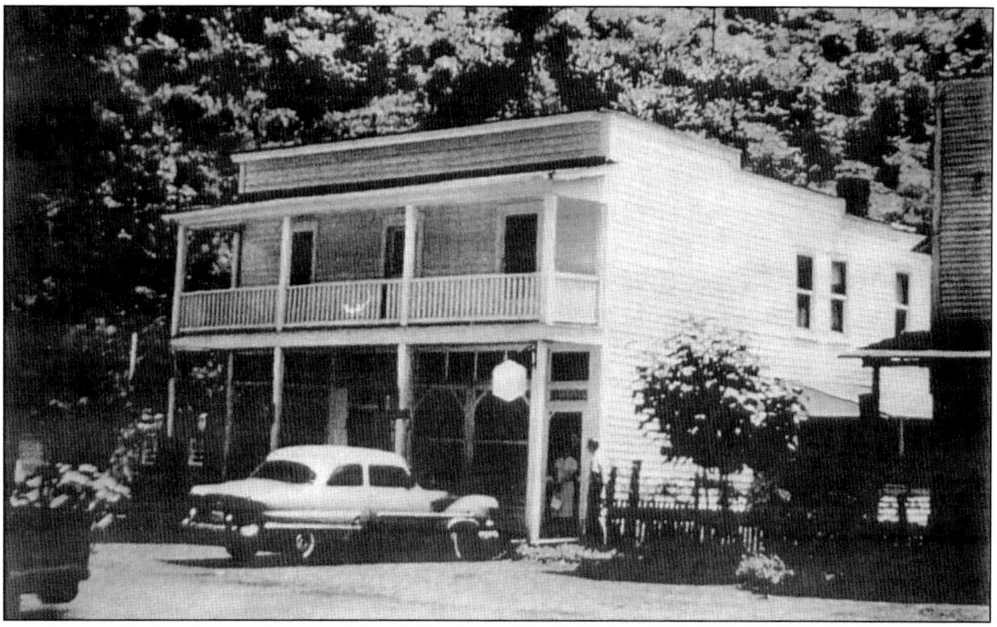

Clifford Miller's grandfather, Martin Miller, owned the Finney Hotel in the 1930s. This picture was taken in 1953. As a child, Miller often stayed here with his grandfather. He remembers Finney was considered by many to be a railroad town. Finney was the drop-off point for railroad crews. It was halfway between Bluefield and Norton. Railroad workers changed crews here, and often people changed trains. The workers would stay at the Finney Hotel, sleeping and taking their meals there. (Courtesy of RCPL, provided by R. C. Sykes.)

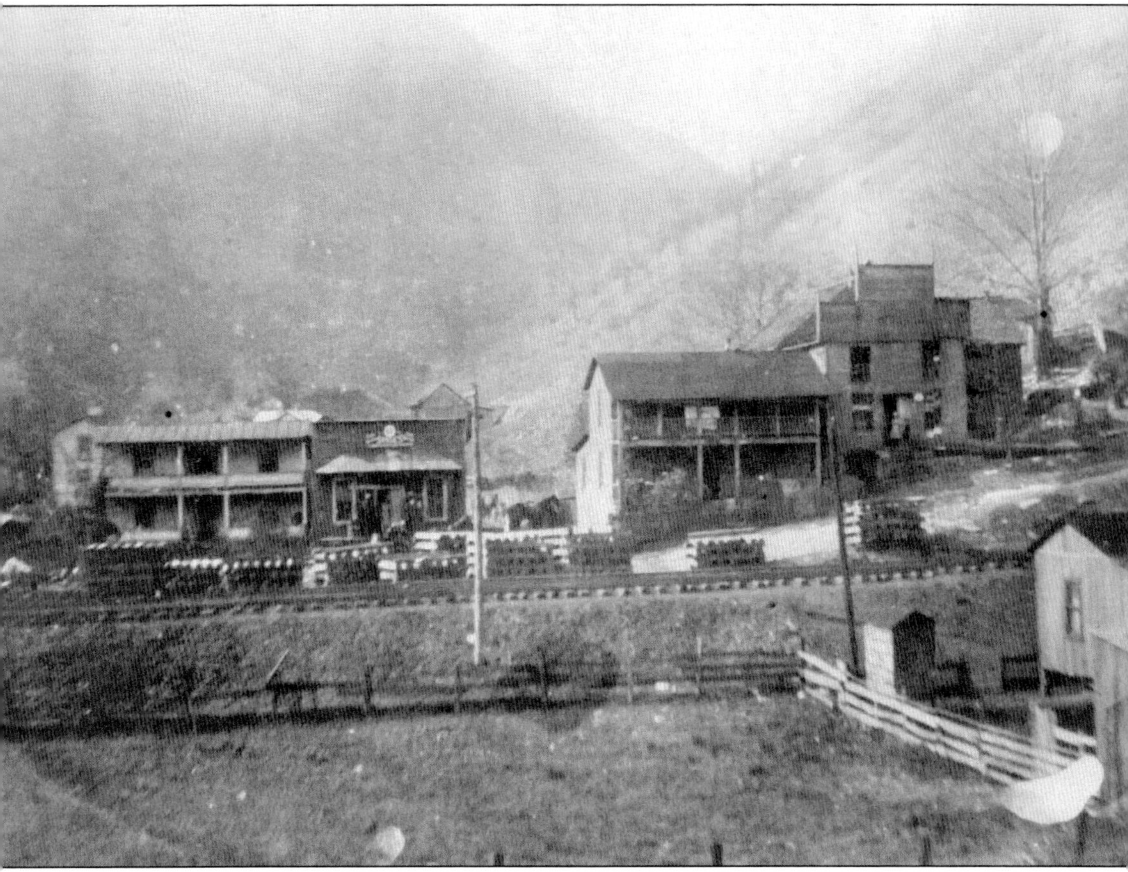

This early-1900s photograph of the town of Finney shows Finney Hardware just to the left of the gap. In the early days, people traveling from "Old Honaker" (New Garden) to the new town that started to develop as a result of the railroad traveled through the gap. (Courtesy of RCPL, provided by R. C. Sykes.)

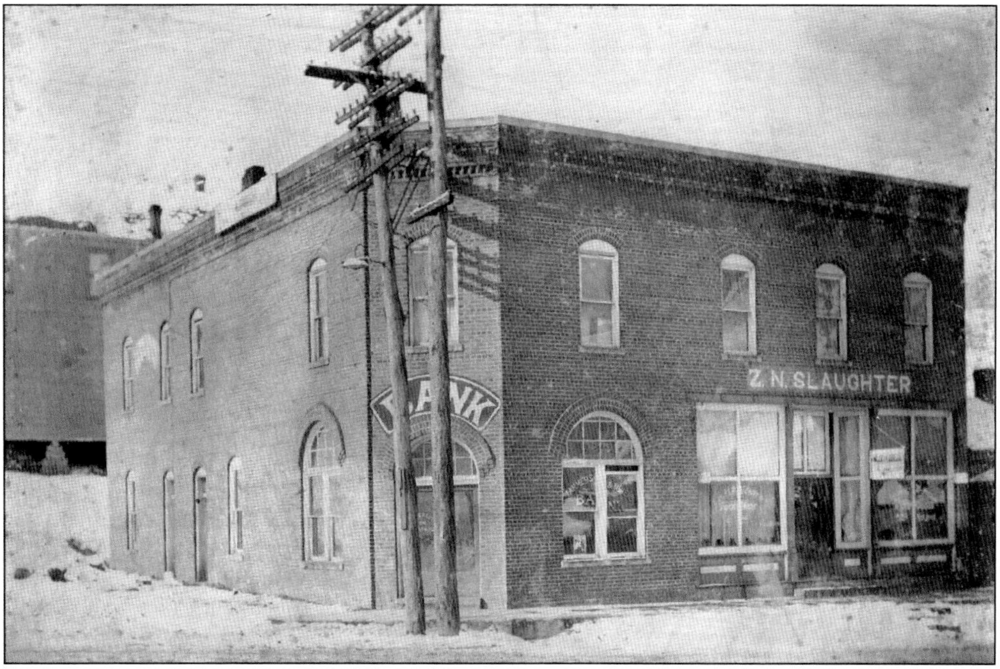

The Z. N. Slaughter building is located on the corner of Main Street and North Railroad Avenue in Honaker. This was the first brick building in town and was built around 1880. It is one of the oldest buildings in Honaker. It has been used as a bank, post office, restaurant, furniture and hardware store, and a factory. (Courtesy of HHM, provided by Kathleen R. Taylor.)

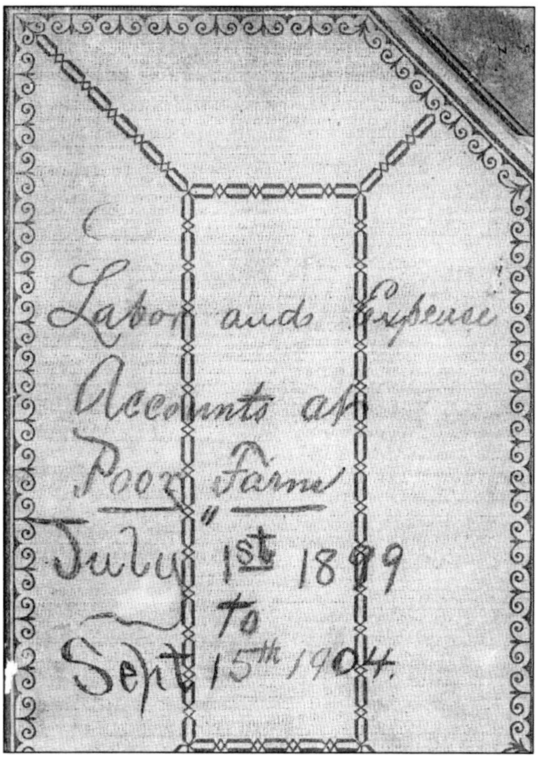

The Russell County Poor Farm was a refuge of safety and security for those who had no other options. This photograph represents the ledger kept of activities and related expenses from July 1, 1899, until September 15, 1904. The residents of the poor farm worked in exchange for room and board. The farm was 300 acres. The residents farmed to meet their food needs as well as raising tobacco, corn, grain, and hay to use and to sell. There were 75 acres under cultivation. Three-year crop rotation was practiced, with corn planted the first year, grain the second year, and hay the third year. They raised cattle and pigs for their use and for sale. They bartered the things they grew to purchase items such as sugar and coffee. Folks did what they were able to do. Everyone had tasks to perform. In 1956, the poor farm was sold at auction for $106,000. (Courtesy of HHM.)

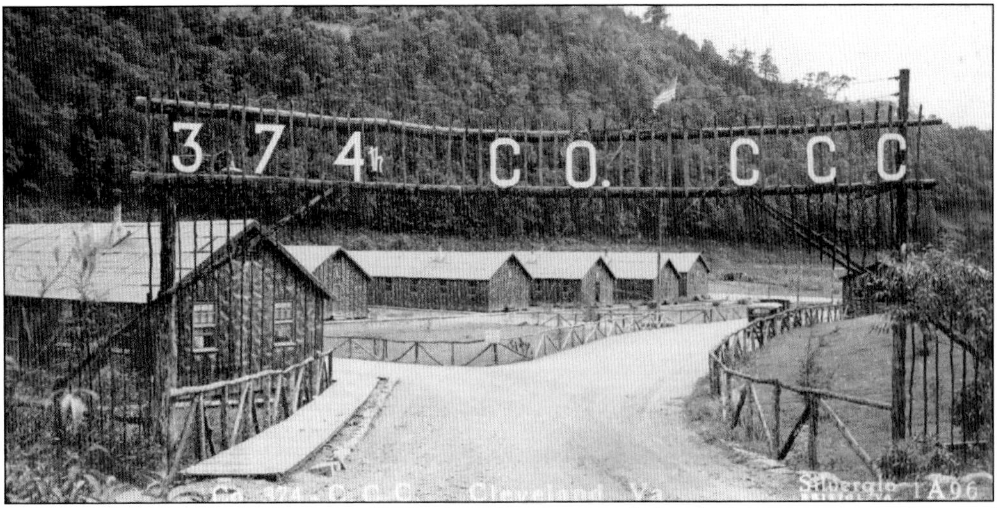

In an effort to combat rampant depressed unemployment coupled with the economic conditions of the time, Pres. Franklin Roosevelt planned an effort to fight declining resources and soil erosion across the country. His plan was to utilize the unemployed. The Emergency Conservation Act became known as the Civilian Conservation Corps (CCC) and was signed into law in March 1933. This is a picture postcard of the CCC Camp, Cleveland entrance in 1935. These camps were home to unemployed youth. Many had never been out of their state before. Some remained in the communities after their service was over. Some took brides back home with them. The camps generally added as much as $5,000 a month to the local businesses through purchases. By late 1942, the federal government ceased the funding and the camps closed. (Courtesy of RCPL, provided by Evelyn Meyer.)

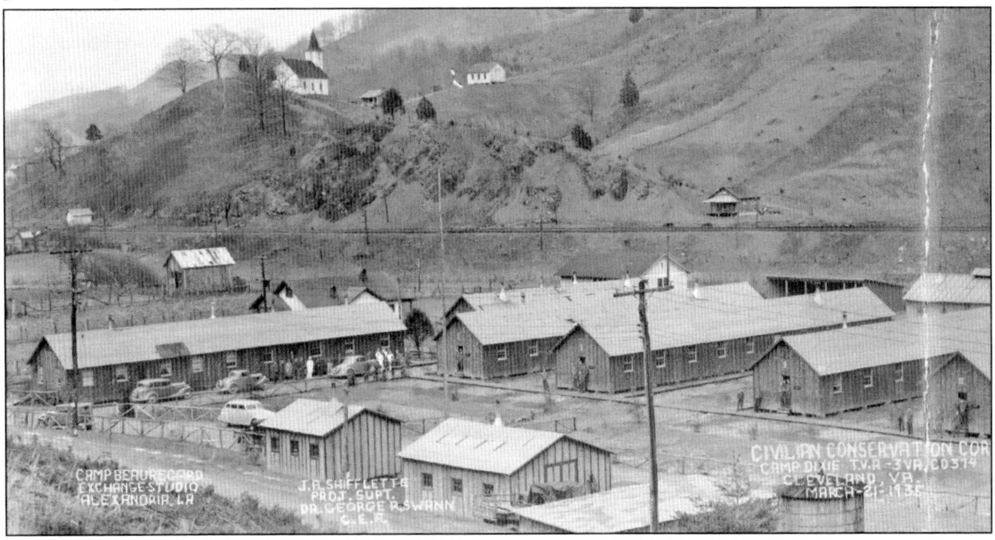

This picture of the CCC Camp in Cleveland was taken in 1935. The CCC was a compound with barracks, a dining hall, and everything required to meet the needs of those who called it home. There was also a community room so the residents could enjoy time together with card games, the radio, and swapping stories of home. Notice the area hillside is in pasture in this photograph. Much of it is now wooded again. During the years of the CCC's existence, 3 billion trees were planted across the United States in an effort to avoid soil erosion. (Courtesy of Russell County Historical Society.)

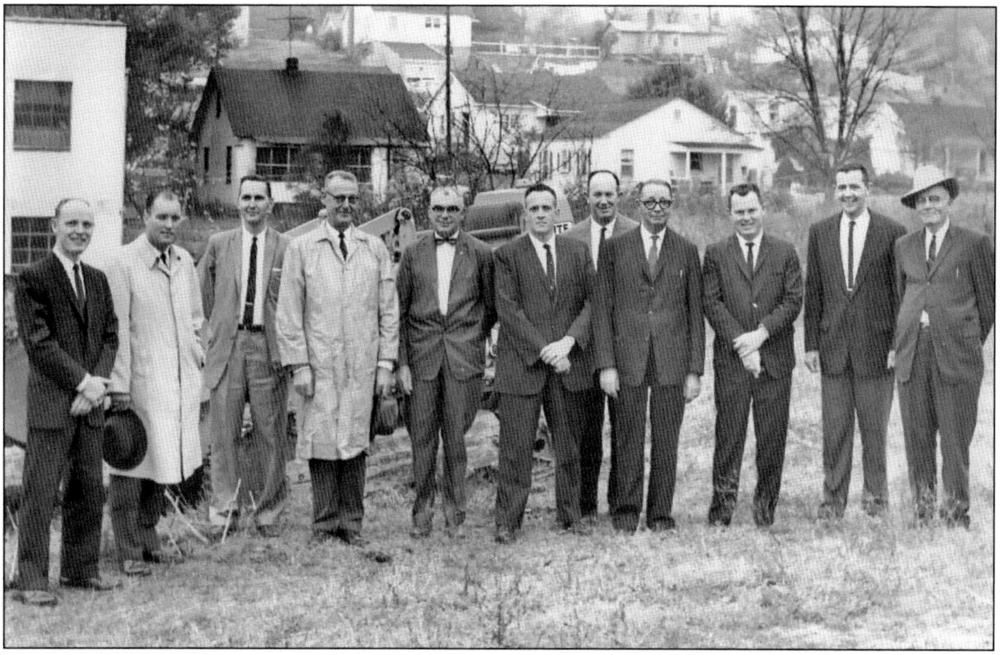

Officials gather for the ground-breaking of the telephone company building in Lebanon in the 1940s. From left to right are unidentified, Herman Puckett, Malcolm Doubles, B. C. All, Clarence Archer, unidentified, Dr. Roy Smith, James S. Easterly, unidentified, Junior Griffith, and Sherman Wallace. (Courtesy of Jim Easterly.)

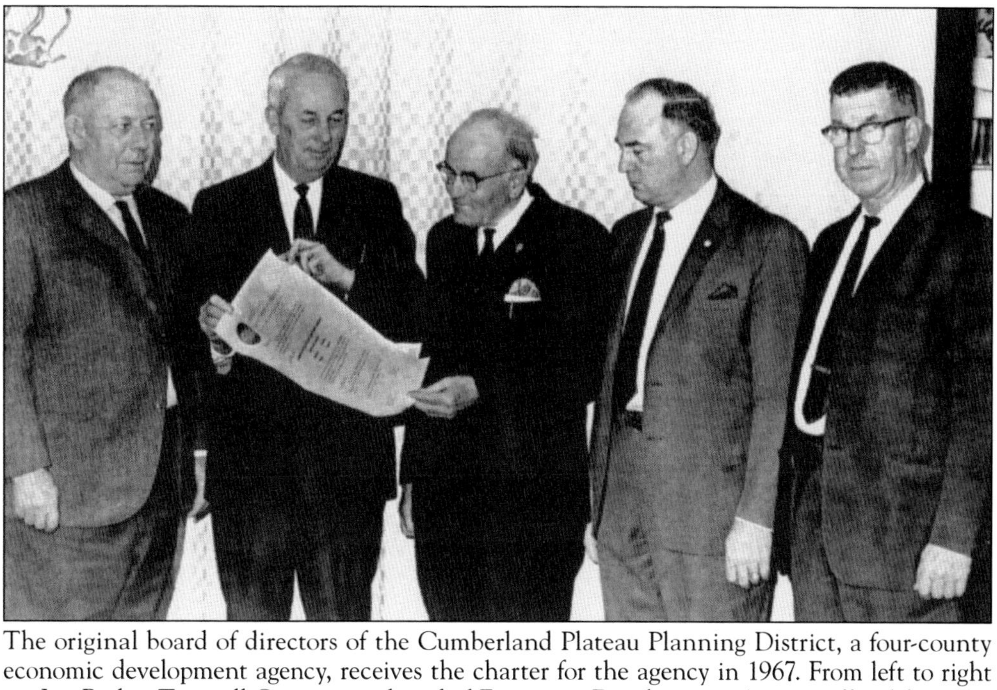

The original board of directors of the Cumberland Plateau Planning District, a four-county economic development agency, receives the charter for the agency in 1967. From left to right are Jim Bailey, Tazewell County; unidentified Economic Development Agency official from the U.S. Department of Commerce; Sherman Wallace, Russell County; Arthur Brown, Buchanan County; and Everett Davis, Dickenson County. (Courtesy of Sherman Wallace Jr.)

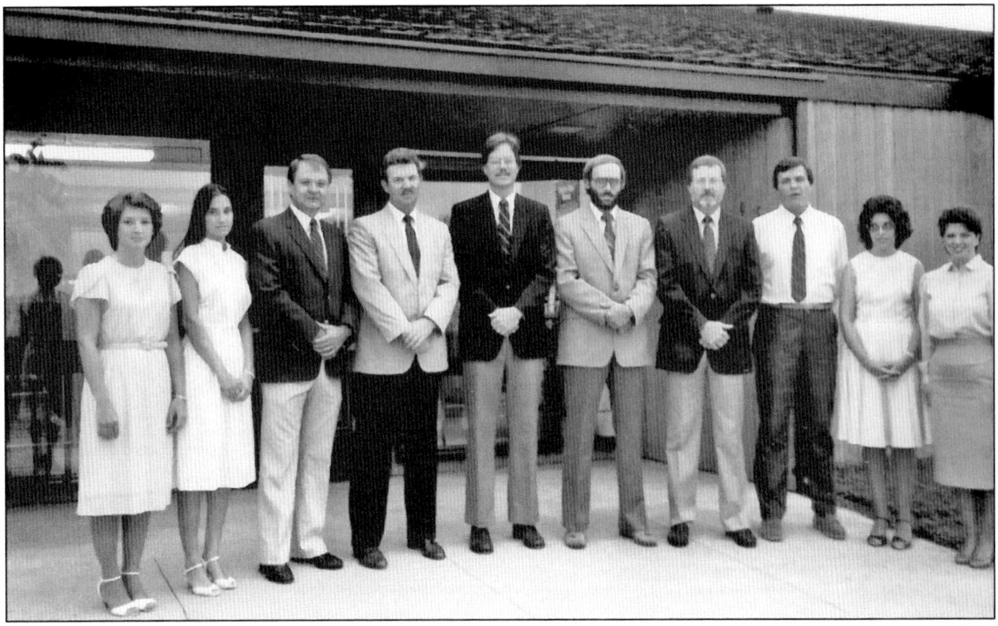

Pictured here is the staff of the Cumberland Plateau Planning District in the 1980s. From left to right are Roseann Jones, Debbie Puckett, Larry Carr, Andrew Chafin, James Baldwin, Louis Ballenberger, Sonny Jones, Jeff Owen, Judy Harris, and Trish Henderson. The planning district is a four-county economic development and planning commission that serves Buchanan, Dickenson, Russell, and Tazewell Counties. (Courtesy of Cumberland Plateau Planning District.)

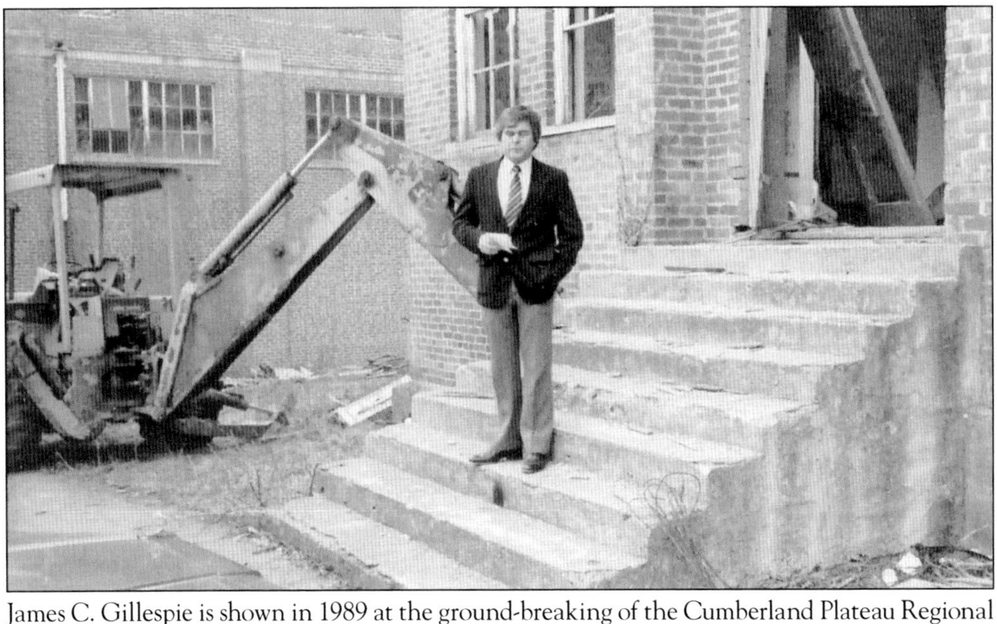

James C. Gillespie is shown in 1989 at the ground-breaking of the Cumberland Plateau Regional Housing Authority's senior citizens housing project in Cleveland. Jim is currently the Russell County administrator. Among his many other jobs, he serves as secretary of the Russell County Industrial Development Authority. Jim has served as Russell County administrator for many years and is regarded as one of Virginia's leading administrators. (Courtesy of Cumberland Plateau Planning District.)

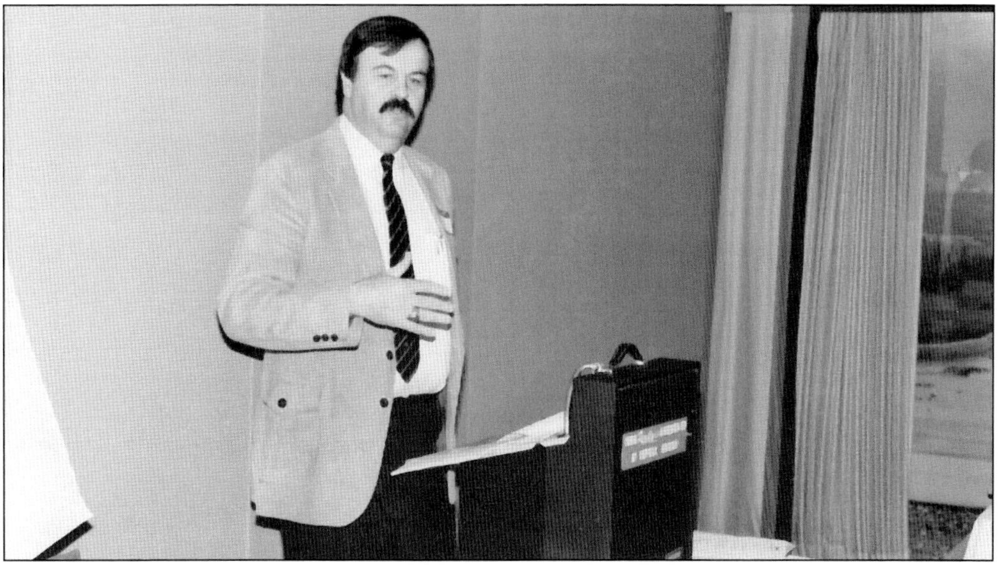

Frank Horton served as chairman of the Russell County Board of Supervisors for 14 years (1990–2003) and was a leading spokesman for economic growth. As of 2008, Horton serves as dean of math, science, and allied health and dean of work-force training for Southwest Community College. He also serves as chairman of the Cumberland Plateau Regional Waste Management Authority, a three-county organization formed by Buchanan, Dickenson, and Russell Counties. Horton resides in Lebanon with his wife, Beverly, and is affectionately known as "Pops" to his grandchildren, Elliott and Arwyn. (Courtesy of Cumberland Plateau Planning District.)

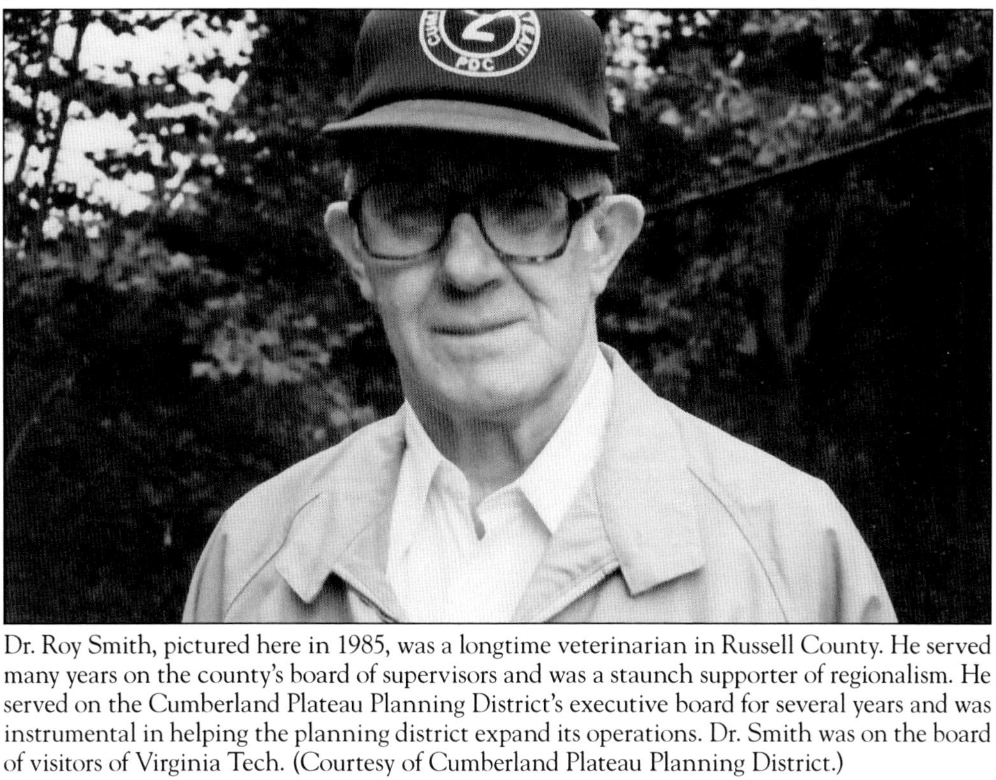

Dr. Roy Smith, pictured here in 1985, was a longtime veterinarian in Russell County. He served many years on the county's board of supervisors and was a staunch supporter of regionalism. He served on the Cumberland Plateau Planning District's executive board for several years and was instrumental in helping the planning district expand its operations. Dr. Smith was on the board of visitors of Virginia Tech. (Courtesy of Cumberland Plateau Planning District.)

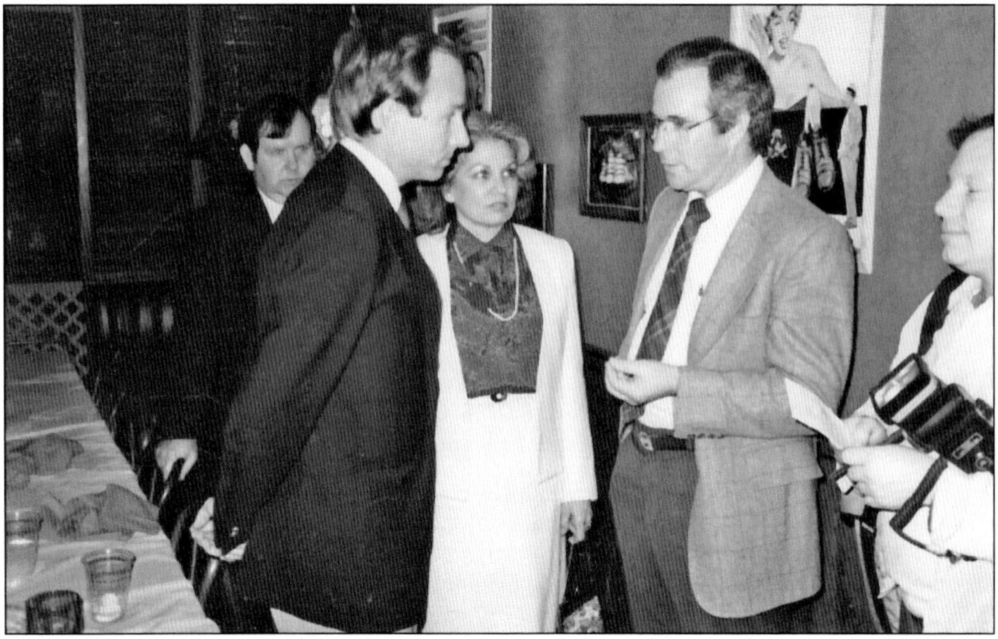

Dr. Charles King, president of Southwest Virginia Community College, speaks to U.S. senator Paul Trible in 1985. From left to right are R. Wayne Bostic, Senator Trible, Mary King, and Dr. King. Dr. King retired as president in 2007 and continued to work with the Southwest Virginia Community College Foundation on a number of new building projects. (Courtesy of Cumberland Plateau Planning District.)

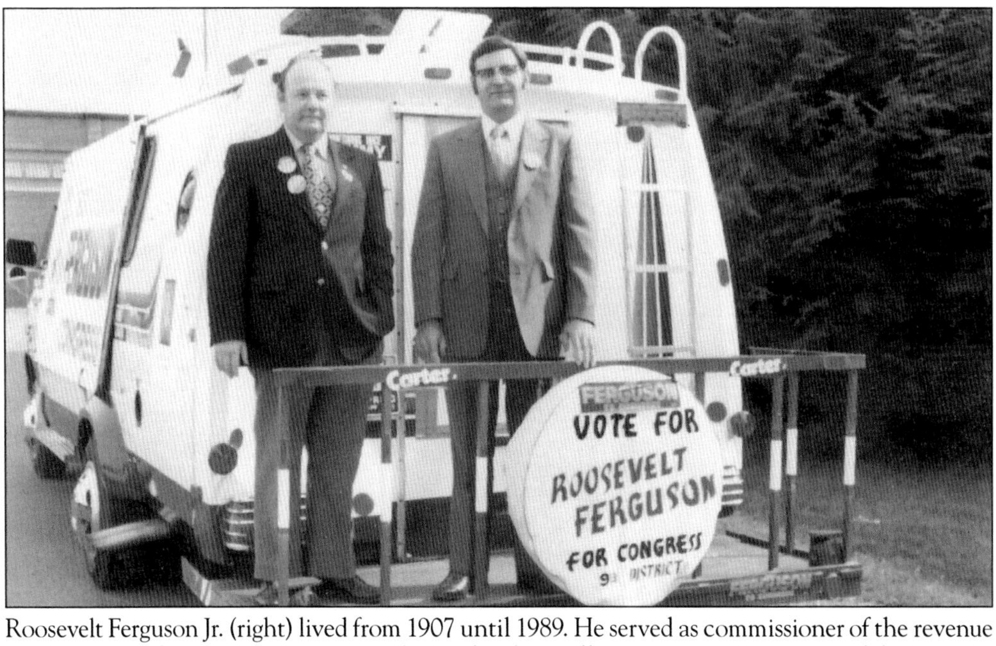

Roosevelt Ferguson Jr. (right) lived from 1907 until 1989. He served as commissioner of the revenue for the county for many years. He was the uncle of Russell County's commissioner of the revenue as of 2008, Randy Williams. Ferguson was active in county politics for many years and ran for congressman of Virginia's Ninth District. The identity of the gentleman to the left is unknown. (Courtesy of Randy Williams.)

Lebanon mayor Harold Mitchell addresses the crowd at the sale of the Cumberland Plateau Planning District's first shell building to Mattaco, a Connecticut company that produced automotive cables, in 1988. Mattaco was later purchased by Teleflex, which employed more that 400 workers before moving to Mexico. (Courtesy of Cumberland Plateau Planning District.)

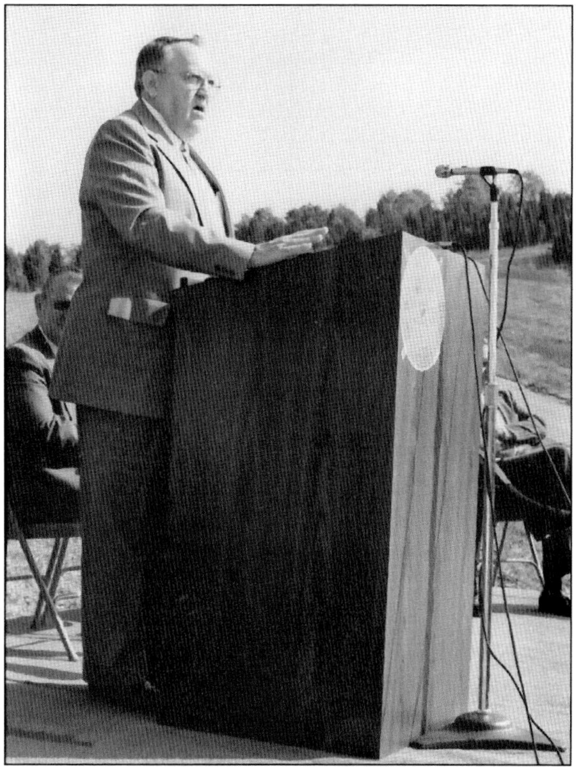

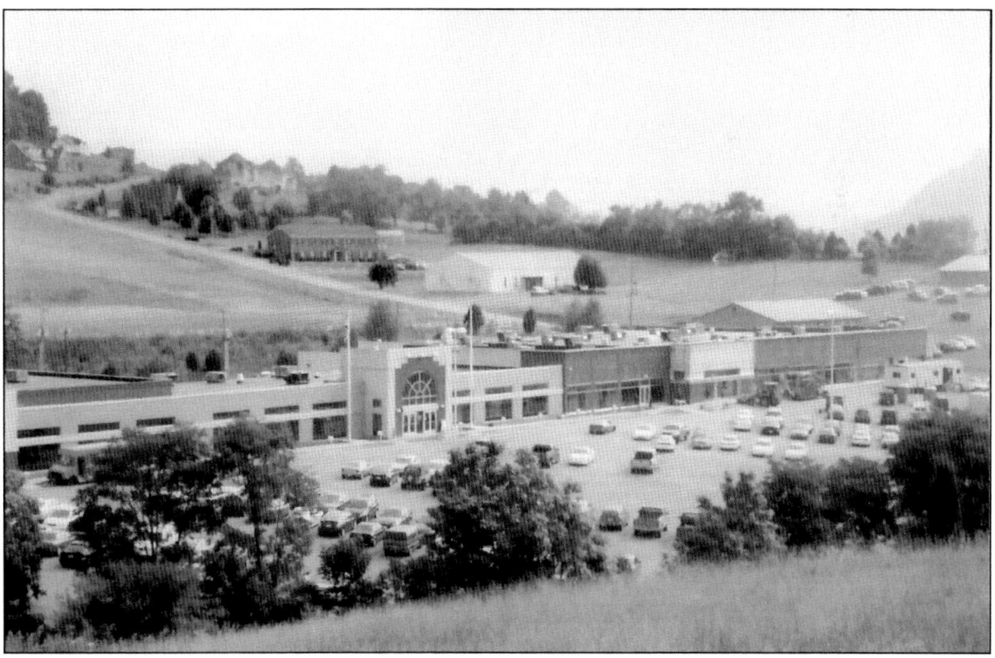

This is the new Russell County Government Center, completed in 2007. The county courthouse was renovated and now houses the county judicial system. The new government center houses the county's constitutional offices, the Russell County Regional Technology Training Center, and a regional conference center. (Courtesy of Russell County administrator Jim Gillespie.)

Consistent with our mission to preserve history on a local level, this book was printed in South Carolina on American-made paper and manufactured entirely in the United States. Products carrying the accredited Forest Stewardship Council (FSC) label are printed on 100 percent FSC-certified paper.

MADE IN THE USA